"They fall, and leave their
Little lives in the air."

—Alexander Pope *Windsor Forest*

FRISBEE

A Practitioner's Manual and Definitive Treatise

By Stancil E.D. Johnson, M.D.

Workman Publishing Company New York

Library of Congress Cataloging in Publication Data

Johnson, Stancil E D
    Frisbee: practitioner's manual and definitive
treatise.
    Bibliography
    Includes index.
    1. Frisbee (Game) I. Title.
GV1097.J64   796.2   75-9881
ISBN 0-911104-53-4

Cover design: Paul Hanson
Book Designer: Paul Hanson
Illustrations: David Cook
Printed and bound by the George Banta Company
Manufactured in the United States of America

Workman Publishing Company
231 East 51 Street
New York, New York 10022

First printing, July 1975

        3   4   5   6   7   8   9   10

The term FRISBEE as used in the
title and text of this book refers solely
to the flying saucer manufactured and
sold by Wham-O under the trademark
FRISBEE®. The first letter or all letters of the word FRISBEE are capi-
talized throughout this book as the
method chosen to signify that this
term is a registered trademark.

FRISBEE is a registered trademark of
Wham-O Mfg. Co., San Gabriel,
California, under U.S. Trademark
Registration No. 679,186, issued May
26, 1959 for goods specified as toy fly-
ing saucers for toss games.

To Harvey J. Kukuk, beloved leader of the world of
Frisbee, and to Kristin, beloved leader of mine

**Only known existing photograph of Harvey J.
Kukuk.**

CONTENTS

PREFACE

"A bad beginning
makes a bad ending."

—Euripides, *Aeolus Fragment 32*

I have this conversation all the time:

Frisbee's a fad, right? I mean, they've been around a few years and will fade out soon.

They have been around since 1947! And there was a metal disc at least a century before.

But it's for kids.

Frisbee's the favorite play for people who don't like organized sports.

There's nothing to it, just throwing and catching.

There are over two dozen games already devised for Frisbee.

Well, okay, Frisbee looks like it's here to stay. Grownups dig it, and you can play games with it, and all that, but how does a psychiatrist get into it?

It's fun, and I don't have to weigh 300 pounds or be seven feet tall to do it well. The difference between the great and the good isn't very much. Although it takes a long time to master it, it takes only a short time to enjoy. But the psychiatrist part of me didn't get into Frisbee for quite a while, not until I came to realize what Frisbee means to people and what it could do for sport in general. Over the years I've made up a lot of one-liners extolling Frisbee, but there's one that says it all: "When a ball dreams, it dreams it's a Frisbee."

This book hopes to fill a long-felt need, a definitive treatise of Frisbee. Although we have had the modern-day Frisbee with us for over three decades, and have seen it grow from a child's toy to a serious nation-wide sport, this work is the first effort to establish a terminology, elucidate the history and describe in detail the basic features and finer points of play. It suffers from bias and, at times, ignorance and idiosyncrasy. Even so, hopefully, the framework will provide a beginning fabric for Frisbee enthusiasts everywhere.

I began this book in 1968 in the musty offices of the International Frisbee Association in its first quarters on Rowena Avenue in Los Angeles. My research has carried me to the crystal shores of Lake Superior, the shadow of the Rose Bowl, the klieg lights of New York City T.V. studios, the dusty cotton fields of southern Missouri, and to carnival-esque Telegraph Avenue in Berkeley,

California. I have interviewed thousands of Frisbee freaks and corresponded with players all around the world.

I wanted a truly complete book with something for everyone, and enough for anyone: a book for beginners and aficionados. The articles and tables in the appendix will appeal mostly to the accomplished and determined players but can greatly aid the neophyte, too. Many have asked me how I could write so much about Frisbee; actually, the problem was how to avoid too much. In 1972 I completed the first draft and spent another two years spasmodically polishing. Finally, in mid-1974, I realized I could never tell it all.

I would like to thank the many who assisted, encouraged and urged me on. A few in specific: Robert Healy, of the International Frisbee Tournament, for providing the historical materials of that premiere tournament; Drs. Jay Shelton and Steve Sewall for much help and advice; George and Charles Gallaway, of Alfa Manufacturing, Los Angeles, for their information about Frisbee making; Ed Headrick, of Wham-O, who was invaluable and encouraging; Jim Boggio and Tom Ellis, of Eagle Harbor and Jon Davis, of Houghton, Michigan, for their help with International Frisbee Tournament matters; and Dr. Robert Vosburg of Dartmouth for assistance with the "Frisby" game; Roger Barrett, the curator of the International Frisbee Association, for much information about exotic discs; Dan Roddick and the staff of the *Flying Disc World* for many areas of advice; James Palmeri, of the Rochester Frisbee Club, for help with Double Disc Court; Irv Lander and Esther of IFA for all their help with diverse things; Goldy Norton for much assistance with records and photographs; Ed Hirst, of Irwin Toy in Toronto, for assistance with Canadian Frisbee; and, of course, Peter Workman, of Workman Publishing, who made the decision to "whelm" the Frisbee book, and his editorial staff, which made it all come together.

Particular thanks to the many who have taught me so much about Frisbee: Dr. David Roberts, one of my earliest Frisbee partners, John Oliveria and Robert Sellers, two of my latest; my brother, Charles, and Steve Young, who helped develop the Goal Line game; my three sons, Christopher, Jeffrey, and Michael and their friends—John Marshall, William and George Armistead, Jim and Phil Booth, and "Fast Eddie" Cahill, with whom I have learned and made up many games, especially Street Frisbee; all the members of the B.F.G., Thor Anderson and the members of the Foul Five, Hugh Anderson, Jack Kaitala, Bob May, Dan Headrick, Paul Richardson, Jim Gabbard, Doug McRae, and Mel Visser; my affable amanuenses JoAnn Belch, Beth DeSeelhorst, Elinore Mezzanares, Sharon Holt, Sally Ransome, Janet Banks and, especially Debbie Legg. Last, and particular thanks to Rick Lowenberg who gave me my first Frisbee.

S.E.D.J.

Pacific Grove, California 1975

INTRODUCTION

"Yes, a man's style o' play
and his swing certainly
reflect the state of his soul."

Shivas Irons in Michael Murphy's, *Golf in the Kingdom*

The ball is dead. It sold out to the consumer ethic. Long live the Frisbee!

Ball sports are now as much a consumer commodity as color TVs, cabbage and colored commodes. Rife with such pollutants as withholding play for television commercials and withholding players from road games so they can establish records in front of hometown crowds, organized ball sports have come a cathode ray tube circus—so many watching so few doing so little for so long. Consumerism and mechanization have nearly destroyed man's capacity to enjoy himself; they now threaten the spirit of sportsmanship.

Frisbee is the hope of sport—it brings back the individual as player. It is unfettered, nonconforming and usually noncompetitive. Even the most accomplished player enjoys tossing with a neophyte; sex and size matter little in proficiency. The disc calls for intelligence, not brawn; coordination, not mass. The difference between the best and the beginner is narrow. Play is once more the thing.

A Frisbee player scoffs at the expensive accouterments of the golfer and the fisherman—all he needs is a disc. He laughs at the organized brouhaha of professional games; almost any ball game can be played as well, if not better, with a Frisbee. Folf, for example, is ecological golf using trees, rocks and other natural landmarks as targets or traps.

But Frisbee is more than a game, a sport, a pastime. It is the thinking and feeling man's fantasy of unencumbered flight. The free spirit of Frisbee gives sport a new awareness—a fresh form of play, where the joy is in the doing, and where the mind and body interact with nature. As the Frisbee wafts skyward, man's spirit is released to soar the heights, to sense and explore the unknown. Man is drawn to the Frisbee with the same urge that led fish to land, the curious quadruped to stand, and the primate to shape his first tool. Its classic design is a further step in the evolutionary process toward the ultimate artifice of man's expression. For nothing befits the hand and challenges the coordinate movement of the arm and body more than throwing a Frisbee; nothing captures the essence of flying more than the disc.

Pick up a Frisbee. Feel it. Join man's greatest tool, his hand, with his grandest dream, to fly. Renew the joy of play.

The Frisbie Pie Company, now Leathermode Sportscraft, of Bridgeport, Connecticut.

1. THE HISTORY OF FRISBEE

"Twinkle, twinkle, little bat!
How I wonder what you're at!
Up above the world you fly,
Like a tea-tray in the sky."
—Lewis Carroll, *Alice in Wonderland*

Frisbee history is divided into ancient and modern times. The latter is well understood, the former a murky sea of mystery. Let us begin, then, not with the beginning, but with the more certain part of our subject.

Modern History

The story of modern Frisbee is a tale of the American coasts; first to the East Coast:

The Frisbie Pie Company

In 1871, in the wake of the Civil War, William Russell Frisbie moved from Bransford, Connecticut, where his father, Russell, had operated a successful grist mill, to Bridgeport, Connecticut. Hired to manage a new bakery, a branch of the Olds Baking Company of New Haven,[1] he soon bought it outright and named it the Frisbie Pie Company.[2] W. R. was the outside man on the routes, while his sister, Susan, did the baking. W. R. died in 1903 and his son, Joseph P., manned the ovens until his death in 1940. Under his direction the small company grew from six to two hundred and fifty routes, and shops were opened in Hartford, Connecticut; Poughkeepsie, New York; and Providence, Rhode Island. His widow, Marian Rose Frisbie, and long-time

[1]One of, if not the oldest bakery, in the United States.
[2]It was located on 363 Kossuth Street. Contrary to popular report, there never was a *Mother Frisbie's Pie Company* in Bridgeport.

Mr. Joseph P. Frisbie.

plant manager, Joseph J. Vaughn, baked on until August 1958[3] and reached a zenith production of 80,000 pies per day in 1956.

In this otherwise simple baking operation we find the origin of the earliest Frisbee! Now the company offered a variety of bakery goodies, including pies and cookies, and therein reside the roots of the controversy. For there are two crusty schools concerning Frisbee's origins: the Pie-Tin School and the Cookie-Tin School, each camp holding devoutly to its own argument.

The Pie-Tin School. The pie-tin people claim Yale students bought Frisbie's pies (undoubtedly a treat in themselves) and tossed the prototype all over old Eli's campus. These early throwers would exclaim "Frisbie" to signal the catcher. And well they might, for a tin Frisbie is something else again to catch.[4]

The Cookie-Tin School. Now the cookie tin people agree on these details save one: they insist that the true, original prototype was the cookie-tin lid that held in the goodness of Frisbie's sugar cookies.

Charles O. Gregory recalls tins in flight before 1920 in the following letter:

When I was around eight or ten years old, we used to go to Cedar Beach on Long Island Sound in Milford, Connecticut. I grew up in Derby, Connecticut. At Cedar Beach there was a store that sold Frisbie's Sugar Cookies—it could have been Mrs. Frisbie's, but I am not sure—and they came in a tin box, round, about

ten inches or a foot in diameter. I clearly remember the cookies; and I also recall that the cover of the tin box was used by the older kids just the same way that "frisbees" are now used. Then, some years later, when I went to college—Yale—I saw students using these same tin-box lids as people now use frisbees. So I assumed that the name came from these sugar cookies and the boxes in which they were sold.

I am now sixty-nine, so that it must have been around sixty years ago that I first saw kids using these box tops as they now use frisbees. And I entered college in 1920, where it was still going on. You attribute the origin to Frisbie's pie plates from a Bridgeport bakery. Well, I never heard of Frisbie's pies; but my home town of Derby and Milford, where Cedar Beach is, are both about ten miles or so from Bridgeport. And of course New Haven is almost as close to Bridgeport. So you no doubt have the right bakery if not the correct confection and container!

Now, which is true? Both have a morsel of truth. Undoubtedly both were flown. Extensive research, including personal conversations with Joseph P.'s widow[5] and the ex-plant manager of the Frisbie Pie Company, Mr. Vaughn, leads me to conclude that the earlier prototype was the pie tin.[6] This humble object springing

from the hands of Yale students led to the Frisbee of today.[7]

[3] At last report the building housed the Leathermode Sportswear Company.

[4] The author has been fortunate, indeed, to try his hand with one of the original Frisbie pie tins! It is a surprisingly stable instrument in flight, as mentioned, requiring extra skill and caution in the catch. Thanks to Miss Nora Frisbie, President of Frisbie-Frisbee Family of America, for the loan from the Frisbie family's museum.

[5] She also recalls that the Frisbie truck drivers were pie-tin scalers and held competitions at the plant. During World War II, they infected military installations all over the U.S.A.

[6] Just to complicate matters, there were *three* Frisbie pie tins—10, 8, and 4 inches in diameter, all bearing the Frisbie Pie stamp. There were also some Frisbie pies in tins without the stamp! More research is needed.

[7] Of course others all about the country were throwing similar objects. Mr. Carl Cope of Sacramento, California, recalls that in the early forties, perhaps in the late thirties (Carl's memory is a bit faulty here), many California youngsters were nearly addicted to throwing things. Camera crews on Hollywood movie lots flipped film lids, while coffee and paint can lids were my earliest "Frisbees."

Miss Nora Frisbie, President of the Frisbie-Frisbee Family of America, and the author compare Master Frisbee and authentic Frisbie pie tin (10-inch size). Note: Six holes in center star pattern.

Walter Frederick Morrison, the Flyin' Saucer and the Invisible Wire

Frisbee playing might have gone on forever in this metallic form, never to reach the pinnacle of popularity it possesses today, but for two happenings of the mid-1940's: plastic and West Coast inventor Fred Morrison.

Walter Frederick Morrison, the son of the inventor of the automobile sealed-beam headlight, returned home after World War II, finishing his European campaign as a prisoner-of-war in the now famous Stalag 13. He worked for a while as a carpenter, but like his father, he had an inventive mind. The time was 1948; flying saucers from outer space were beginning to capture people's imagination. Why not turn the concern into a craze? As a Utah youth, he scaled pie tins, paint-can lids, and the like. He remembered those pleasurable moments and his mind turned to perfecting the pie tin into a commercial product. First he welded a steel ring inside the rim (in Toejam's recess—discussed later) to improve the plate's stability, but without success. In a surge of serendipity, he adopted the child of the times—*plastic*. Plastic was the ideal stuff for Frisbee. It seems impossible to imagine anything better. And, perhaps, Frisbee is plastic's finest form.

Initially Morrison used a butyl stearate blend. He recalls: "It worked fine as long as the sun was up, but then the thing got brittle, and if you didn't catch it, it would break into a million pieces! We worked that out. We offered to replace any broken one with a brand-new one, *if* they brought back every piece! I think we probably replaced three or four all told."

Morrison scraped together enough money for an injection mold, ran off a batch, and opened a booth at the Pomona Fair (the county fair of Los Angeles). Here he introduced the "invisible wire pitch." Morrison and a comrade would stride through the fair crowds holding an invisible wire high above their heads. "Make way for the wire," Morrison would bellow. Crowds would part like a zipper as Morrison brought the wire to the booth and attached it to posts. Then he would sail the saucer along the charlatan string. The crowd, agape and amazed, would press forth asking how did this new-fangled gadget work and could they buy it. "Why, the saucer is free, but the wire costs a penny a foot and comes in lots of 100 feet!"

This original Morrison's Flyin' Saucer was his *arcuate vane model*,[8] named for the six topside[9] curved spoilers (vanes). They were designed to improve lift by facilitating the Bernoulli principle,[10] which they didn't. Curiously, the spoilers were on backwards; that is, they would theoretically work only for a counterclockwise spin.

Flightwise, the original Morrison is poor by today's standards. It is still available in a modified version[11] at Disneyland shops, where the

Fred Morrison, the plastic Frisbee inventor, showing his form outside his hardware store in La Verne, California.

Disbee, which is worse, is also sold. The big difference between the Disneyland Morrison and the original is the plastic—a soft, polyethylene. The peaked cupola of the original Morrison is absent. See page 35 for more information.

The Pluto Platter. In 1951 Morrison vastly improved his model, and the design, unchanged, served as Wham-O's legendary Pluto Platter. The Pluto Platter is the basic design[12]

---

[8]Morrison also called it the Rotary Fingernail Clipper!
[9]Flight plate.
[10]See Frisbee Physics.
[11]The Republic Flyin' Saucer.
[12]There was an 11-inch-diameter model—the now quite rare Sputnik—that posed for the Master Model.

for all succeeding Frisbees. Credit Fred Morrison for this farsightedness. The outer third of the disc, his fundamental design feature,[13] is appropriately named the Morrison Slope.

The Morrison Pluto Platter had the first true cupola (cabin in Morrison's terms). The UFO influence colored his design. The cabin had portholes! The planet ring hinted an extraterrestrial origin.

Pluto Platter is still a useful Frisbee. Vic Malafronte's Super Frisbee is a Pluto Platter with a Pro rim[14] melted to the cheek. He claims throws of 115 yards! Wham-O modified the Pluto Platter several times before it developed the new standard with Headrick's lines.

Wham-O. Rich Knerr and A. K. "Spud" Melin fresh from the University of Southern California were making slingshots in their fledgling toy company when they first saw Morrison's flying saucers whizzing around southern California beaches. They were interested in this exciting, simple thing that employed the basic principles of physics, primary ingredients in all their products to come. In late 1955, they cornered Morrison while he was hawking his wares and tying up traffic on Broadway in downtown Los Angeles. Just before he was asked to break it up by the local gendarmerie, the dynamic duo invited him to their San Gabriel factory and made him a proposition.

Thus, flying saucers landed on the West Coast in San Gabriel, and on January 13, 1957, they began to fly out from a production line that has since sent over one hundred million sailing all over the globe.

"At first the saucers had trouble catching on," Rich Knerr reminisces, "but we were confident they were good, so we sprinkled them in different parts of the country to prime the market." On a trip to the campuses of the Ivy League, Knerr first heard the term "Frisbee." Harvard students said they'd tossed pie tins about for years, and called it Frisbie-ing.[15] Knerr liked the terms Frisbie and Frisbie-ing, so he borrowed them. Having no idea of the historical origins, he spelled the saucer *Frisbee*, phonetically correct, but one vowel away from the *Frisbie* Pie Company.[16]

Since 1957 Wham-O has made sixteen models of Frisbees (see Chapter 2 for a more complete description of the important ones). Almost from the beginning there have been rival renderings, but to date, none as successful as Frisbee (Chapter 2 describes some of these).

Sachnoff Hypothesis

There are other theories of the origin of the modern Frisbee; the Frisbee Potato-Tin Lid School, or the Sachnoff[17] Hypothesis, heads the field. The following is a letter from that gentleman with his claim:

Yes, it all happened at Harvard College, Leverett House, in the fall of 1949. And, yes, as Ed Fagen (my college roommate) reports, at times I was a champion swimmer of enormous strength, but then again at other times, I found myself barely surviving for days on end in a weakened and debilitated state. My plight is hardly news to anyone who ever fought to survive solely on Harvard food, solely that is, with one notable exception. My blessed mother, aware of the dearth of proper edibles for me, her baby boy at Harvard, would indeed (albeit sporadically) send emergency rations in the interest of my survival.

One particular week, the situation was dire. Monday, Tuesday, Wednesday, Thursday passed and no ration can had arrived—no crumbled cookies, no salami, no bagels or lox—all jam-packed in another pair of galoshes for me. (Lox! Do you know what happens to a lox, an angry fish in its own right, after a week in mail transit stuffed in the toe of a galosh?) I was growing weaker each day, when finally, on Friday, Ed came racing up the entry stairs to our room, a brownpaper wrapped package in hand. Ed gave me the package to open—he knew about the old lox risk. With my waning strength, I tore off the wrapping paper and string and found a round (approximately 10 inches in diameter) metal can of "Frisbee's Potato Chips." The lid was tightly affixed, but with a last burst of energy, I pried it off and with the same desperate upward movement of

---

[13]The new Fastback model of Wham-O offends this design with its indentation in the outer third—the Gillespie Groove. Fastback was an interesting idea but an unstable flyer and is already dropped from the Wham-O line.

[14]A Pro's rim has a third of the total weight of the saucer.

[15]In a small way, this complicates the Eli Theory of Frisbee origin.

[16]Today there is a very active organization called the Frisbie-Frisbee Family of America, headed by Miss Nora Frisbie. It has some three hundred active members, and is one of the best genealogically studied families in America.

[17]Note in Lowell E. Sachnoff's letter Frisbee is his spelling. Perhaps the years have dulled his memory, or more likely we are dealing with a different manufacturer, named Frisbee. Joseph P.'s widow doesn't remember making potato chips!

my arm, the lid skimmed off in the direction of the bedroom window (which was slightly raised) sailed out the open window, and arched a graceful parabolic curve through the crisp autumn air in the Leverett House courtyard. Though my soma was weak, my psyche was uplifted gloriously at that splendid sight. Yes, at that moment, Dr. Johnson, Frisbee was born.

Everything else Ed says is true. We played regularly after that, Ed and my other roommates. Jules Garelick and Bill Klein and several other Leverett House men including Jim Ross, who had great technique and controlled the Frisbee with the same crisp authority that Horowitz masters a Chopin sonata. From that fall on at Harvard, the banks of the Charles became the center of Frisbee activity, and with delicate arches, tantalizing hovers, swift skimmers and all the subtle, splendid variations on these basic themes, metal-top Frisbee-type tins graced the air.

We scattered after graduation in 1952 and, like so many delights of our youth, Frisbee, as we knew it then, passed from the scene. Until one day, years later, I saw my first commercial plastic Saran-wrapped discounted Frisbee on a Walgreen's counter. I was overcome by a flash of nostalgia and wrote the manufacturer, Wham-O, Inc., the whole story. I got back a form letter telling some incredible origin yarn of Yalies frolicking on the banks of the New Haven & Hartford Railroad flinging manhole covers, or was it a collection of pie (in the sky) plates or something equally preposterous. Don't be gulled by these apocryphal tales, Dr. Johnson; the Sachnoff Theory of Frisbee Origin is gospel.

The Coming of Age of Frisbee

As we have seen, the 1940's and early 50's hatched and nurtured the plastic flying disc. By the mid-1950's, isolated tournaments and the gathering together of dedicated players began. Along with this, attempts at organized games with Frisbees appeared (see Games chapter). However, the toy flying saucer, as Wham-

O called it in those pre-Frisbee days, still seemed destined to be just another passing fad; and when Wham-O introduced its biggest fad of all, the Hula Hoop, in 1958, the saucer was nearly done in by its swirling plastic cousin. The flying saucer was aground at the San Gabriel manufactory. Then Wham-O discovered the name Frisbee, trademarked it in 1959, and hopes ran high that this catchy sobriquet would at last bring success to the toy flying saucer.

In the early 1960's the real motive force came in the form of Ed Headrick, general manager and vice-president of Wham-O. He envisioned Frisbee as a sport, not just a toy, and developed and introduced the Professional Model in 1964 to test the idea.[18] Hoping to stabilize its flight, he developed and patented flight rings, now called Lines of Headrick. The Pro did it! Frisbee was a toy no more. Headrick went on to found the International Frisbee Association and then helped to organize the legendary California Masters Guts team, which defeated all comers at the IFT in 1968. Headrick's dream was complete: Frisbee was a sport and the best players were in California, where the sport originated.

In the late sixties, Frisbee-related events occurred fast and furiously. Ultimate, another serious Frisbee game, was developed in late 1969. The first Moonlighter Frisbee appeared, and the Navy began secret studies with Frisbee-like discs molded into battlefield flares to be launched from low-flying airplanes.[19] Although the Navy spent nearly $400,000, the Frisbee refused to be drafted. When ignited, it flew up and away, AWOL forever!

Maturity in the Seventies

The seventies seem to be the golden era for Frisbee. Many new tournaments have sprung up; new models have been made not only by Wham-O but also by the first serious competitors in flying discs. The first 100-yard distance throws, like the four-minute mile, were reached and have now become commonplace in premier tournaments. In 1974 the *Flying Disc World*, a bimonthly Frisbee journal "of, by, and for flying-disc enthusiasts," was introduced. Later, two Frisbee champions toured the country with the Harlem Globetrotters, demonstrating flying-disc expertise. The Rose Bowl World Frisbee Championships in the late summer of 1974 brought together for the first time nearly all the great and late-great Frisbee players in a quintessential display of Frisbee prowess that led to the crowning of the man and woman champions of the world. This

---

[18]In years to come this model will no doubt be known as *the Headrick*.

[19]The Navy also developed a mechanical Frisbee launcher, reported to be the world's most powerful thrower. Jon Davis, tournament director of the IFT and coach of the world's Guts champions—Library Bar team—has issued a challenge to the Navy to test their thrower against his champion catchers.

Discobolus, thought to be by Myron.

event signified Frisbee's maturation. Ten years after Headrick's dream, Frisbee is regarded as a serious sport and promises to become a major one.

Ancient and Apocryphal Theories of Frisbee Origin

In this realm there are many vague ideas. The credibility factor is small, but for completeness' sake the outstanding theories are described below.

The Discobolus Legend

It is alleged that the famous bronze statue Discobolus, reputedly by Myron, is actually a young Greek lad about to execute an overhand wrist fling[20] on an oversize Greek Frisbee. Some authorities feel that Myron had a bad day at the Eleusinian Brass Rail and was too stoned to chisel out the undersurface of the Frisbee.

The Elihu Frisbie Story

In this version, popular on the Yale campus, Elihu[21] in 1827 revolted in chapel against the passing of the collection plate, seized the platter, and sailed it mightily in the direction of the university quad. The custom caught on, to the collective chagrin of the college clerics.

---

[20]Note the poor thumb placement.
[21]Elihu Frisbie was born in Connecticut in 1805 and is no. 912 (of over 5000) on the Frisbie family tree.

Toejam Diggings

There was much excitement several years ago when archaeologists, on a dig near Toejam, Utah, unearthed Indian artifacts resembling mud-pie tins. They were fragmented for sure, but an inscription on one shard in a near-forgotten dialect was translated to read, "Play catch, invent games, fly-flip away." This musty piece of preposterous apocrypha cannot be given serious regard, particularly when we remember that it was Fred Morrison who wrote that still succinct script on the undersurface of his Pluto Platter.

Roman Frisbee Shields

And then there are the reoccurring reports of Roman soldiers in phalanx hurling their razor-sharp, Frisbee-shaped shields in 202 B.C. at the Battle of Zama to defeat Hannibal and the might of Carthage.

Neanderthal Man, Frisbee, and the Wheel

There is some sketchy evidence that Neanderthal man made a baked clay Frisbee similar to the artifacts found at Toejam, Utah (q.v.), and when one of them rolled, unbroken, along the ground the idea occurred to him, "Now, if I put a stick between two of these. . . ."

Albert J. Fall[22] (Robert de Roos Hypothesis) — The Jake Newhouse That Became Frisbee

Mr. Robert de Roos of the *San Francisco Chronicle* is responsible for the following account of Frisbee's origin, and it is reproduced by his permission. Suffice it to say, there is no firm evidence for his argument at the present time.

When Albert J. Fall, the inventor of Frisbee (then known as "the Jake Newhouse")[23] sat down to ponder upon what he had wrought, he recognized a great truth. He had found another, a new way to use a great natural force: Reciprocal Action. He had devised a new utilization of the principle of Back and Forth, which drives engine—and thus, stationary engineers—motor scooters, outboard and inboard motors for boats of various sizes, lawn mowers, mechanical saws, graders, scoopers, tugs of war, ice hockey and other sports, love, war and commuters. Back and forth. Here and there. To and fro. The samba. Bells ringing in the nighttime. Tit for tat.[24]

Now, when he thought of all this, Albert J. Fall realized that his invention, "the Jake Newhouse," had one irreparable fault: it was useless. Of all the reciprocal motions in the world, "the Jake Newhouse" did no good, saved no soul, earned no dollar. And although he knew he would take a tongue-lashing from his wife, Imelda, he destroyed "the Jake Newhouse" prototype. "Although I know I will catch billy hell from Imelda for wasting my time, I will not be responsible for subjecting the world to this useless device," he said. And he broke the prototype of "the Jake Newhouse" into small pieces and thrust them into his backyard Bessemer.[25]

It was just as well, for that first visionary, "breadboard" model of what finally became the modern, ovable Frisbee was made of iron and weighed forty-two pounds.[26] It was not until the invention of high-tensile-strength, low-density, medium-grade, light-weight, low-cost inherent-color plastic that the true Frisbee could be perfected. So, I say to you, "Let us toss our Frisbees gaily as we go through life but let us remember that we would be less than human if we do not acclaim the sacrifices suffered and the deep insights contributed by Albert J. Fall of Inveterate, Mass., so long ago (circa 1860)."

Imelda, his unfeeling wife, left Albert J. Fall less than a year later. "I have married a tinkerer," she told a close friend, "but I will not be tinkered with."[27]

There are dozens of other theories even less promising. Time and patient research must unveil this shadowed area.

---

[22]Not to be confused with Albert B. Fall, Secretary of the Interior in Warren Harding's Administration.

[23]How this name came to be associated with Fall's invention is not entirely clear. It is known that a Jacob Neuhaus once lived for a time near Inveterate, Mass., where he operated a small pea-shelling factory. It is probable that he was called Jake, but Fall would never have corrupted Neuhaus's last name. Fall was known to be meticulous about things like that.

[24]The generally approved spelling.

[25]See David Carnegie and S. C. Gladwyn, *Liquid Steel, Its Manufacture and Cost,* second edition (1918).

[26]This was the lightest model Fall ever constructed. His first "Jake Newhouse" weighed eighty-four pounds (six stone).

[27]Private revelation in a letter (dated September 5, 1861) to Sarah Nevada, Imelda Fall's girlhood chum, said by some to be her second cousin. Mrs. Fall married Ernest Barch, an upholsterer's assistant, in 1863 and moved into Imberry Transfer (Conn.? R.I.?) and dropped out of sight.

2. THE FRISBEE AND OTHER FLYING DISCS

"No bird soars too high if he soars with his own wings.
—William Blake, *The Marriage of Heaven and Hell*

The Frisbee[1] lay dormant until the coming of plastic in the 1940's. In plastic, the Frisbee reached its apogee.

The modern Frisbee still resembles a pie tin. The essential differences are the slope of Morrison and the lip. The lip tucked in[2] enhances stability. Have you ever tossed a pie tin? Take one out and give it a twirl. It is more sailable than you might imagine.

The Wham-O Company makes sixteen different Frisbees. Concept Products, Inc., of Minneapolis makes five discs; Northern Pacific in Bend, Oregon, three; and Skyway Products of Brooklyn, three. There are several dozen other manufacturers in the United States, plus a number of others scattered throughout the world.

Material

With unnotable exceptions[3] all flying discs are made of polyethylene plastic. The ideal plastic is pliable and not subject to breaking.[4] Rigid plastics have not been successful. Surprisingly, they are too firm for distance throwing.

In early 1969 Wham-O changed to a softer, higher-melting-point polyethylene.[5] This made a less breakable but poorer distance Frisbee. Throwers abhor these "bubble tops"[6] and cling to the older models.

Production

The injection-mold method is the most practical. In this process, the mold halves are pressed together and molten polyethylene is injected into it. Pressure is maintained for one to

---

[1]Frisbee is a registered trademark of the Wham-O Company; therefore all Frisbees *per se* come from them. Plat Volante (French), Disco (Mexican), Flygende Tallerken (Norwegian), Whrympl Platte (Ivy League), Flying Saucer, Discus Plasticus, Plastic Plate, Flying Disc, Friz'Bee, and Whizgig are a few other disc names.

[2]Several models—Hasbro-Glo, the Nerf Disc, the Psychedelic—offend this dictum, and they suffer for it.

[3]The Nerf Ring and the Bozo Flyer are made of Styrofoam.

[4]Fred Morrison made his original flying saucer in cold unstable butyl and stearate plastic. It broke into smithereens every time the sun went down!

[5]This corresponded closely in time to the dropping of the five Olympic-like rings from the cupola label. "Olympic Frisbees" are prize possessions. Frisbees made in Canada until recently carried the "Olympic label." An Olympic-label, Mold 1 disc, has sold for as much as thirty dollars.

[6]Because the flight plate flaps in flight.

two seconds,[7] then released (creating the parting line—the line of Shelton) —and the new Frisbee is born. At this point, still hot, it will warp as it cools unless the flight plate is supported by pegs. Wham-O contracts with a half dozen plastic molders in the Los Angeles area. They also lease molds to other countries, including Canada, Great Britain, South Africa, Belgium, Australia, Denmark and France. Foreign Frisbees are not so different from their American counterparts. The plastic is shinier and a bit less pliable, and Canadian Pros for some reason have a longer lip and inferior hot-stamping.

The mold itself is in two pieces, called concave and convex. After the liquid polyethylene is injected through the *sprue*,[8] into the *gate*,[9] and across the *puddle*,[10] it flows into the mold *cavity*. Injection to separation and finished product takes only a few seconds. Since a mold costs about $20,000, large runs are needed to amortize the cost; so thousands of Frisbees are made in several hours. Five percent is the average spoil per run. Most of the bad spots can be cut out and the remainder remelted[11] and run again.

The raw polyethylene comes to the factory as *nibs*, translucent white bits of polyethylene an eighth of an inch in diameter. For colored Frisbees, the nibs are dyed in rotating drums. The Moonlighter's luminous dye is so heavy that smaller, more expensive nibs must be used.[12]

Ornamentation and Packaging

The finished product is embellished with labels, colored rings[13] and designs put on by the hot-stamping process,[14] and glue-ons.[15] The top of the Frisbee is stamped with a heat press that transfers the color from a mylar sheet. The All-American model with stars and bars is the quintessence of this technique.

I usually peel off labels if I want a streamlined Frisbee.[16] The owner's-identification-number label on the Wham-O Master is hopefully good for its intended purpose, so leave it on. Glue-ons such as the spiral on the newer models of the Psychedelic Disc[17] are ugly and impede air flow.

of little importance to the sportsman but for one exception. Because cer-

Vic Malafronte surrounded by one of the world's largest Frisbee collections—over 500 flying discs.

---

[7]Under approximately 22,000 pounds *per square inch.*
[8]Becomes The Bead of Barrett.
[9]Later the navel.
[10]The nipple.
[11]Some experts feel remelted plastic, for a chemical reason, makes a stronger Frisbee. Research is needed here.
[12]The Moonlighter plastic is the best polyethylene yet used in Frisbee making. See Chapter 10 for its use in the repair of cracked Frisbees.
[13]Color bands first appeared on the Pro model.
[14]The first use of hot-stamping I know of was on Empire Plastic's late fifties Zolar.
[15]The glue-on replaced the original colored spiral and is on backwards. The psychedelic spinning effect occurs with a counterclockwise spin only.
[16]However, I write the date of purchase on each disc.
[17]Eagle Rubber Company, Ashland, Ohio.

Professional Model Label

Inspector's Label for Balance

Olympic Ring Professional Label

Fastback Label—Premium Version

All American Label

Olympic Ring Mini Label

Special Mini Label for the 12th IFT.

Master Label

Master's Identification Label

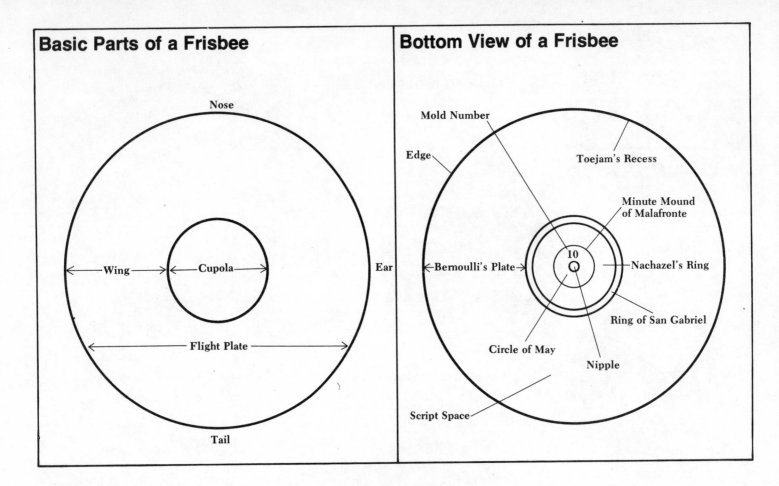

Basic Parts of a Frisbee

Nose

Wing — Cupola

Ear

Flight Plate

Tail

Bottom View of a Frisbee

Mold Number

Edge

Toejam's Recess

Minute Mound of Malafronte

Bernoulli's Plate

10

Nachazel's Ring

Ring of San Gabriel

Circle of May

Nipple

Script Space

tain molds[18] are better than others, especially for distance, the mold number should be visible. It is a demonstration of commercial crassness to cover it with the package. This hinders a person from completing his collection.[19] Wham-O has not yet responded to collectors' pleas on this problem.

The Basic Model and Nomenclature

The following is a long-needed nomenclature for the Frisbee. You will note that the same part or place often has several names. The first is the preferred or the more widely accepted name. Most of the terms are derived from great Frisbee masters and champions or promulgators of the sport. As much as possible this nomenclature will be used to describe other flying discs. If noteworthy modifications exist on other flying discs, they will be identified.

[18]Wham-O insists their Pro molds are standardized, but there are differences. Mold number 1 is probably the best all around. Look out for the late-comer reversed numeral 1—bad. Mold 10 is good, and 14, usually. (See Table of Wham-O Pro Molds in Appendix.) Mold 4's are almost all gone, and just as well. The original number 1 mold was later used in Canada and South Africa.

[19]The best Frisbee collections? John Kirkland has over 700 discs, followed closely by the combined Dan Roddick-Gary Seubert collection. Malafronte has over five hundred flying discs.

The Pro Model

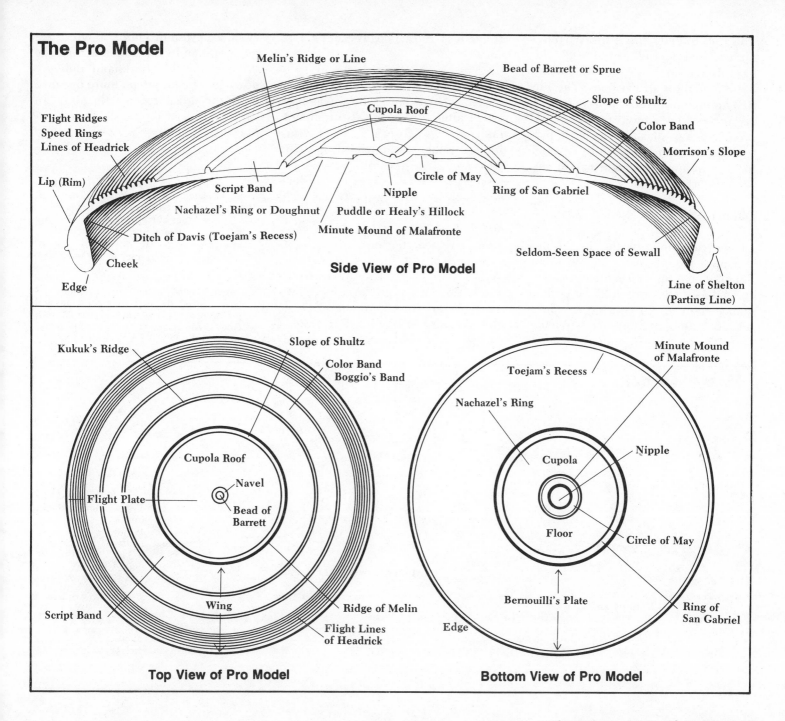

Melin's Ridge or Line

Bead of Barrett or Sprue

Slope of Shultz

Cupola Roof

Color Band

Flight Ridges
Speed Rings
Lines of Headrick

Morrison's Slope

Circle of May

Lip (Rim)

Script Band

Nipple

Ring of San Gabriel

Nachazel's Ring or Doughnut

Puddle or Healy's Hillock

Ditch of Davis (Toejam's Recess)

Minute Mound of Malafronte

Seldom-Seen Space of Sewall

Cheek

Edge

Line of Shelton
(Parting Line)

Side View of Pro Model

Kukuk's Ridge

Slope of Shultz

Color Band
Boggio's Band

Cupola Roof

Navel

Flight Plate

Bead of
Barrett

Script Band

Wing

Ridge of Melin

Flight Lines
of Headrick

Top View of Pro Model

Minute Mound
of Malafronte

Toejam's Recess

Nachazel's Ring

Cupola

Nipple

Floor

Circle of May

Bernouilli's Plate

Edge

Ring of
San Gabriel

Bottom View of Pro Model

The Pro. I have chosen the Wham-O professional model (the Pro),[20] the best all-around Frisbee extant, as the basic model for all Frisbees. The Pro first appeared in 1964. It has come to us from seven molds, in six colors, three types of plastic, two basic patterns of hot-stamping, and a special form with luminous dye called the Moonlighter.

Other Wham-O Models

In comparison with the Pro, other Wham-O models have less to offer. Several have interesting features and special uses (see appendix for performance ratings). Of course, this does not include the Super-Pro—Wham-O's 1974 souped-up, larger, heavier, cupola-less Pro. Also, the cupola is gone.

Master Frisbee. The large 150-gram Master, in black and white, was patterned after the earlier Tournament model and was designed to be the supreme Frisbee. It appeared in 1970. It has excellent lines of Headrick on the top surface as well as the underside[21]—to improve grip. It has *two* color bands and a cupola like the Pro model. The Master fails as a topnotch Frisbee because the flight plate is too soft for the mass and "bubbles" in flight. The lip structure is only fair and needs more weight. Many players find its diameter (27.4 cm.) awkward to handle. For underhanders, it's almost impossible to avoid a Thwart of Thor.[22] If winds are moderate and very favorable and the thrower has his backhand delivery down pat, he might get more distance with the Master than the Pro. In strong winds at the beach, it is superior,[23] although not as good as an old

---

[20]The label calls this a *sport model*. The term never caught on. Each Pro mold has been reworked at least three dozen times.

[21]Called the Rings of Hellring. Buzzy Hellring was the prime author of the Ultimate Frisbee game rules. He was killed in a car crash in early 1971; a great loss to Frisbee.

[22]Discussed in Chapter 3.

[23]There are two Frisbee crowds: grass and beach. Beach Bees are style-conscious and prefer heavy plates such as the Master; Grass Bees are distance and game freaks and nod the Pro.

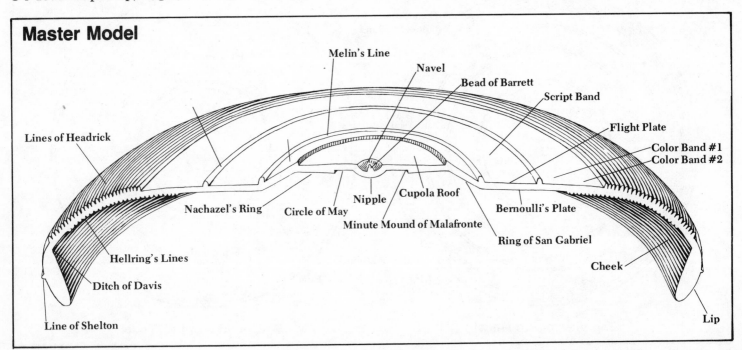

Master Model

Melin's Line
Navel
Bead of Barrett
Script Band
Lines of Headrick
Flight Plate
Color Band #1
Color Band #2
Nachazel's Ring
Circle of May
Nipple
Cupola Roof
Bernoulli's Plate
Hellring's Lines
Minute Mound of Malafronte
Ring of San Gabriel
Ditch of Davis
Cheek
Line of Shelton
Lip

Tournament model (especially the Y model). Is the Master used in tournaments? Not in any tournaments I've seen. It has not replaced the Pro and is not the design to do so.

Regular Frisbee. For years the regular Frisbee was the Pluto Platter, and it was an adequate performer. Regular I replaced the Pluto Platter with lines of Headrick on Morrison's slope. Now the Regular II has a more sloped cupola with flight rings on the cupola roof.[24] Neither is better than the old Pluto Platter. (Incidentally, the way to tell an original Morrison Pluto Platter from Wham-O's Pluto Platter is quite easy: the original Morrison does not have Wham-O in the script.) Regulars are best for children.

All American. The All American was Wham-O's attempt to improve their Pro model. The cupola is deleted. In its place on the undersurface is a flat plate[25] of reinforcing plastic 2 millimeters thick. On the topside is an array of hot-stamping in red, white, and blue with elaborate script. The label shows an American bald eagle, talons clutching Frisbees, with the saying, "E Pluribus Frisbee." There is mixed opinion about the All American model. It is heavier and performs well, but it is not as stable as a good Pro. So far, molds 10 and 14 lead the field. The garish design offends the dedicated player, although it is eye-pleasing and an aid to commercial success.

Fastback. The Fastback is Wham-O's newest offering, and it is their widest departure in design in years. Dick Gillespie, director of Frisbee design at Wham-O, heated the flight plate of the Pro with a blowtorch, lowering its height, and made a faster Frisbee. His original purpose was to develop a speedier missile for the Guts game.[26] Gillespie's final model has a pronounced groove on the top surface—a reversed Morrison slope

---

[24]No advantage in them, baroque decoration only.

[25]Plate of Blake.

[26]It is not needed in the minds of most Guts players. The Pro's capacity of 85 mph plus is enough. Throwing is ahead of catching in the game. Improved catching techniques, e.g., the Headrick Claw Catch, are needed now.

Regular Model

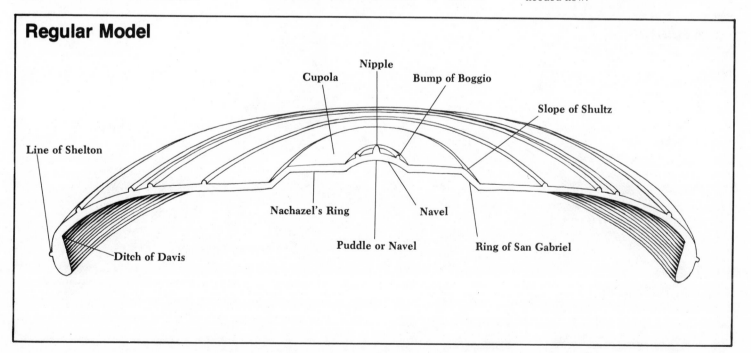

Line of Shelton · Ditch of Davis · Cupola · Nipple · Bump of Boggio · Slope of Shultz · Nachazel's Ring · Navel · Puddle or Navel · Ring of San Gabriel

All American

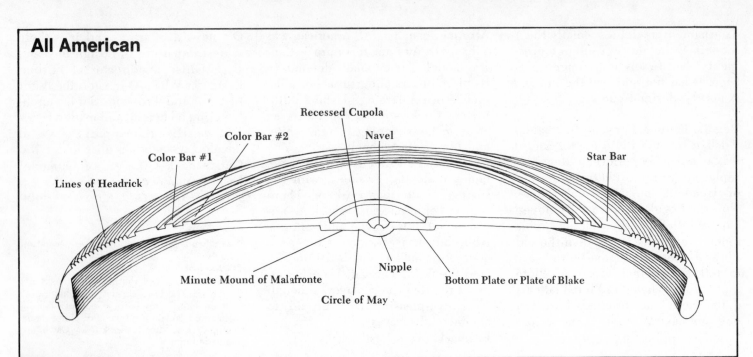

Recessed Cupola

Color Bar #2

Color Bar #1

Navel

Star Bar

Lines of Headrick

Minute Mound of Malafronte

Nipple

Bottom Plate or Plate of Blake

Circle of May

Horseshoe

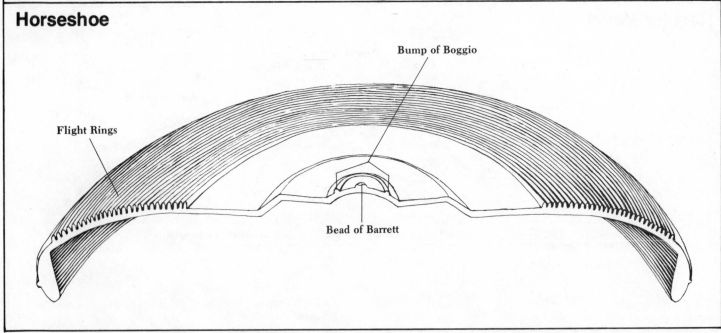

Bump of Boggio

Flight Rings

Bead of Barrett

called Gillespie's groove. Beginner players will like this indentation; it gives them a place for their thumb on the top surface in the common grip. But sidearm throwers, particularly two-finger stylists, hate this bulging undersurface. Nor do distance throwers like the Fastback, since it turns over very badly after 25 yards. It does go faster, but it also has greater impact in the catch. I can't recommend it for the Guts game in top-flight competition. It also has a tendency to break where the flight plate joins the lip (the Seldom Seen Space of Sewall). Fastbacks rip in Sewell's space because of the inherent structural weakness of Gillespie's groove.

Horseshoe (Speedy) Model. This Frisbee is a lightweight copy of the old Speedy model (now extinct) and found only in early versions of the Horseshoe game. The Horseshoe, for all the world, looks like a shrunk regular. It is a fun Frisbee, best indoors, but not as safe as the mini-model. Nor is it as good an overall performer as the older, heavier Speedy; although the Speedy, with higher-density polyethylene, cracked easily. The game is played like regular horseshoes with ring stakes for targets, but the Horseshoe saucer is too light for outdoor play. The game was improved several years later by substituting with the Regular.

Tournament Models. There were three models in this group: Tourna-ment, Sailing Satellite, and the Mystery-Y. All were big rascals and, therefore, good for beach play. The Tournament was one of the first Frisbees made[27] after the Pluto Platter, and in 1968 the Tournament mold was retooled to make the Master Frisbee. The Sailing Satellite was a lighter and softer version of the Tournament plate and therefore a poor actor for the theater of the berm.

The best was the Mystery-Y.[28] It was heavier with a firm flight plate showing two players, one with a Y (Yale?) on his tee shirt. The mystery: Who really made it? Wham-O packaged and sold it but admits it was one of their "adopted" Frisbees, i.e., they bought someone else's mold and "adopted" its offspring. Whoever fathered it made a superior plate. It has fantastic hovering qualities and sufficient weight with a sharp edge to cut through offshore gusts. It is the best beach Frisbee. Another mystery: Directions for a one-on-one Guts game are on the under surface. Could the Mystery-Y maker also be the father of the heretofore fatherless Guts game?

Mini-Frisbees. The Mini's[29], designed for indoor play and rainy days, were an effort to cash in on the popularity of their outdoor uncles. The original looked like a miniature Pro and, designwise, was very pleasing. Mini-II imitates Regular II with flight lines on the cupola roof. The Mini is strictly an indoors plate. I have used them to test aerodynamic theories in windless conditions. They are excellent for indoors Frisbee golf and basketball. Because they are so small, they are difficult to catch one-handed. All of the usual throws can be done with a Mini and the outside spider throw is unique to it.[30]

Other Flying Discs

"Oh Hamlet,
"What a falling off was there!"

—William Shakespeare

Most people will pick up any plastic flying saucer and call it a Frisbee. Not so! Only Wham-O's saucers can be called Frisbees. Roger Barrett, curator of Wham-O's Flying Disc Museum, The Wall of Fame, estimates that there may be as many as two thousand different *flying discs,* the now accepted generic name for plastic flying saucers. And, if one counts all the premiums,[31] knock-offs,[32] colors, and mold numbers, there may be as many as twelve thousand.

The number of discus plasticus producers is unknown. Too often companies will contract the same

---

[27]Circa 1961.

[28]Just to complicate things, I now know of a smaller, Pro-size Mystery-Y.

[29] White Mini's replaced the traditional rice at the wedding of Sue Bullman and I.F.A. Master Jim Randa in Chicago.

[30]Unless you have hands like Wilt Chamberlain.

[31]A premium is an advertising disc such as the Kool-Aid (I-2) or Keds (I-6). As a class they say much more than they do.

[32]A knock-off is a toy term for an imitation or facsimile of the original.

plastic manufacturer to make their model. All these cousin saucers will bear strong resemblance to one another except for minor ornamental details. Many toy makers want a flying disc in their line, but do not want the expense of developing their own model. For the serious Frisbee player, this practice is not enthusiastically received. It is not cheap imitations and minor variations we need, but serious design improvements based on sound physical principles and streamlining concepts. We hear about rocket-powered Frisbees and biodegradable plastic discs, and these are interesting: but the genuine advances will come from applying basic flying-disc research, such as in the ill-fated naval flare study in designing the discus plasticus of the future.

The table below lists seventy-four flying discs in nine categories.

FLYING DISCS (other than Wham-O's)

A. Antique

1. Frisbie Pie Tin
2. Tenite
3. Arcuate Vane (Pipco)
4. Flyin' Saucer (Pipco)
5. Lil' Abner (Pipco)
6. Y-Models
7. Dartmouth
8. Sky Pie (Hall)
9. Zo-lar (Empire)
10. Saucer
11. Scalo
12. Space Saucer
13. Cow That Jumped Over the Moon
14. Angel

B. Serious

1. Saucer Tosser (CPI)
2. All Star (CPI)
3. Twirl-A-Boom
4. Flinger II (Skyway)
5. Flying Saucer (Cossom)
6. Whizz (Reliable)
7. Tosserino (Oregon Novelty)
8. Super Saucer (Amsun)

C. Toys

1. Explorer II (Cox)
2. Nerf Disc (Parker)
3. Bozo Fun Flyere (Brooklyn Products)
4. Flinger I (Skyway)
5. Psychedelic Disc & Comet (Eagle)
6. Hasbro-Glo
7. Flapjack (Fun Stoff)
8. Flying Bottlecaps (Potter)
9. Whirl-King (Sock-It)
10. Giant Saucer Tosser (CPI)
11. M-R
12. Brand X
13. Catch-It (Remco)

D. Experimentals, Variations and Mysteries

1. Tee Bird (Allentown Scientific Associates)
2. Tee Bird Tournament (ASA)
3. Gyrospin Gee Whizzer (ASA)
4. Whiz Ring (North Pacific Products)
5. Master Whiz Ring (NPP)
6. Mini Whiz Ring (NPP)
7. Atlantis

E. Knock-Offs (Domestic)

1. Sportcraft [B-5]
2. Super Zinger (Chem Toy) [B-1]
3. Scaler (Whiffle) D-4
4. Zing Wing (Azrak-Hamway) [B-8]
5. Gold Medal Winner
6. Scaler (Vercal)
7. Best Ever [I-12]

F. Knock-Offs (Foreign)

1. Boom-A-Ring (Hong Kong) [D-4]
2. Disco (Hong Kong) Wham-O Pro
3. Disc—Voll Mod. Inho

G. Licenses (Foreign)

1. Irwin Toy—Canada, Whom-O
2. S.S.F.—Germany, Whom-O
3. Manu S.A.—Belgium Wham-O
4. Wembley—England [D-1]
5. Venor—Norway [C-6]
5. International Games of Canada—CPI Products

H. Foreign Originals

1. Plasticum Flying Saucer (German)
2. P.P. Swing Poletten (German)
3. Spiel Sport Freiten (German)
4. Mego—Hong Kong
5. Foreign Flying Saucer
6. Harlem Globetrotter Flying Whiz (Larami, Hong Kong)
7. Belly Button (Barrett, England)

I. Premiums

1. Firestone
2. Kool-Aid (Amsun) [B-8]
3. Fly Navy (Amsun) [B-8]
4. Burger Chef (Amsun) [B-8]
5. Herfy's (Republic Tool and Mfg. Co.)
6. Keds (J.V. Zimmerman)
7. Oreo
8. Diz-Bee
9. Cap'n Crunch (CPI)
10. California (Oregon Novelty) [B-7]
11. Hang Ten (Brand X) [C-12]
12. Saucer Tosser—Single Cupola (CPI)

Legend:

( ) = manufacturer or country of origin, if known.
[ ] = disc in bracket is original disc.

Antique Flying Discs

Flying discs made before 1960 are considered antiques by collectors. The Frisbie Pie Tin, the Arcuate Vane, the Flyin' Saucer, and the Y-models have already been described. The story behind the Tenite and the Lil' Abner discs reveals a bit more about the making of the discus plasticus.

The first plastic disc was hand-carved by Fred Morrison from a solid block of tenite.[33] It was a crude prototype for a Frisbee. But it flew better than pie tins. Morrison took his whittled saucer to Southern California Plastics Company of Los Angeles, headed by Mr. Edward S. Kennedy.[34] The Arcuate Vane mold was made there, and it was produced in two versions: hard (butyl stearate) and soft (polyethylene). The hard version—sometimes called a Pipco[35] crab—was also made up into Lil' Abner discs.

The Lil' Abner would have been the first premium disc if the arrangement with Al Capp had gone through. It didn't; Pipco's hard Arcuate Vane with a Lil' Abner label pasted on is a disc collector's dream.

The Dartmouth. The Dartmouth is a legendary plate. None are known to exist. Ex-Dartmouth students flushed with excitement over their Guts Frisby Game (see page 75) allegedly made and sold a 1959 plastic disc in the Chicago area. Numbers A-10 through A-14 are known to me but I haven't examined one yet.

Two antiques representative of the group are described below.

The Zolar (Empire Plastics, New York City). A late fifties disc (probably 1958), Zolar apparently had the first silk-screened design on a disc—a white, three-pronged surrealistic ring around a shallow cupola. There's a large nipple, no navel, and a sharp Francioni angle. My Zolar is flimsy by today's standards, but considering its day, it's a worthy disc.

Sky Pie (Hall Manufacturing, Los Angeles). Sky Pie may be older than Zolar; it's certainly different. They must have thrown away the mold, for no one has made anything like it since. The plate is flat and soft with a large central hole (the disc was apparently caught on a triangular wire on the end of a stick), and the lip, its strangest feature, is flat and thin and extends equally above and below the flight plate. This weird rim is open every ninety degrees—perhaps for gripping.

The most interesting thing about Sky Pie is its name. Does it relate to the Frisbie Pie Company? I don't know.

Serious Discs

These are good playing flying discs. Some in the G and H foreign group (see table) are good performers too.

The Saucer Tosser. The Saucer Tosser is produced by Concept Products, Inc., of Minneapolis. Its outstanding feature is simplicity. There are no flight lines, the script[36] is kept to a minimum—the name, nothing else. The nipple-navel pattern is an imitation of Wham-O's Pro model. The lip structure is well done, with adequate thickness. Morrison's slope is weak and needs improvement. A weak Morrison's slope leads to turn-over problems, and this is the ST's greatest fault. There is double-cupola design,[37] which seems unnecessary and should be eliminated.

[33]A plastic compound from Eastman Kodak Chemical, usually used in making extrusion parts.

[34]In personal correspondence, Mr. Kennedy told me Morrison had a compeer, Warren Francioni. Kennedy said that they had created the tenite model together. I traced Francioni to Norway in 1973, where he was serving as a colonel in the U.S. Air Force. He confirmed Kennedy's story and said he would fill in the rest of the story when he retired from active duty in 1974. Colonel Francioni died suddenly in 1974, several months before he was to have returned to the United States. I have named a vital feature of Frisbee design in his honor—the angle the lip (rim) makes with the flight plate as it toes in toward center—the Francioni angle. I asked Colonel Francioni if the original tenite disc still existed; he feared it was discarded in the excitement of making Arcuate Vanes. If it's still around it's probably hiding on some musty shelf or bargain box in a thrift shop in San Luis Obispo, Francioni and Morrison's home at the time.

[35]Morrison's company. John Kirkland paid $57 for his "Pipco Crab"—the highest price ever paid for a flying disc.

[36]Wham-O started this scribbling business on Frisbees, and it does nothing for the streamlining effect. Serious players have even resorted to sanding their models smooth.

[37]CPI makes a single-cupola model Saucer Tosser but just for "premium" plates; consequently it is poorer in quality.

CPI All Star. The Saucer Tosser was a promising start from this midwest company. Perhaps a good, serious disc would soon be launched from Minneapolis.

In the spring of 1972, CPI released their best model to date—the All Star. It is larger and heavier than the Saucer Tosser or, for that matter, Wham-O's Pro. A remarkable thing about the All Star is its resistance to breakage. (All Star is the best of all discs with a breakage score of 94 —see Flying Disc Performance Table, page 202).

There is only one cupola, no flight lines or bars, and minimum script and hot stamping. The Morrison's slope is much steeper than the Pro's, and the flight plate is twice as thick as an All American. It may be the best distance model available today, but it's too heavy for Guts competition (see page 75).

Twirl-A-Boom. The rare Twirl-A-Boom! I only know of one—in the Malafronte collection. It has the best plastic of any disc, bar none. And the best Morrison's slope and greatest stability of all flying saucers, save the CPI's All Star. Who made it? Where's the mold? All unknown.

Malafronte has thrown his Twirl-A-Boom in distance meets rarely and only over soft ground. The beast is too rare to risk. Where did you come from Twirl-A-Boom?

The Flinger. The Flinger is manufactured by Skyway Products, Brooklyn, New York. The original Flinger was a crude model, 22.5 centimeters in diameter, without a cupola or any nipple or navel structure. The Flinger I had crude flight rings (lines of Headrick) very wide apart. It gave promise of something better despite an atrocious turn-over tendency. It had an excellent Morrison's slope, clean lines, and good workmanship. The coming of the Flinger II was anxiously awaited. There were two significant changes. The flight lines were replaced by flight bars. These are circular bands alternately raised and lowered on the flight plate. The second change was the plastic. Instead

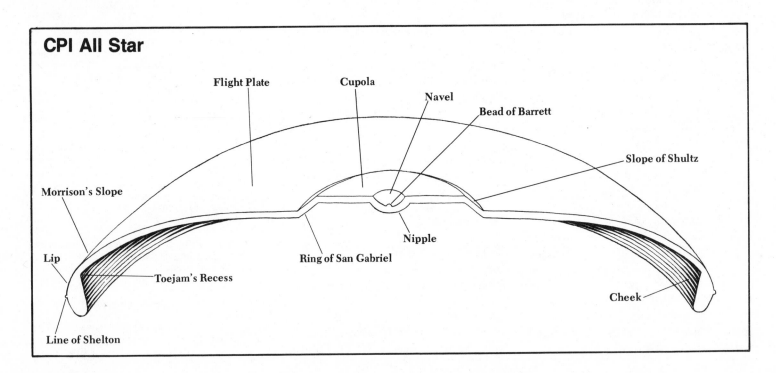

CPI All Star

Flight Plate

Cupola

Navel

Bead of Barrett

Slope of Shultz

Morrison's Slope

Lip

Toejam's Recess

Line of Shelton

Ring of San Gabriel

Nipple

Cheek

of brittle, near-clear stuff, Flinger II came in a tough and flexible form as good as Wham-O's best. Still, Flinger II is an inferior model. If the diameter were increased and quality control enforced, it would definitely benefit.

Tosserino. This slick-finish, straightforward plate is hard to find. The mold is usually cranking out premiums like "California" and "Sailors have more fun." The manufacturer, Oregon Novelty, has the dubious distinction of being the greatest premium maker in the disc world. The Tosserino is a low-profile plate with a relatively huge cupola.[38] It's a decent disc but can't compete with an All Star or a Twirl-A-Boom.

Toys

Some flying discs are nothing more than toys. Many will have an amusing feature, such as electric lights or psychedelic streamers, or will fold in a pocket. Some examples follow:

The Cox Lighted Model. The L. M. Cox Company makes the only lighted flying disc. Housed in two wing nacelles are triple A pen-light batteries and the tiniest light bulbs you can find.[39] Centrifical force of the whelm (see page 56) presses the contact plates shut, resulting in in-flight illumination!

The script band calls it the Explorer II. The cupola is a huge, boxish, transparent affair covering a hand-painted space cockpit with two astronauts sitting back-to-back, gazing at a rocket control panel. This disc is so pretty I never throw it; moreover it is almost impossible to find the wee bulbs. The Cox is rare. I found mine around Christmas, 1969.

The Nerf Disc (Parker Brothers). This Styrofoam disc cousin to the Nerf Ball is the lightest and softest saucer around. It can be thrown on either

---

[38]For stamping on those little messages like "Eat at Joe's."
[39]Try Hk 1.2 volt size.

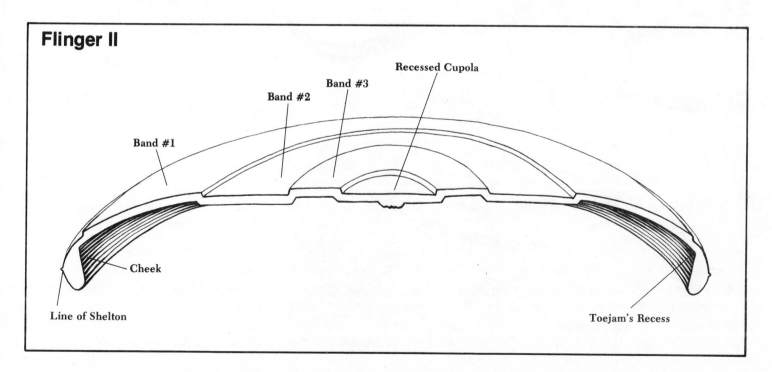

Flinger II

Recessed Cupola

Band #3

Band #2

Band #1

Cheek

Line of Shelton

Toejam's Recess

side. The recounting of its virtues is concluded.

Psychedelic Disc (Eagle Rubber Company, Ashland, Ohio.) This is an exceptionally thick plate. It takes its name from a red and blue spiral pattern glued[40] on the top. This decoration is backwards for the psychedelic effect and only appears with counterclockwise spins. As in the Hasbro-Glo and Nerf Disc, the lip is flat. The Psychedelic Disc recently appeared with four 18-inch-long ribbon streamers pinned to a central revolving ring. This whirling dervish is called the Comet.

The Hasbro-Glo Model. The only saucer with an upside-down cupola. Otherwise, it has little else worth noting. The lip is flat like the Nerf Disc, which ruins it for running. I recently saw a Hasbro-Glo without the glo, from Norway.[41] Bought in a small shop in the hinterlands by American students, it had lain in a hardware store for months, and no one knew what it was until the American seized it, delighting the Norwegians with saucer tosses in the streets. I commend Hasbro for their unique design efforts, but it's back to the drawing board for a better flyer.

Flapjack (Fun Stuff of Santa Monica, California). The absolute worst flying disc in the world, it's made of rub-

---

[40]Older Psychedelic Discs had the spiral pattern silk-screened.
[41]The UFO, Flygende Tallerken, by Venor.

bery stuff, wads up in your hand, droops when you grip it—it's impossible. The only use I can imagine for it would be as the pocket handkerchief in your tux at the Marquis De Sade's dress ball.

The Giant Saucer Tosser (GST). This is the biggest saucer of all—nearly eleven centimeters larger than Wham-O's Master. Otherwise the GST is virtually identical to its little brother, ST. Because of its exceptional weight and volume, this plate shows some very unusual features in flight. It develops more momentum, an increased period of waft (see page 61), and is a rascal to catch. With its surprising momentum, it disrupts

timing and can even hurt your mitt. It's quite awkward to handle and throw. It is tempting to throw it two-handed "a la Pancho Segura." It flies quite well, perhaps better than its little brother, and turns over less. I do not recommend serious play or practice with the GST. I have seen many good players baffled by the giant as it flies by them, surprised by its velocity and prolonged waft. It is an excellent beach model. If it were a bit heavier, it would be even better. A still larger model? I can't see the use for it. This giant is also known as the Garbage Can Lid.

The Catch-It. Remco toymakers make this unusual-looking disc. The flight

rings radiate like spokes[42] and occupy the outer fifth of the top surface. It has the largest cupola relative to diameter of any disc. There is disagreement about whether the center is a small cupola or a huge exaggerated nipple. I favor the latter. The Catch-It is as intricate in design as any model. The plastic, as in the Cox lighted model, is rigid polyethylene. It should break, but I haven't broken one yet. But I use it so seldom, since it turns over ferociously.

---

[42]Somewhat like Morrison's Spoilers on the Arcuate Vane model.

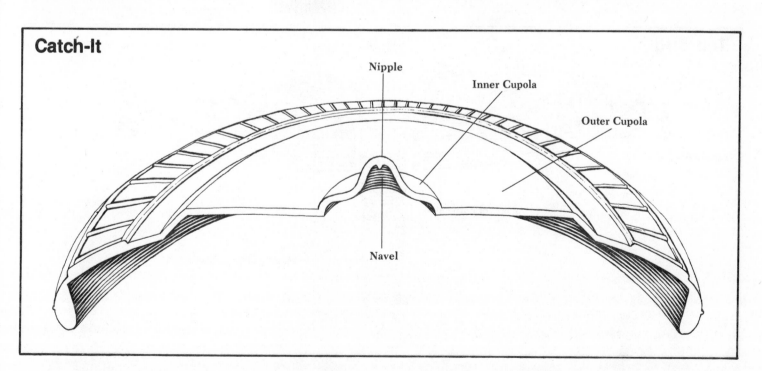

Catch-It

Nipple

Inner Cupola

Outer Cupola

Navel

Experiments, Variations, and Mysteries

This is a mixed bag of way-out discs, including the difficult-to-categorize Flying Rings. The D Group in the table is certainly innovative, but they are not good flyers.

The Tee Bird. This silly saucer deserves its name. The navel drops eleven centimeters below the flight plate to form a center handle for catching. This "tee" spoils the skipping game but introduces a potential new catch—*the one-fingered upside-down navel catch.* The Tee Bird has nice plastic, Hellring lines and spokes. The Allentown (Pa.) Scientific Associates Makers are to be congratulated for their design. The dolphins at the San Francisco Aquarium are entranced by the Tee Bird: it fits their snouts nicely, and they are becoming avid players. Quality control is excellent, but the Bird is not a serious flying disc; turn-over is outrageous. The Tee Bird also comes in a larger model, actually two: the Tournament and the Gyro-Spin Gee Whizzer with four and eight flight-plate holes, respectively.

The Whiz Ring (North Pacific Products, Bend, Ore.). Perhaps the most unusual flying saucer of all. It is not a flying saucer in the usual sense, but a ring—a very skinny, hard plastic ring. It earns the nickname, *The Halo,* with a diameter of only 3.8 centimeters (1½ inches) that leaves a central open space of 16 centimeters. How does it fly? Well, it does, and the secret is, it is more than a ring. It is an airfoil. The 1½-inch wing develops lift according to Bernoulli's theorem. I have called it a circular flying disc, that is, a half a disc drawn into a circle, if you can visualize that. It is too light for fast and distance throwing, and is made of brittle stuff. It has a frightful turn-over which can only be remedied by a hyper-Hyzer release. A special point for the Whiz Ring, it is excellent for training the young player to catch. (see Performance Table catching score in Appen-

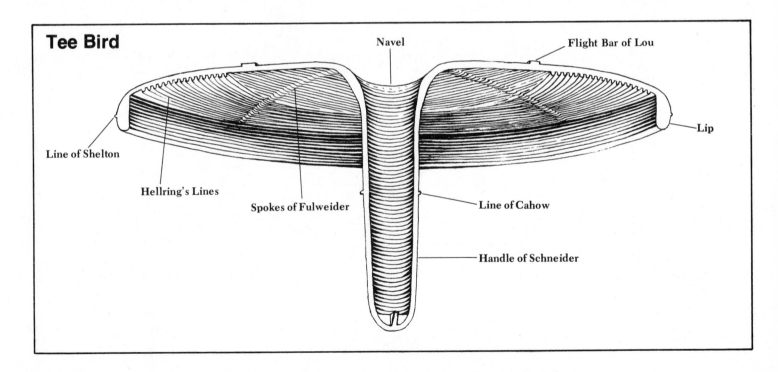

Tee Bird

Navel

Flight Bar of Lou

Lip

Line of Shelton

Hellring's Lines

Spokes of Fulweider

Line of Cahow

Handle of Schneider

dix). The Pro Whiz Ring is a considerably better flyer. I carry one in my folf bag for overhead throws in strong crosswinds. North Pacific also makes the Mini Whiz Ring, which might make a nice bracelet for a large-wristed girl.

The Atlantis. This disc is the rarest I have; actually it's on loan to me from the forest ranger who found it washed up on the shores of Point Lobos, just south of Carmel. I call it the Atlantis, for I fancy it came from that fabled place. No disc expert can identify it. It's 8¾ inches in diameter, with a four-inch rounded cupola rising almost half an inch above the flight plate. There is one large Headrick line in the middle of the flight plate. The cheek width is very small—one centimeter, with a sharp Francioni angle. Mine is red, medium hard, and a collector's dream.

Knock-Offs—Domestic

These simulacrum saucers are the bane of Frisbee.

Identified Flying Object (IFO Flying Saucer). The House of Sportcraft is well known for sporting goods. The souls of Frisbee players warmed with the expectation of a Sportcraft saucer. However, the product did not live up to hopes.[43] It had one good feature—

---

[43]It turned out to be identical to the *Cossom* of Minneapolis and is, apparently, made by them for Sportcraft. The Cossom is a decent enough disc but not in a class with the All Star of CPI.

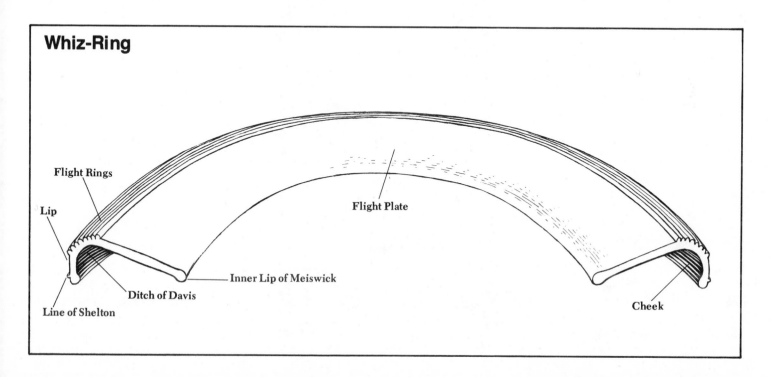

Whiz-Ring

Flight Rings

Lip

Flight Plate

Inner Lip of Meiswick

Ditch of Davis

Line of Shelton

Cheek

not a single mark of identification. The only script on the beast was "made in U.S.A.," plus a mold number, inconspicuously stenciled on the underside. This trend is commendable and should be imitated. It's the only way to achieve a perfectly balanced disc. The Sportcraft had good plastic, with a double-cupola design, which is more ornamental than optimum: The Morrison's slope factor is poor and the lip, sorry to say, weak and shallow.

Superzinger (Chemtoy). The Superzinger appears to be identical to CPI's Saucer Tosser (double-cupola model) except that it's thinner and made of cheaper plastic.

The Bozo Fun Flyer. (Brooklyn Products, Brooklyn, Mich.). A knock-off of the Nerf Flying Disc, and a poor one at that. It is a little larger in diameter and made of cheaper foam. It reminds one of a circular artificial household sponge. The undersurface is sculptured to simulate the lip. Of all the discs tested, the Bozo has the poorest performance number. Like the Nerf Disc, it is a harmless household saucer, nothing else, better employed for washing the car.

Knock-Offs—Foreign

Foreign knock-offs are usually cheap imitations of successful domestic discs.

Disco. A rock-hard imitation of an early (circa 1968) Wham-O Pro, com-

SPONGY

NON TOXIC

THE BOZO

FUN FLYER

H98

FF-2

BOZO the CLOWN © Capitol Records, Inc.
Licensed by: LARRY HARMON PICTURES CORP.

BROOKLYN PRODUCTS INC. BROOKLYN, MICHIGAN 49230

plete with an oriental version of an Olympic ring label. This Hong Kong disc is the classic example of the old adage, "Anybody can make anything cheaper."

Licensees. At least four U.S. disc producers have licensed foreign companies to make their plates: Wham-O, CPI, Hasbro, and Allentown Scientific Associates. Wham-O leads with six outlets. The differences are subtle. Often old molds are sent abroad. Wham-O's famous Pro 1 mold performed in Canada until it was recalled to San Gabriel to become mold 10.

Foreign Originals. There is no Nikon or Mercedes-Benz in the Frisbee world. A few non-U.S.A. discs are interesting, even adequate, but to date no challenge to American plastic flying saucer supremacy.

Swing Poletten. This is a fine-looking, solid, 106-gram regular-size saucer. The flight plate has three distinct ring sections. The outer ring is stippled and grips well, the middle ring is smooth and flat, and the inner ring actually slopes down about three millimeters to join with a shallow cupola. The rim is thick and a bit too flat. It's the best of the foreign originals I've tested.

Big Prof Disc (Der Big Spiel Warenfabrik). A hard plate like Catch-It, the Big Prof Disc is from West Germany. It has all the flight faults of other rigid discs. Appearance-wise, it looks a bit like a Wham-O Pro.

Harlem Globetrotter Flying Whiz (Larami, Hong Kong). A little flying ring within a larger one, joined by eight sprues, the Flying Whiz is the crudest-made disc I've seen. Fly 'em together, take 'em apart, take your pick—together they are original, apart they are knock-offs of the Whiz Ring.

Premiums

Some discs are designed to be premiums, e.g., Keds, Firestone, and Oreo. Others are modified from another company's stock, such as Kool-Aid (Amsun's is Super Saucer). Finally, a few companies make a special disc or rework an old one, such as CPI's single-cupola ST, and now Wham-O's modified Fastback.

Kool-Aid (Amsun). This resembles the Flinger II with the recessed script bands. Quality is better than average; I have seen it a few times in tournament distance events. The luminous Kool-Aid is a special find—extra heavy. It is identical to Amsun's Super Saucer.

Keds (J. V. Zimmerman). This is a handsome medium-size disc about the size of Wham-O's Speedy. Zimmerman molded an authentic-looking flying saucer with portholes and rocket exhausts. It's cute, small—and good for tossing to the Pekingese.

Herfy's Hamburger Baseball Cap Disc (Republic Tool and Manufacturing Company, Los Angeles). Matters sank low, even for the premium disc world, when the Herfy/Republic Cap Disc appeared. It comes with a plastic chin strap to wear at the game on Little League day. Then home, snip off the little loop, and *violà!* A flying disc? Well, sort of. It flies about as well as a Herfy Hamburger, but I like the idea of luring the Little Leaguers away from that dangerous ex-national pastime.

3. THE THROW

"The weakest kind of fruit drops earliest to the ground."
—William Shakespeare, *The Merchant of Venice*

Many would-be players put their Frisbees on the top shelf of the closet, unable to make the thing go. Anyone can throw a ball, but throwing a Frisbee takes study and practice. *Al primo colpo, non cade l'albero.*

Basic Grips

Any way you can hold a Frisbee you can throw it. There are five basic grips[1] and three trick ones. Each grip leads to a characteristic throw, which will be described. Grip number one is for beginners and has three throws. Grips two and three each have two throws.

No. 1 — The Common Grip

This grip and its three modified

[1]See Appendix for an advanced system of throws.

The common grip.

forms are primarily for backhand and underhand throws. The thumb is on top, fingers two, three, and four fanning underneath; the fourth finger is pushing against the cheek, braced by the others. The index finger runs along the lip, hooking over the edge. In Frisbee language, this hooking is known as Nortoning.

The Clark-Shelton Modified Common Grip. Separately, the two Frisbee greats, Al Clark and Jay Shelton, developed the first major modification of the common grip. The fingers are pulled away from the lip in the swing. Jay aids this with his power cuff. The thumb above and second finger below pinch the Frisbee, the index finger slides lightly along the rim. This grip increases the arc curve of the throw, and enabled Jay in 1968 to set a world's distance record of 84 yards with his backhand.

The May Modification. Former world distance champion Robert P. May has a grip that's very difficult to imitate; it features maximum stability. All four fingertips press firm against the cheek. The lip rides on top of the palm pads. The thumb bears down on the rim. This grip appears to lack wrist flexibility, but with practice it returns, and the added stability is worth the initial cramp.

The Berkeley Power Grip. The May grip is further modified in the Berkeley power grip. Here the lip slides over the palm pads and rests in the

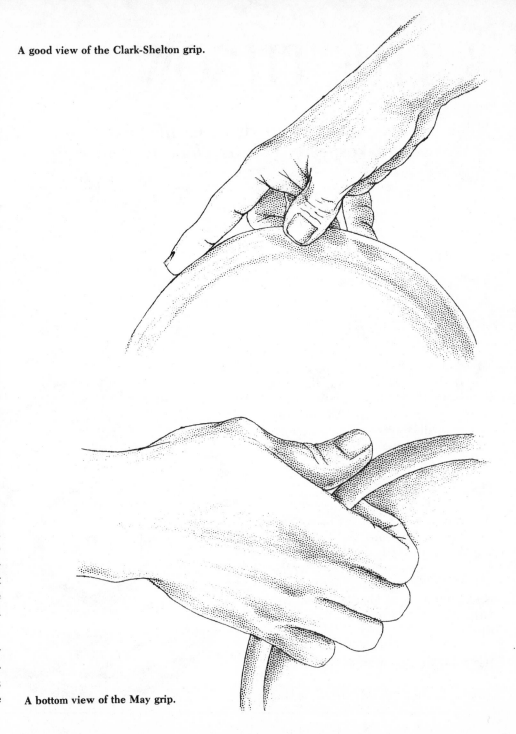

A good view of the Clark-Shelton grip.

A bottom view of the May grip.

Uncurling and whelming in a Steve Sewall backhand delivery.

palm itself; the thumb presses hard on Morrison's slope; all four fingers grip and curl in the cheek. This grip maximizes power; control is its major bugaboo.

The Common Grip Throws

The backhand throw is the favorite of most distance and accuracy throwers, although in power games such as Guts, it is losing favor to forehand throws.

The underhand throw (basic or bowling) is very popular but not as strong as the backhand. It is always done with a common grip or any of its three modifications. (See Question Mark Skip of Pitt, page 64, for the "upside version" of the underhand performed with Grip No. 4.)

No. 2 — The Sidearm or Two-Finger Grip

Any or all of the fingers may be placed on the underside in this grip. The favored form is two, hence it's

The sidearm or two-finger grip.

called the two-finger grip. The release rolls off the forefinger. The thumb is above the line of Shelton and, in the two-finger form, fingers three and four are usually braced against the lip. The index finger braces against and slightly on top of the forefingers.

The Sidearm (Forehand) Throw

The most powerful throws are delivered sidearm style (also called forehand) with either grip No. 2 or No. 3—the thumb. All forehand throws are characterized by the absence of follow-through, like popping a whip. Any follow-through ruins the insertion. The wrist is the key. Extend your right hand in front of you. Now turn it palm side up.

Turn your arm clockwise as far as you can, and now a little farther. That's hypersupination of the wrist,[2] and the better you do that, the better you will throw sidearm.

Behind-the-Back Throw[3]

The sidearm grip can be used with another throw—the behind-the-back, which is one of two throws with a thwart problem (the other is the underarm). It is not just a trick throw. Malafronte of the Berkeley Frisbee Group can get distances of 85+ yards with it.

---

[2]Known sometimes as Johnson's wrist.
[3]The BTB is the principal *stern* shot, i.e., throws from the rear. The others—behind-the-head (BTH) and between-the-legs (BTL)—share the throwing dynamics and difficulties of the BTB.

The behind-the-back throw.

Victor Malafronte shows the side-arm throw. Note thumb on top, index and first finger underneath, with the other fingers bracing the rim. Elbow precedes arm in swing. Hyzer angle developed.

Two views of the thumb grip.

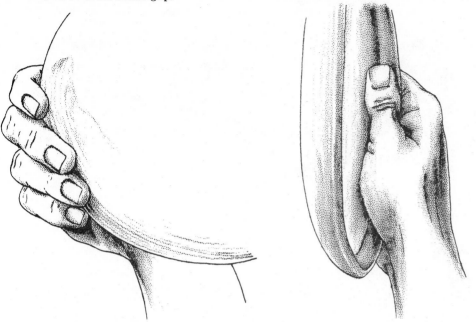

No. 3 — The Thumb Grip

In this grip, the Frisbee is spun off the thumb. The thumb is underneath, the rim, pressing against the cheek, and the four fingers are curled over and around the rim on the top side.

The Thumb Throw and Weyand's Variation

The thumb throw is rapidly becoming the main weapon in Guts games.[4] Its tendency to sink at the line makes it a very hard shot to catch. Thumbers are a bit easier to throw than sidearms or two-fingers, and their effect is probably greater. The thumb grip also gave birth to a variation—the upside-down or Weyand's throw. Named after John Weyand of Berkeley, California, who developed this most unusual throw in Frisbee, it will, in his hands, travel 60 to 70 yards, all upside down. John will use his throw for accuracy if tournament directors allow. Like Kékulé, the upside-down throw occurred to John in a dream.

No. 4 — Overhand-Wrist-Fling Grip (OWF) or Bodá Grip and Throw[5]

This is a slight modification of the thumb grip. The thumb is off the

The upside-down or Weyand throw performed by the originator.

[4]Bob Hanson of the Library Team is the country's leading thumber, with close contention by Joe Essman and John Hodges.
[5]Not to be confused with the simple overhead throw. Sometimes called the overhead, this is a little-used or needed toss off all basic grips. See Folf, page 97, for the overhead throw's usefulness.

Tom Boda demonstrates his overhand-wrist-fling form. Between the second and third photograph, Tom spins completely around. Note the blurred Frisbee's extreme angle of Hyzer, necessary for wafting in this delivery in the third photograph.

cheek and moves into Davis's Ditch or even onto Bernoulli's plate. The fingers are on the top side of the Frisbee and spread for stability. (Note grip in second photograph)

The OWF or Bodá is a throw of the future. Seldom seen in Guts games, it could be a devastating weapon. Ultimate players use it when closely guarded. A Frisbee stylist must have a good OWF—it is the most beautiful throw of all.

No. 5 — Hooked-Thumb Grip[6]

This is the OWF, backhand style. The thumb hooks under the lip and presses against the cheek as the four fingers curve around Morrison's slope. The hooked-thumb grip can be used for a fast return of a thumbs-up catch. It's extremely versatile and lends itself to a powerful underhand throw, a strong overhand, a weak backhand, and a sidearm upside-down.

Trick Grips and Throws

Trick grips aren't truly grips of the Frisbee but rather weak pressings of hand(s) to plate. Their distance and power potential are very limited because the ones with enough "grip" don't have enough curl (see page 56) and vice versa.

---

[6]Believe it or not, there is a hooked toe grip and throw. Slide your big toe into Toejam's Recess and try curving toes one and two over Morrison's Slope. Now, with your back to your unbelieving partner, deliver your toss from the forefoot side. It works, sort of.

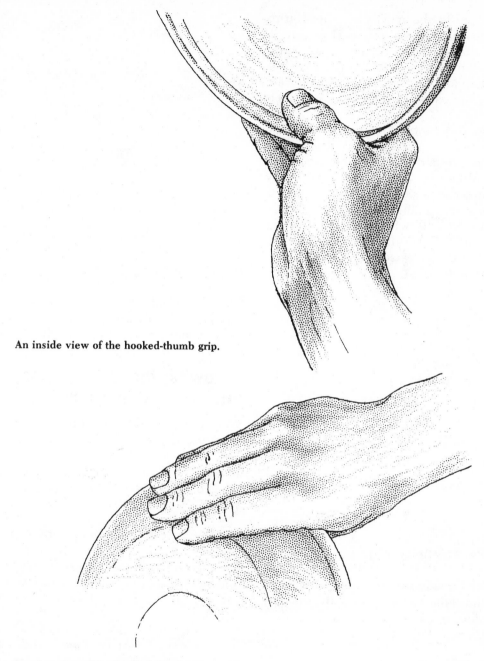

An inside view of the hooked-thumb grip.

Another view of the hooked-thumb grip.

For the most part, these grips are for style and dazzle. However, in Folf (see page 97) in certain traps and roughage—like *inside* a bush!—a cautious finger flip or a delicate inside spider may be your only shot.

No. 6 — Finger Flip and Throw

The finger flip is self-explanatory and can be accomplished with any finger or a pointed object, but it is best with the index finger. You should cuff with the non-throwing hand for stability. The flip can be either clockwise or counterclockwise. Finger flips are snappy throws.

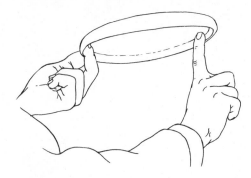

The finger flip grip.

No. 7 — Spider Grip

The inside spider is shown above. If the palm is flat against the concave side of the Frisbee—this is a palm grip or a flat spider. An outside spider requires either small Frisbees or very large hands.

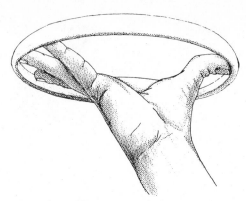

The spider grip.

No. 8 — Hamburger Grip

This is the only two-handed grip in Frisbee. It's really a double spider grip and can be fairly powerful in a backhand throw.

Throwing the Frisbee — Dynamics

We will now find it useful to consider how to put power into the throw and, at the same time, produce a smooth uncurling. The different kinds of throws may be disregarded, since they have the same dynamics.

The Body's Contribution to Throwing

For distance throwing, nearly everyone will use a *run* varying from a few yards to as many as 10 yards. The length of the run seems to contribute little to the flight's distance (unlike in broad jumping). Instead, the run is an exercise between the body and the throwing arm to put maximum coordinated power into the Frisbee at the time of release. The run should be smooth and reproducible. At the end of the run, the body muscles, particularly the long muscles of the legs and back, should have added their maximum force to the throwing arm. The backhand throw lends itself to a greater body power input than the sidearm or the underarm throw. The Bodá may be the equal of the backhand in body power.

The Stance. Accuracy throws are usually delivered without a run and are characterized by ritualistic stances and deliveries. The player usually stands sideways, with his throwing arm toward the target (as in darts). The feet are spread approximately shoulder-width. The free hand is

Steady Ed displays classic stance in accuracy competition at the 12th IFT. Note Frisbee flag high above George Gipp Memorial Pagoda on Eagle Harbor Ballyard.

either trailing for balance (as in fencing), or holding other Frisbees for fast feed and quick throws to find the "groove," or cuffing the wing to lock in the Hyzer and Mung angles.

Cuffing is especially effectual in the backhand throw. It increases the curl, prolongs the moment of uncurling, and heightens the *acceleration* of uncurling, creating a hyper-torque throw.

In the run, Jay Shelton cuffs wing of Frisbee to enhance his distance throw. He uses cuffing to an advantage.

Sighting. Sighting the throwing arm to the target before the swing is a maneuver for accuracy. It enhances concentration. Remember, in Frisbee as in other sports that involve aiming, don't just try to hit the target, aim for

Fred Morrison, father of the plastic Frisbee, positions young player for proper sighting technique.

the small center of it; force your maximum effort.[7]

The Swing

There are two fundamental arm-swings; one for power, the other for accuracy.

The Curve Swing

The curve swing, also called the arc, has greater potential power. Rule: the longer the arm of the thrower, the longer the potential arc swing. And the longer the arc, the greater the potential force, the greater the Frisbee speed, the longer the Frisbee flight. For these reasons, it has been popular lately to note the *ape index* of Frisbee distance throwers, i.e., the length of their arms divided by their height. Bob May has an ape index of 1.041.

Straight Swings

Straight swings, without arc, sacrifice power for simplicity and therefore have more accuracy. The underhand (bowling) throw is essentially a straight swing. However well it has done in distance throwing, the underhand owes to its extra "hours of curl".

Follow-Through

A vital part of the swing of most throws is the follow-through. The only exceptions are the sidearm and thumb deliveries. A developed follow-through will add 10 percent more distance to your throws.

Thwart of Thor

When the swing accidentally strikes the body it's a *thwart:* primary, if the Frisbee hits; secondary, if the hand hits. This dastardly occurrence was named for George "Thor" Anderson, captain of the Foul Five Guts Team of Gary, Indiana, who first displayed this affliction. Besides the underarm, the only other delivery that thwarts is the behind-the-back.

A good straight swing.

"Thor" accepts the new Julis T. Nachazel trophy from the 13th IFT Queen, after Foul Five won the 1970 Guts championship.

The Contribution of Arm and Hand Anomalies to the Swing. There are several curious examples of anomalies of the upper extremity of the body that merit description.

"Fling" Hyzer's flutter ball terrorized the International Frisbee Tournament from 1959 to 1963, and was attributed to his curious six-fingered right hand. Lately the IFA has learned of an Australian Aborigine with two thumbs on his throwing hand and an uncanny degree of accuracy. Finally, there are unconfirmed reports of an Arkansas lad with Ehlers-Danlos Syndrome— "elastic joints"—who has been winning all the local tournaments in the Southwest.

[7]Jim Stowe, self-styled accuracy champion of Birmingham, Alabama, describes his accuracy concentration as "flying with his Frisbee." Jim has two other claims to fame in Frisbee: first to attempt Frisbee play while sky diving, and first to try (still trying) to throw over Little River Canyon in Alabama!

The curve swing featuring Jay Shelton

(1) Throwing arm fully extended, wrist curled, other arm is cuffing. (2) Left leg is moving into throw, back and shoulder muscles are beginning to draw Frisbee forward. (3) Right leg is now moving into throw, elbow is bent, wrist still curled. (4) Wristing begins. Note Frisbee wing across from hand is down. This makes the angle of Hyzer—approximately 20 degrees in this shot. Also notice the Shelton grip—two fingers and thumb holding the rim at whelm. (5) Whelm, wedge and away. Frisbee is already out of the picture.

Letting Go of the Frisbee — Wristing (uncurling)

Wristing, the last part of throwing, is the uncoiling of the wrist. This spins[8] the Frisbee, producing a gyroscopic effect in flight. It must be done smoothly, with as much spin as possible. A weakly spinning Frisbee will quickly fall into a warp.

The O'Clock System. This system describes the amount of curl in the windup in terms of hours. The hand holds the Frisbee at three o'clock; as the hand rotates around the center of the Frisbee, it winds through the number of hours of curl. For example, in the standard backhand, nine *hours* of curl is usual, but in the underhand, as much as twelve hours is possible. The following table lists the potential hours of curl of each delivery.

"HOURS OF CURL"

1=		0
2=		3
3=		6
4=		9
5=		9
6=		6
7=		3
8=	wristing ⟶ whelm	

THROWS	POTENTIAL "HOURS OF CURL"
Backhand	9
Underarm	12
Sidearm	6
Overhand Wrist Fling	6
Thumb Throw	12

Hours of curl. Also shows good backhand throw form.

Frisbee in late whelm and early wedge periods of flight. Note Frisbee is bent from force of release—a possible cause of early wobble or dip. (See Chapter 4).

Whelm (Release, Hatch)

Whelm is the first period of flight;[9] for practical purposes we will consider it briefly here. It is the moment the Frisbee is released from the hand. The critical element of whelming is the *angle* of Hyzer. Release and hatch are other names for whelm.

[8] A *Paradox* throw spins in the *opposite* direction of the expected: in the wristing the plate is twisted in the reverse direction. Uncommon except with backhand and underhand throws.

[9] See Chapter 4.

Angle of Hyzer[10]

This is the angle the Frisbee makes at release in relation to the ground. Hyzer problems are the bane of the beginning player. Rule: the unheld (9 o'clock) side (wing) of the Frisbee is lower at release than the held side. The angle will vary for curve throws and cross and against winds.

Wedge (Insertion) and the Angle of Mung[11]

Wedge is the second period of flight,[12] immediately following whelm and characterized by the angle of Mung, the second vital angle of throw. The Mung angle, sometimes called the angle of attack, is the nose-to-tail angle with the horizon. It is at a 90-degree angle to the Hyzer and is easily seen in the photograph of Steve Sewall. Unlike the Hyzer, the Mung may be absent in short flights, or even be a negative angle, e.g., in skips and dips. Hyper-munging is a common fault seen in distance throwing: the Frisbee wells too much, making a delayed waft and a shortened flight.

Like whelm, wedge is very brief. In short, flat flights whelm may proceed directly to waft without any significant wedge.

---

[10]Named for H. R. "Fling" Hyzer, father of the "Flying Flutterball." It is also called the angle of roll.
[11]Named for Y. E. Mung, Chinese Frisbee great of the early years of IFT.
[12]See Chapter 4.

The Hyzer angle.

Figuring out the correct Mung angle.

Throw Table

Throw	Grip	Spin*	Other Names for Throws
Backhand	One	C	Crossbody, Classic, Graeco-Roman
Underhand	One	C	Bowling, Basic
Sidearm	Two	CC	Sider, Scaling, Forehand, Skimmer, Two-Finger, Radical
Behind the Back	One Two	C CC	Stern Shot
Behind the Head	Five	C	
Behind the Legs	One Two Three Four Five	C CC CC C → CC[2] C → CC[2]	
Upside Down	Three	C → CC[1]	Weyand, Dream Shot
Overhand	One Two Three Four Five	C CC CC CC C	Overhead
Overhand Wrist Fling	Four	CC	Bodá, Discus
Thumb	Three	CC	Underhand-Wrist-Fling, Thumber
Hooked Thumb	Five	C	Reverse Overhand-Wrist-Fling, Backhand-Wrist-Fling, Bird Wing, Corkscrew
Finger Flip	Six	C or CC	
Spider	Seven	C or CC	Palm, Inside and Outside
Hamburger	Eight	CC	
Paradox	One	C or CC	
Flutterball of Hyzer	?	N/A	

*Legend
C=Clockwise
CC=Counterclockwise
(Reverse for lefthand deliveries)

→ = changes to

[1]An upside-down flight rights like a warp curls. The Frisbee always rights in the opposite direction to spin. The remaining spin will be opposite to the original.
[2]An upside-down flight. See note 1.

Flight Periods of Frisbee

Opening Phase

1. Whelm
   (release, hatch)
2. Wedge
   (insertion)
3. Well
   (climb)

Middle Phase

4. Wax
5. Waft
   (float)
6. Wane

Closing Phase

7. Waste
8. Warp
   (turn, curl)
9. Was
   (touch)

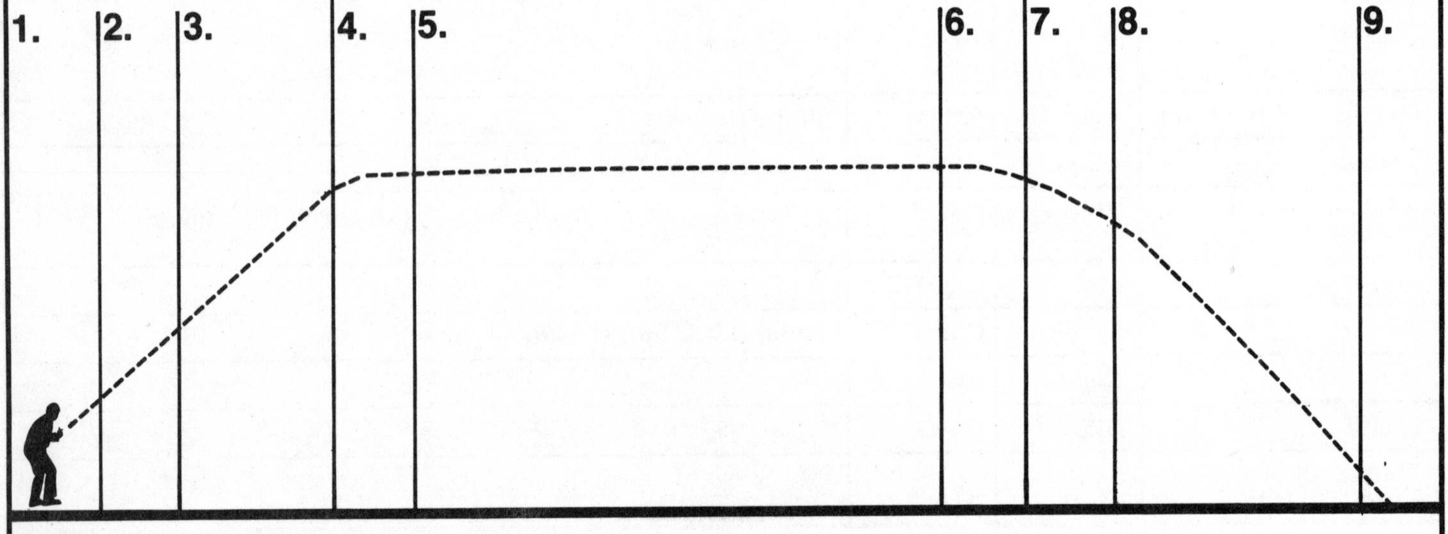

1. 2. 3. 4. 5. 6. 7. 8. 9.

4. FLIGHT

"And seem to walk on wings and tread in air."
—Homer, *Iliad*

"E'en like the passage of an angel's tear
that falls through the clear ether silently."
—John Keats, "To One Who Has Been in City Pent"

Flight, like chess, is divided into three phases—the opening, the middle, and the closing. Each phase of flight is subdivided into three periods, each with a name (often several). The periods may blend imperceptibly, but only distance flights will display all nine periods.

Opening Phase

Whelm and Wedge (described on pages 56-57)

Well (Climb)

Well is the last and longest period of the opening phase. In well, flight stabilizes as the Hyzer angle levels off.

Short flights have little or no well; skip throws have well and waste turned around; and return flights (imprecisely called boomerangs) have the greatest wells of all.

An outstanding distance thrower must master the well. In the distance throw the greatest single fault is excessive well, caused by a hyper-Mung angle in whelming. This occurs when too much force is applied, ruining a smooth and coordinated whelm. The Frisbee rises too high, shortening the waft, and lessening the distance.

Middle Phase

Wax

Wax is very brief and is characterized by the loss of the Mung angle. Return flights obviously do not wax.

Waft (Float)

Waft is the quintessence of a distance flight, taking the longest amount of time, and causing the most joy to the thrower. If the ingredients of flight up to this point are balanced, a superb and lengthy waft follows. (See waft variations, pages 64)

Wane

Flight is a function of force and spin acting in the wind. The moment of wane usually marks the beginning of flight failure.[1] Although the question is unsettled, most Frisbee physicists feel that force fails first. Waning is the

---

[1]An important exception, nose gliding, a premature wane phenomenon (see page 119).

Flight Periods of Frisbee

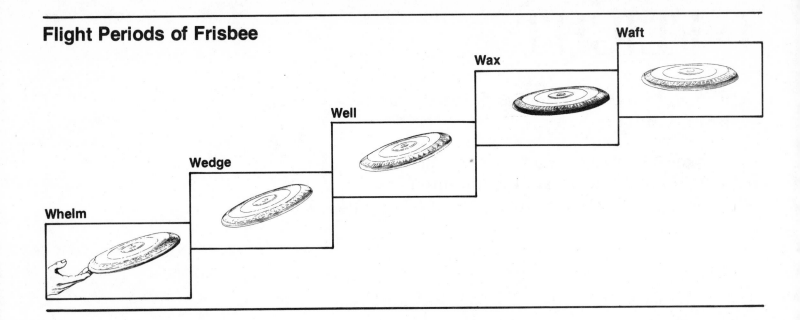

Whelm   **Wedge**   **Well**   **Wax**   **Waft**

sign of force failure, whereas wasting, the next period, and, particularly warping, signal declining spin. Remember: force fails first and spin shows second.

Closing Phase

Waste

The first period of the closing phase begins when the plate distinctly begins to decline. It is not easily divided from the next longer and more significant period—warp.

Warp

The longest and most significant period of the closing phase, warp gets its name from the sideways curl, which is always in the opposite direction of the Frisbee's flight spin.

This warp curl results from spin failure. Remember Newton's second law about equal and opposite forces? A right-handed backhand delivery produces a clockwise spin and will end with a warp curl to the left.

Was

The was is the end of flight—the downing of the disc.[2] Wases don't interest throwers much, except to say "Where *was* it?" when searching for their missing missile.

Special Kinds of Flights

Curves

Baseball buffs will harangue endless-ly about whether their *objet d'art* curves, but Frisbee devotees *know* theirs can.

Right and left curves refer to the side the flight turns *at the end*. Throwing a curve requires a special kind of wedging—a very high Hyzer and just a bit extra Mung. Remember

[2]For a discussion of a post-was event, the roll (running), see page 119.

Right curve flight.

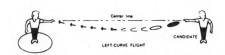

Left curve flight.

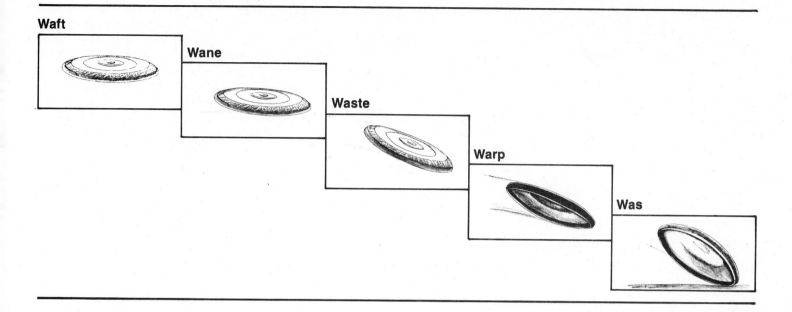

Waft

Wane

Waste

Warp

Was

when spin fails, the warp—a natural curve—occurs in the opposite direction of the spin. In other words, a left curve with a clockwise spin will warp *into* the curve, while a counterclockwise left curve will warp out of a curve, i.e., tend to slide right again.

The curve occurs because wasting begins before the Hyzer is smoothed out and gravity draws the Frisbee down into a curve.

Curve flights[3] are the most accurate when the directions of spin and curve are opposite. The Frisbee Master takes this into account, especially in the Medley Accuracy Contest, which includes curve flights.

[3]Certain models will hold a curve better than others. Longer lips and smooth flight plates make for good curving plates.

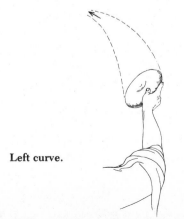

Right curve.

Left curve.

Hover Flights

Hover flights are straight hyper-Mung, hyperspin (extra torque) throws that settle with little or no warping. Because of the hyper-Mung

Hover flight.

wedge, the Frisbee will tailskate and the middle period (wax, waft, and wane) will be slight or absent. The increased torque postpones the warp of the closing phase. Hover flights are the most fun in beach play. They are easier to do against the wind. If the waste's fall is soft and the warp delayed, fingertip catching, tipping, and other trick catches are possible.

Boomerang flight.

Boomerang Flight (Return Flight)

The boomerang is a combination of the curve and the hover, and it requires a modest headwind. The more headwind, the less Mung (pitch) angle needed. An ideal boomerang returns exactly to the point of whelm. This requires exquisite timing of wind speed, wind direction, whelm thrust, torque, and Mung angle. The return speed and momentum of the boomerang can be fantastic. Accurate boomeranging is a mark of an accomplished player. The maximum Time Aloft (MTA) tournament event, develops an appreciation of the boomerang in competitive play.

Skip Flights

Skips flights are hypo-Mung (negative angle) throws that bounce off a hard surface[4] and rise.

There are two basic kinds of skips: the straight skip, where the Frisbee bounces off its nose; and the curve skip, where the Frisbee ricochets off its ear and may make multiple skips.[5]

Skip flight.

Any throw can skip. If the skip is too shallow move your bounce point closer to you. On the average, ten to twenty feet in front of you is a good skip point. Many players find the underarm delivery easier to execute the skip.

Flight Peculiarities

Dip

The dip[6] is an early flight occurrence with backhand deliveries. This is a pre-well event characterized by a small downward flight just after wedging. It happens because of an insertion close to a *negative* Mung angle. When the lift forces of flight occur (the Bernoulli-effect), a sharp well results. This is further enhanced by the gyroscopic rebound executed on the wind face itself. Unlike wobble, a mid-phase event, dipping is always in the opening phase.

The Wobble (Rattle, Flutter)

Wobble is a special characteristic of shorter flights. Rattling occurs in longer flights, but usually goes unnoticed unless it develops into major forms described as *lifts, drops,* and *siders* (see waft variations, below). But in shorter, player-to-player throws, wobble is a vertitable bane. Nearly every Frisbee player has experienced that disquieting moment when, just about to make a catch, he finds his Frisbee darting eccentrically up and down, to one side, or sometimes in all three directions at once. This is *wobble* (originally called rattling, to describe the catcher's state of mind). It is a wind phenomenon, especially noticed in upwind throws. When a beginning player is striving to develop his catching skills, he should never stand in a heavy upwind position. I recommend the delayed technique described on page 73 as the best antidote for rattle.

Waft Variations

Lifts

Lifts are always delightful in distance flights and occur when aloft winds alter the waft (float) into one or more higher flight planes. These re-

---

[4] Even water! Try a swimming pool, but be sure the surface is very still.

[5] Often called dancing skips. A complex skip requiring special practice is the Question Mark Skip of Pitt (Chuck). It's an overhand-wrist-fling thrown bowling style with hyper- Hyzer. The bounce point is the ear and more on Morrison's slope than the lip. The Frisbee bounces into a curve skip and finishes with a "question mark" curl. Excellent point maker for the game of Street Frisbee.

[6] Also known as the Air Bounce of Spyder Wills.

newed upward surges, with usually (though not necessarily) increased velocities can make for fantastic distance marks. Aground winds do not accurately reflect these prized upper currents. They can be *thermals,* that is, heated air arising; *reflects,* moving air bouncing upward from, say, a building or a hill; or *waves,* special currents of faster flowing air streaming into the Frisbee's flight (see Appendix for a detailed description).

Drops

These are dastardly events, usually resulting in abortion of flight when a sudden down air current forces the Frisbee to the ground.

Siders

There are two kinds of siders—positive and negative. A positive sider occurs when a sideways wind is in the direction of the spin, producing a heightened flight force and usually a greater distance. Negative siders, like drops, are woeful and occur when a lateral wind gust acts against the Frisbee's spin direction, resulting in a shortened float and a premature closing period.

Tailskating (Dragging Your Tail)

This is a major catastrophe of climb and occurs when the angle of Mung is too severe in a strong with-wind. A very strong favoring wind will offer less than ordinary resistance for lift, the tail will not rise, and the Frisbee tailskates downfield; waft does not occur, distance is shortened. After the eleventh International Frisbee Tournament, Jay Shelton, distance winner that day,[7] his playing companion Steve Sewall, Ken Headrick, and I were throwing a few in a late evening seaward gale. They were using their backhand deliveries while I stuck to my underhand (bowling) style. We measured off their better efforts to the tune of 150 yards plus! With my underhand style, I tailskated every throw. The underhand delivery is especially susceptible to tailskating because the release is closer to the ground and the few extra degrees of Mung angle needed for the climb is disastrous in high winds. In such extraordinary winds, a high release around the shoulder is best. (See height of release and nose-gliding in tournament chapter—Distance Throwing).

----

[7]Jay's winning throw that day was a respectable 73-yarder, but it would have gone farther had it not bounced off the Justus Henry Rathbone Memorial Pylon, which commands the north corner of the Eagle Harbor ball yard. J. H. Rathbone founded the Knights of Pythias and taught in a one-room schoolhouse beside the field.

Tailskating.

5. THE CATCH

"I hold you as a thing en' skyed and sainted."
— William Shakespeare, *Measure for Measure*, Act 1, Scene 4

O n the other end of a well-thrown Frisbee is a well-caught Frisbee. No aficionado neglects this aspect of the game, for one of the most spectacular moments in the sport consists of bringing in a high one with a last-second fingertip snag.[1]

Unless you're a seal, catching a ball is more or less putting your paw around it and holding on. Not so with the Frisbee: its shape, slow terminal speed, and parachute potential invite a variety of seizing styles. We will consider both the easy and the esoteric, and give pointers on execution.

Basic Catches

Thumbs-up versus the thumbs-down catch? It's one or the other, but

which is best? The argument still rages, but the thumbs-down people now have the upper hand, so to speak.

Proponents of thumbs up focus their attention on the mammalian thenar fat pad—in nontechnical terms, the palm-side base of the thumb. They argue that when the Frisbee strikes this fat pad, the grasping reflex is brought into play through primary nerve pathways, automatically quickening the grasp and catch.

Not so, say the thumbs-down people. They maintain that the grasp reflex is found only in neonates and

---

[1]The almost but not quite catchable flight that seems to elude as though sighted is called a "gollum," in honor of another slippery beastie of literary fame.

Thumbs-up catch, noting correct impact point.

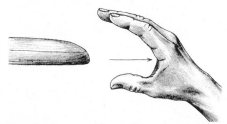

Thumbs-down catch, noting correct impact point.

brain wastees.[2] Accordingly, in the thumbs-down catch, the Frisbee first contacts the hand across the metacarpal-phalangeal junction on the palm side—a zone rich in highly myelinated nerve endings—the swiftest nerve conductors, hence a quicker response, touch, grasp, and catch.

I urge the beginning player to catch in whatever way is the most comfortable. The best catchers seem to favor the thumbs-down method, until the Frisbee comes below the knee, where it then becomes awkward. Expertise with both techniques is ideal in Guts competition. I am convinced the thumbs-down is superior! The thumb can curl around[3] and secure the catch better, while the four fingers stabilize the flight plate.

Excellent positioning for thumbs-up catch.

Behind-the-Back (BTB). A sheep-from-the-goats catch, but simple compared to the *spinning* behind-the-back (SBTB).

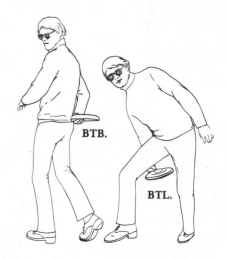

Between-the-Legs (BTL). This is a self-explanatory catch simpler than the behind-the-back. There is, however, a refinement known as the Guillotine—a between-the-legs catch of a boomerang flight!

Behind-the-Head (BTH). A tricky catch that calls for extra confidence in the old mitt.

Tail Catch. The Frisbee is almost always caught on its nose, but wing and

Good form for thumbs-down catch.

---

[2]There have been scurrilous rumors suggesting that this has led to the apparent success of some of the thumbs-up devotees.

[3]If the fingers and thumb are curled, it is called the Headrick Claw Catch, designed especially for Guts games. Ed Headrick discovered this catch in 1969 growing Venus Fly Traps, while recovering from the Twelfth International Frisbee Tournament.

Behind-the-back catch.

tail catches are also possible and fun to try. The tail catch—either thumbs up or thumbs down—can be done as the Frisbee goes by you, on the side, over your head; or the trickiest of all—the *Clarkerina*[4] where the catcher has his back to the thrower and snags the tail of the Frisbee as it passes over his head.

Finger Catch. The simplest of the special catches. Best perfected on head-

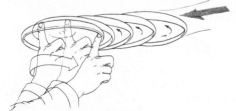

Finger catch with ideal finger counter rotation.

high hover flights. The finger must go in the opposite direction of the spin in order to slow the Frisbee down and stabilize the catch.

Special Catches

Tipping

Tipping is not a catch but a way of setting one up. The Frisbee is deflected by the hands or feet so that it will fall softly to the tipper or another catcher. Double and triple tips can be done in combination of hand to foot to a behind-the-back catch, or other spectacular arrays.

The basic tip is with one hand striking the center of the underside;[5] the Frisbee pops straight up and settles slowly down for an easy catch.

Tipping the Frisbee.

Foot tips[6] are tougher but are done the same way.

The Laguna Jam

The quintessence of the tipping game is on Laguna Beach, California, where Oak Street runs into the water. Here Spyder Wills and the Laguna gang do their thing. Their style is unique in all the world. It is two-man ballet with Frisbee. Called a *jam*, it's a precision drill—not fast, not hard, but dancelike, with the emphasis on complex catches. They tip the incoming Frisbee with either hand and then, reaching behind the back, catch it just as it is falling by the waist,[7] or they will tip it with both hands, catch it between their legs and the like. They are the masters of tip catches!

The Laguna throw is designed for accuracy, not speed, and a thrower is valued for his ability to place the Frisbee exactly where his partner wants it in order to complete the drill. At Laguna, players will stand fifteen to twenty yards apart and throw for several hours in rhythmic exercise.

---

[4]Names for Al Clark, IFF great.
[5]The cupola floor or plate of Blake.
[6]The toughest foot tip is the backwards somersault, where the tipper rolls over as he kicks the Frisbee behind him to a second catcher.
[7]Laguna players have a special way to catch waist-high throws—the Will's waist catch. They move their bodies into the incoming spin, then reach behind their backs with the opposite hand and make the catch. To absorb the force, clockwise spins are cushioned on the right side; counterclockwise on the left, as the Frisbee spins into their hands. This sets up for a quick, smooth return of a thumbs-up catch into a No. 1 grip underhand toss.

A between-the-legs catch.

The Frisbee is held shoulder high, the armswing is straight from the shoulder, the hand is palm up after wristing with the index finger pointing at the target. They put a few extra degrees of Mung into their wedging to make the Frisbee tailskate so they can tip more easily.

Pointers on Catching the Frisbee

The hands are the most important element, but the catch actually begins in the toes. Plant your feet well apart, about the width of your shoulders, perhaps slightly more, especially if you're prone to asthenia. Now, up onto the balls of your feet. This places you in a good pivoting position for quick movements to either side. Knees should be bent slightly for comfort and springing. Look straight ahead, with your upper limbs loose and gangly.

Positioning for the catch is one of the trickiest actions in the sport and easily distinguishes the master from the novice. The alert player catalogues a wealth of information at the onset of the throw. He notes which hand is throwing and the style of delivery—backhand, sidearm, underhand—to determine spin and warp. He notes wind direction and the relative speed of the Frisbee. The expert will study the opening, whether it's a curve, straight, or hover flight. Now he can begin to position for the catch. In the middle period of the flight he will move to a tentative position. At this time it is a thing of near beauty to watch a truly accomplished player pick his way deftly through the shrubbery, tricycles, and babes in arms to reach this tentative position. In the last period of flight, the closing, fine adjustments are made in accordance with contending wind changes, birds in flight, etc., as the would-be catcher makes the last critical decision for a thumbs-up or thumbs-down or even a trick catch.

Don't begin to catch too soon! The Frisbee in flight is constant inconstancy, invariable variation, and an effort begun too soon will befuddle the delicate sensomotor apparatus of the eye-brain-hand system. I recommend bringing the hand to a catching position *just* before the moment of contact. This eliminates unnecessary and confusing midcourse corrections.

Many players are initially baffled in timing the Frisbee's flight. *Wait*, and wait a little more. The Frisbee in its last third of flight is slow, approximately two-fifths of its initial speed. Practice will reward you with spectacular results—smashing fingertip snags in midair.

A final suggestion: learn to catch with your non-throwing hand, not exlusively but predominantly. This specialization[8] will spare your whelming mitt from unnecessary trauma and add years to your game.

---

[8]Not to mention the advantages gained from cerebral hemispheric specialization. Look for a breakthrough in research in this area from the Institute of Frisbee Medicine soon.

6. GAMES

It is not strength, but art, obtains the prize
And to be swift is less than wise.
"Tis more by Art, than force of num'rous strokes."
—Homer, *Iliad,* Book 23

The Frisbee is ideally suited for the human hand and applicable to any game with a throwing element. Little surprise that Frisbee improves many existing sports.[1] Frisbee is not just a new sport but, in a larger sense, a new *medium* in sport.

Ancient legends tell us that football began in cemeteries. Bored grave diggers would kick skulls into convenient holes.[2] Frisbee players can breathe a relieved sigh. The human has no Frisbee bone. Man has designed the Frisbee as his sports missile for the new era.

Outdoor Games

Frisbee, the child of the wind, is naturally at its best out of doors. First, some original outdoor games:

Guts Frisbee[3]

The granddaddy of all Frisbee games and *the* tournament game, Guts may become the stardard game for Frisbee. Although it appears simple at first, Guts can be as complicated as a world series baseball game.

Its origin is mysterious. The Healy brothers introduced Guts in the first International Frisbee Tournament in 1958, and a description of one-on-one Guts is described on the undersurface of the Y-tournament model. But it is not clear who devised the game.

An ancestral version called Frisby was played with cookie-tin lids on Dartmouth campus, where the first international match took place on November 7, 1954, between

---

[1] Geoffrey Wong, self-exiled potentate of the island of Yanuca in the Fiji archipelago, declared Frisbee the national sport of the island in 1970.

[2] Never kick a Frisbee! There is no more unseemly sight in sport! The four excusable times are in Street Frisbee, Goal Line Frisbee, Hock-Bee (see p. 101), and foot tipping (see p. 71).

[3] The Guts game seems paradoxical. Frisbee—the tender, fluttery thing it is—being hurled at speeds that would excite a highway patrolman. Yet, it is appropriate that the first Frisbee game would attempt to bring sense to competitive athletics. Guts is extremely competitive. I can think of no other vis-à-vis sport where players square off and constantly attack each other in complete abandon and with all-out force from start to finish. The slowing down of the flight of the plastic disc operating between two ultimately aggressive forces allows this total war to occur and be stable long enough to experience as a catharsis.

the Blossom Brothers Five of Omnicron Deuteron Charge of the Theta Delta Chi and the Tweedy Free-Throwers of Montreal, Canada. The Greeks overcame their guests 21-16 after three and a quarter hours of toss and tussle. Obviously in those early days defense was the forte of the game. (See page 35 for more details.)

Players. Team Guts is played five to a side. The players are named as follows:

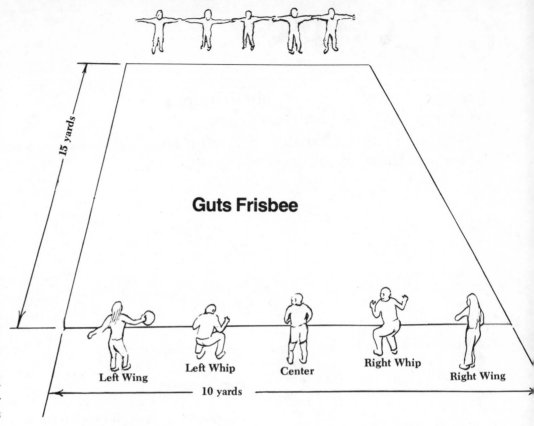

Guts Frisbee

Naming Scheme				
Left Wing	Left Whip	Center	Right Whip	Right Wing

But the Guts game can be played with any number per side. In the Wilmette Invitational tourneys, three is the usual number; one per side is popular in small West Coast meets. Reduce the width of the field six feet for each deleted player. In one-on-one Guts, players defend a six-foot-wide space.

Equipment. The Professional Model Frisbee is always used. Heavier discs are undesirable. Catching gloves are usually allowed in tournaments.

    The Team Guts field is 15 yards long and 10 yards wide (the width of five players with arms outstretched). The upper limit is the upstretched arms of the players at the goal line, about 8 feet. Any throw that passes through this 30-by-8-foot goal space is good, and there is no behind-the-goal limit. (Catches can be made any distance behind the goal line.)

Object. Throw the Frisbee in the air through opponent's 30-by-8-foot goal space *uncaught* for a score. Twenty-one points is a game. On 20-20 ties, winner must win by two points.

Scoring. Uncaught toss in goal space equals one point to throwers. A throw above upstretched arms of receivers, or outside lateral bounds, or into the ground in front of the goal is one point for the receivers.

    Game officials are called gamesmen and number up to five in the following positions:

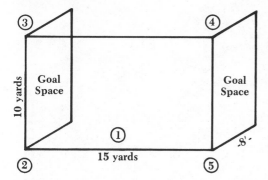

① Head Gamesman
② Linesman I
③ Goalsman I
④ Linesman II
⑤ Goalsman II

Goal Space
Goal Space
10 yards
15 yards
8'

Teams may play a gentleman's game and call their own faults.[4]

There are four difficult calls in Guts. Since catches must be made one-handed, a catch made by holding, pressing, or squeezing the Frisbee against the body is a *trap*. Any number of players may each catch the Frisbee one-handed. I have seen a three-person one-handed catch, and a Frisbee come to rest atop a fallen player—all good catches.

Grounders are throws that touch the ground before being caught. The difficult decision is with catches that strike the ground during the catch; possession is the key.

The *out-of-bounds* call is a tough problem, especially with high throws. Would-be catchers *must* extend their arms but need not jump. Touches count as drops unless caught.

The last and perhaps most difficult call is the *turnover*. Tradition-ally the game rule is that the Frisbee must not exceed a 90-degree change in *roll*[5] during flight. For practical purposes, if the Frisbee is straight up and down (i.e., perpendicular when it crosses the goal), a turnover is called, and a point is awarded to the receivers. This rule eliminates such throws as the upside down.

Play: The game begins with a coin (or Frisbee) toss for goal to defend; sun and wind are the main factors in goal choice. Favoring winds are usually desirable, so teams change sides every eleven points (e.g., 6-5, 15-7).

The player who first touches the Frisbee returns the throw unless it is caught by someone else. Untouched or out-of-bounds throws can be re-turned by the best thrower. In Guts the weakest catcher is the man to throw to unless he is an exceptionally strong thrower. Throw to his weak hand. Use the wind to advantage; vary the timing of the returns and speed of throws. Low throws, especially sinkers, are the toughest to catch.

Less than half of the Guts throws are caught by the first man to touch the Frisbee; a Guts team wins on its scrambling ability. In scram-bling the players back each other up and play for a deflected catch.[6] In keen competition I have seen fourteen deflections between all five team members result in a successful catch. Master scrambling teams like Library Bar and Diamond Mike's of Keweenan Peninsula practice *con-trolled scrambling*. They keep tip-ping the plate up until their *best* thrower can catch it.

Strategy. Wing players are tradition-ally weak catchers but accurate throwers. Their forte should be throwing at their opposing wing. Ideally, the right wing should be a left-handed thrower,[7] his coun-terclockwise spin will bounce to the opponent wing's left side, and out of bounds. The opposite is true for the left wing. And all of this is reversed if the wing player is a forehand thrower. An accurate wing who can make the sideline wing shot is a valu-able asset to a Guts team.

When a team will "storm the wings," i.e., throw at weak catching wing players, the defending *whip* will need to cover his wing. The whip should have his best catching hand toward his wing.

Keeping the spin strategy, the left whip should be a strong clockwise thrower, but a good left-hand catcher, and vice versa for right whip.

Whips are often the best throw-ers on the team, but the best catcher should be the center. He should

---

[4]Ideally the Guts game should be played with-out referees. Younger teams have difficulty with this and need a kind of officiating that can only be described as therapeutic. A mature Guts team learns to blend absolute aggression with impeccable honesty—an admirable accomplishment.
[5]The term "roll" is used here in the aero-nautical sense—lateral rotation.
[6]Sort of like trying to catch a bar of soap in the shower.
[7]Assuming his delivery is the standard backhand.

The 1969 Foul Five Guts Team at Eagle Harbor. From left to right: Hugh Barry Anderson, Jack Kaitala, Dan Headrick, author, Thor Anderson.

Center Tom Bodá makes high thumbs-down Guts catch. Whips Sewall and Shelton play for deflection.

A "gollum" in a Guts game pursued by Steve Sewall.

Jim Sharp and WABX team of Detroit. Jim, a top flight competitor, plays Guts on crutch.

A close save in Guts match.

California Masters show winning scrambling form in successful defense of their Guts championship at the 12th IFT. Left to right: Captain, Ed Headrick, Steve Sewall, Ken Headrick, Jay Shelton, Tom Bodá.

Guts Player's Strength

Throw (spin)	Clockwise Thrower accurate	Clockwise Thrower	Either	Counter-clockwise thrower	Counter-clockwise thrower accurate
Catch	Average catcher—left stronger	strong left catcher	ambi-dextrous catcher	strong right catcher	Average catcher—right stronger
Position	Left Wing	Left Wing	Center	Right Whip	Right Wing

catch well with both hands, to cover both whips, especially when they extend themselves to the wings.

The line-up has to be juggled to a team's strengths and weaknesses in both catching and throwing. Playing percentages, the table summarizes each position's needs.

Street Frisbee[8]

This is one of my favorite games. I developed it on a steep hillside street in Morgantown, West Virginia.[9] It was a natural development of two simpler well-known games often played with a ball, but better with a Frisbee: Keep-away and Dodge.

Players. It's a team game. I suggest sides of three or four, handicapped for balance. An adult or two can match against a multitude of neighborhood kids.

Equipment. One or two Frisbees, e.g., a Superpro and a Pro. A street, preferably with curbs. Goal lines (street cracks) 10 to 15 yards apart.

Object. To dead-stop the Frisbee behind the opponent's goal without their catching it.

Scoring. The Frisbee must be dead still on the street for a point. Game to 11 or 21. Ties played like Ping-Pong. In the 3-2-1 variation, stops closer to the goal line make more points. For example, using street cracks, stops in the first section beyond the goal line receive three points; the next two, and all beyond, only one. This puts a premium on the most difficult shots to make.

In Double Street Frisbee, two[10] Frisbees are used—the big one over the smaller, and thrown together to split and score. (Avoid jamming or

they won't separate.) Both can make points. If both stop on street, three points; only one, one point. Catching is tougher in Double Street Frisbee, so catching points are usually awarded. If both Frisbees are caught by the same person, five points! This is really hard to do. If both are caught by two or more, two points are awarded. Singleton catches may or may not count for points, depending upon players' pre-agreement. In the regular game, catching points can be awarded, but I never recommend it; in doubles, even though two are flying, catches are harder for either one.

The third version of Street Frisbee is Double 3-2-1. This is wild and best played after the other forms are mastered.

Play. Street Frisbee, like Guts, is played without a rear boundary. Strong throwers may try to overthrow the defense, but they can usually run under long throws, and a long throw must be accurate to stay within the narrow boundary lines of the street.

---

[8]An early version was played on a grass field 20 × 20 yards. Hedges and a street were the goals, 21 points a game, change sides every 11 points. Usually four players to a side. The game was hard on hedges, so we changed to streets, and used the pavement for skip shots.

[9]It is better on flat streets with tall curbs, but I've played on narrow paved alleys and wide suburban Los Angeles boulevards.

[10]There's no limit to how many Frisbees can be thrown, but four is a practical limit. There are special skills to throwing two at a time. By varying the grip and how the two are held together you can change the time and nature of their split. Experts can make one go high or both wide, or not split at all!

Street Frisbee

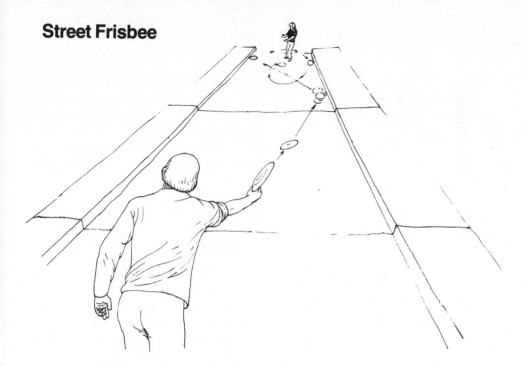

Many throws are made hard and low to slide through or bounce off the goal tender's legs.

Strategy. Vary throws to keep defense loose. Look for defenders' weaknesses. Use skips, corners, and curve skips to skirt a tight front-line defense.

Conversion (Goal-Post Frisbee)

This field game, devised by Roger Barrett, is very challenging and requires a lot of hard throwing and running. The following is Roger's description.

Players. Two (four would be possible, two per side, but the defense would be so strong that the game might not be interesting).

Equipment. A Frisbee (Pro Wham-O model is probably the best all around), one standard football goal post, and preferably about 50 yards of running room in all directions.

Object. Throw the Frisbee above the crossbar and between the uprights so your opponent will not be able to catch it one-handed.

Scoring. One point for the receiver on a bad throw (does not clear crossbar between uprights) and one point for the thrower on an uncaught good throw. Game to 11 or 21. Ties at 10 or 20. Use same rules as in Ping-Pong.

Play. Each player has a free-throw point straight away from the goal post; distance depends upon the player's ability and the wind conditions, average 30 yards. Play begins with a throw from free-throw point. If throw is good, the receiver throws from point of hit (Was). If bad, he has a choice of throwing from the Was or his free-throw point. Throws that hit the goal post and go through are good; bounces off are returned from the free-throw point.

Strategy. Shot curves are better than long, straight shots—particularly into the wind. If you have the good fortune to throw near the goal post, don't waste it with a short one. Though it gains a point, it will lose the game. The opponent will then push you all over the field. Players should switch sides frequently, particularly if there is a strong wind.

Double Disc Court

A unique game developed by the Rochester, New York, Frisbee Club—and one of the two events in their Annual American Flying Disc Open each August—Double Disc Court features two discs in play at all times, and calls for timing and finesse. It is a much more sophisticated form of Double Street Frisbee.

Players. Two.

Equipment. Two identical discs; Wham-O Pros or similar discs are

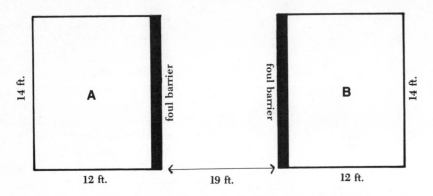

14 ft. | A | foul barrier | foul barrier | B | 14 ft.
12 ft. | 19 ft. | 12 ft.

probably the best. The grass field is as shown.

Foul barrier is $2'' \times 2'' \times 14'$—a wooden foul stick. Only the area within A and B courts is in bounds—the foul barrier is considered out-of-bounds.

Object. To drop disc(s) in opponent's court without touching court lines or foul barriers. Rolls, or bounce-ins, from out of bounds do not count for a score. Defend own court to prevent score. Two-handed catches are allowed.

Play. Play begins with coin (or disc) toss for court of choice. If wind is a factor, players change courts every 5 points.

At signal from referee, players begin attack of opponent's goal.

Play proceeds until referee stops play after score or "break" (see Scoring, below).

Scoring. A dead stopped disc within court limits gives one point to thrower.

A disc that touches out-of-bounds areas in flight, or as a conse-quence of a failed catch, gives one point to opponent of player who *last* touched the disc.

If disc touches would-be catch-er and he fails to catch it, thrower gets one point.

If player touches both discs at the same time, opponent gets one point.

Only one point per volley is awarded; i.e., if one player places both discs in opponent's court—he receives one point only. If both discs thrown in sequence by one player re-sult in one-point situations for each player, only one point is awarded.

Referee *halts* play after each ap-parent score for determination of score. Only referee may pick up scor-ing disc.

If throws of both players in a volley result in points for each, it is called a *break*. Referee calls halt and restarts game. If discs collide in air, this is also a break; play restarts. Throws delivered before halt is called are played.

Players at all times remain in their respective courts. Referee can award one point to opponent of a player who leaves his court, throws after halt is called, or picks up disc in goal area before halt is called.

Strategy. The essential strategies in-volve either timing or placement. An accurate thrower can spread his op-ponent's area of defense to both sides of court and score with a well-placed corner shot. Or using the "lob," a soft floater, he can create a time lag in de-fense and opponent will be unable to defend against both discs.

Field Games

The perfect field game for Fris-bee may not yet have been devised. Frisbee field games differ from Guts and Street in that they have larger playing areas and emphasize strate-gic passing. Purists might argue that the next two games are adapta-tions of soccer or rugby, but I feel they should be considered original.

Ultimate Frisbee

Ultimate Frisbee began in Columbia High School in Maplewood, New Jersey, and is rapidly spreading to colleges. Ultimate freaks aspire to make their game *the* college Frisbee game.

Joel Silver started it at CHS in 1967 and graduates Larry Schindel, Irv Kalb, Geoff West, Johnny Hines, and others have developed an inter-collegiate league of thirteen colleges including MIT, Tufts, Rutgers, Princeton, Yale, Cornell, Holy Cross, Clark, and Hampshire. Rutgers is

The original Ultimate Squad.

Ultimate player waits for gentle hover to settle into his waiting hands.

Running two-handed catch in Ultimate game.

usually the champion.

In the first Ultimate college match, Rutgers met Princeton and won 27-25 in 1972. This was a nostalgic updating of football's first game, played 103 years earlier to the date and on the same spot (now a Rutgers parking lot).

Players. Two teams, any number per side. Teams of seven play in organized games.

Equipment. Wham-O's Master is the traditional disc—one for play. The official field is 60 yards long with 40-yard-wide goal lines. End zones should be endless (as in Guts and Street). Lateral boundaries are not absolutely necessary.

Object. Gain points by scoring goals. A goal is scored when player successfully passes to teammate beyond opponent's goal line.

Scoring. One point per goal. Teams switch sides after each goal.

Play. Following coin (or Frisbee) toss to determine choice of throw (or receive) and goal to defend, play begins with the throw-off from behind the goal line. All players stay behind respective goal lines until the Frisbee is in the air. Receiving team either catches—in Ultimate, two-handed catches are allowed—or allows Frisbee to fall within bounds, untouched, to obtain possession. If touched but not caught, throwing team gains possession at that spot. In Ultimate, the Frisbee is advanced *only by throwing*. In attempting to stop after a catch, a player is allowed a few steps. If Frisbee is grounded uncaught or touches any object in flight other than a player, possession goes to the defending team. Defenders also take possession on interceptions. Guarding is allowed, but no contact with the thrower of the Frisbee is permitted.

Fouls are called by officials, if present, or else by gentlemanly agreement. Defensive fouls such as inappropriate contact with the thrower result in plays being taken over. Offensive fouls such as pushing defenders give possession of Frisbee to defenders at the place of foul.

If defenders gain possession of Frisbee in the end zone, they may throw from that spot or advance to the goal line to begin their attack. Goals are not awarded for interceptions or possessions gained in the end-zone play; instead, play begins just outside end zone.

Time in official contest is two 24-minute halves with a 10-minute half-time rest. Second half begins with throw-off by team that received throw-off in first half. The clock runs during active play as in football. In less formal contest, teams can agree on a fixed period of play such as one hour.

Tie-breaker overtimes are 5 minutes in length with throw-off determined by new coin (or Frisbee) toss. Time-outs can be called by an offensive team at any time or after goals by either team. Each team has three time-outs per half and one per overtime. Substitutions can be made only after a goal, for an injured player, or when the clock is not running.

Strategy. Guarding is an important part of the game and prevents or slows rapid advancement of Frisbee to the goal by the attacking team.

Throwing is usually for short gains but always with the possibility of completing the long pass to a receiver breaking toward the goal. Throwers must be able to deliver accurately and with a variety of tosses—the Bodá throw is an especially useful weapon in closely guarded situations.

Ultimate is a very fast game that requires stamina, accurate throwing, and the development of evasive running tactics. One of the highlights of the game is high jumping for Frisbees in flight.

The Frisbee Game® (Netbee)

The International Frisbee Association introduced this field game in 1974 and hopes to popularize it at sanctioned tournaments. The game differs from Ultimate in that there are cages defended by a goalie, there is one less player per side, there are foul throws at goal cage, there is less running and guarding, and more emphasis on strategic short passes.

Players. Six per side; one goalie, two backs, and three fronts. A nine-player squad is the maximum.

Diagram of Frisbee Game

A composite to show dimensions, goals, player positions, field markings, zones of players and player positions at throw-off.

Players:
B=Back
F=Front
G=Goalie
Action Marks:
△=Throw-off Player
○=Receiving Player
□=Defending Player

Range of Players:
Backs can range from their front line to opponent's back line.
Fronts can range from their front line to opponent's front line.
Goalie can range from his goalie zone to his back line.

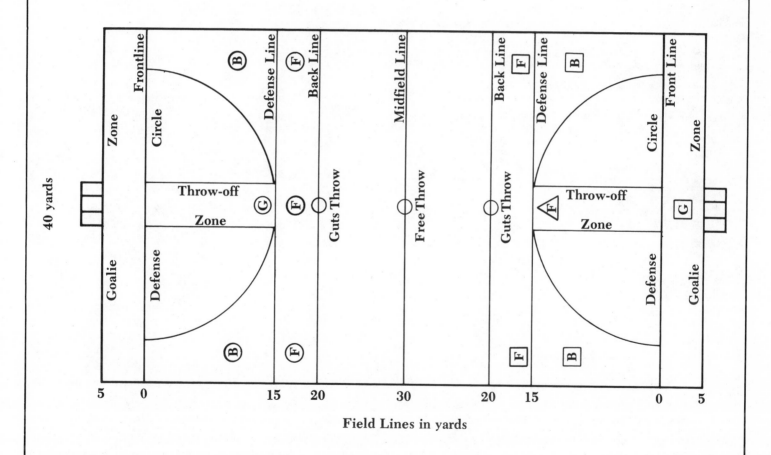

Field Lines in yards

Mark Danna readys shot at goal in the Frisbee Game. Other players are, left to right: Irv Kalb, Tom Bodá, Dan Roddick, and Sky King Richardson.

Equipment. A Frisbee, 8 to 10 inches in diameter and 100 to 130 grams in weight. Two goal cages 15 feet wide and 8 feet high. The goal sits 18 inches above the ground and is in three sections: 1 yard wide on either side and 3 yards wide in the middle. The field is 60 × 40 yards. (See drawing.)

Object. Score points by attacking opponent's goal and placing Frisbee within. Defend own goal to prevent score.

Scoring. Goals within smaller outer areas of goal count 5 points; middle area, 3 points. Free throw anywhere into goal receives 3 points. Guts throw uncaught receives 3 points. Guts throw uncaught anywhere into goal counts 5 points. Throw-off gone astray, i.e., not into throw-off zone, gives one point to receiving team.

Play. Following coin (or Frisbee) toss for throw-off (or receive) and choice of goal, any player of defending team makes throw-off from the appropriate zone. If throw-off does not reach goalie in opposing throw-off zone, it is repeated (see Scoring, above). Receiving team's goalie must catch throw-off to begin their attack; if dropped, receivers must then throw-off (see field diagram for position of players and range of each player on attacking team). After attempting shot on goal, the front may enter into defense circle.

Attacking players can only pass Frisbee; two steps after a running catch are allowed. Any throwing style is allowed, except that Frisbee may not be vertical or upside down in flight. Once attacking team has crossed midfield, they have 30 seconds to make a shot on goal. Player cannot keep disc longer than 10 seconds. Only one throw back to goalie is allowed before crossing midfield line. Throws from behind the back line across opponent's back line are not allowed. Guarding without contact is allowed. Defending team obtains disc through interceptions and when Frisbee falls to ground untouched. If disc is touched by defenders but not caught, offense retains possession at spot where disc was touched.

Only goalie can be in goal zone. Goalie may run with disc but must adhere to 10-second rule. Frisbee goes to other team at midfield if this rule is violated.

If disc goes out of bounds, possession is turned over to defending team at that spot. Offensive plays such as running into opponent result in disc's going to defenders at spot of infraction. Defense fouls such as body contact or holding result in offensive team's taking a Gut's style free throw from the Guts spot (20 yards from goal). Goalie and any two other players defend goal (see Scoring, above). All other fouls, such as blocking, leaving assigned zones, etc., result in offended team's getting a regular free throw from midfield line. On these free throw, goal is not defended.

Play is four 8-minute quarters. Clock runs during active play but not during foul throws. There is one one-minute time-out per half, a 10-minute half time, and 2 minutes between quarters. Substitutions may be made after score, between quarters, and at half time. Three referees, one in charge, maintain continuous action.

Strategy. Develop offensive plays. Take advantage of curved flight path of Frisbee for set-ups for short goal shots. Goalie play is key to defense.

Circle Frisbee

Circle differs from Ultimate in several important respects: the circular field, 30 yards in diameter; a single goal in the center; five players a side; and the Frisbee can be carried, but only backwards or around the circle, never forward.

Plays are set up to pass the Frisbee to an unguarded player for a shot at the goal, to score by hitting the goal—a member of the defending side standing in the center of the circle. He may dodge a throw but must pivot on one foot. Or if he can catch the Frisbee one-handed, he then throws out of the circle to a teammate, and sides change. Dropped, uncaught, or intercepted Frisbees change sides also. The new goalie will be the member of the attacking team closest to the center at the change of sides.

Successful strikes on goal are awarded points according to distance of thrower from goal, i.e., a 10-yard strike is 10 points. Strikes less than 10 yards receive no points. Game is to 100 points or one hour.

Goal Line Frisbee

This is an old field game, usually played with a football or soccer ball. It is a simple game but calls for all-out effort.

Players. Two teams, any number. Can be played well with one per side.

Equipment. One Frisbee, any size—the larger ones such as the Super Pro or Master are preferable. Field can be any dimension; a football field is ideal. Lateral boundaries are desirable; natural boundaries can be used, such as a row of trees, two rocks, three Frisbees, or the like. Goal lines are necessary. End zones can be limitless, as in Ultimate, or defined to ease the task of defense.

Object. Throw Frisbee over opponent's goal line in the air uncaught for score.

Scoring. One point for Frisbee crossing goal line in air uncaught.

Play. Following coin (or Frisbee) toss to determine who will make throw-off and defend which goal, throw-off point is at two-fifths points on field (40-yard line on football field). Any technique is allowed, including upside-down and rolling-along-the-ground throws. If throw is caught, catcher takes five running steps ahead of catch point (shorten this if field is small). Otherwise, throw is returned from where Frisbee stops (not

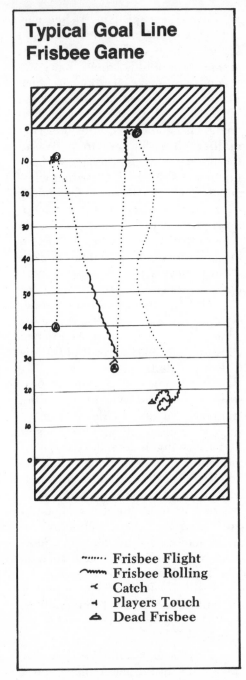

Typical Goal Line Frisbee Game

```
······· Frisbee Flight
〰〰〰 Frisbee Rolling
  ⊰   Catch
  ⊣   Players Touch
  ⏢   Dead Frisbee
```

lands) or is touched in flight or roll. If touched in the air behind goal, return throw is from goal line. If caught in air behind goal line, throw is the five steps (or adjusted number) in front of goal.

Play continues for a predetermined period of time or usually to a point total of 7 or 11.

Strategy. Goal Line is a no-contact field Frisbee game, with fast action and spectacular dives for rolling Frisbees and high leaps for goalward flights. Strong distance throwers can be overcome with rolling throws or handicapped by throwing against-wind throughout the contest and/or defending a limitless end zone.

Style Games

The current trend in Frisbee is toward style and grace. The next three games are designed to demonstrate these qualities.

Trick Catch, or the Millersville Game

Millersville, Pennsylvania, and its namesake state college is a hotbed of Frisbee activity, especially each May when they hold the annual Pennsylvania Frisbee State Championships. Dan Roddick, a graduate of Millersville, and his father devised this game.

Players. Two.

Equipment. One flying disc, Wham-O Professional preferred. Two 6-foot-diameter ground circles 25 yards apart.

Object. One player inside each circle throws back and forth. Thrower delivers toss within the receiver's circle and receiver tries to make as complex a catch as he can.

Scoring. Two points to receiver for any standing (feet on ground) trick catch: finger, behind the back, head, or between the legs. If feet are off the ground in catch, the receiver is awarded 3 points. If receiver drops throw, thrower receives 2 points. Receiver gets 3 points if throw is outside 6-foot circle or above receiver's outstretched arms. Receiver may elect to catch a throw outside his circle, but forfeits his 3 points for a bad throw. He otherwise scores as above or may give points to thrower if he drops a catch. Winner is declared when a player maintains an 11-point lead after his throw.

Play. Ability to catch with both hands is a great asset. The distance between circles can be adjusted for powerful throwers.

Strategy. Thrower will seek catcher's weak areas.

Courtsbee

This is the first Frisbee game devised by Canadian players—namely, Ken Westerfield and James Kenner. Courtsbee is similar to Trick Catch but adds the features of skip shots, team play, a larger field, and faster action.

Players. Two teams, one or two persons each.

Equipment. One Wham-O Professional Frisbee. Field should be a hard surface to allow skipping, with two lateral boundary poles (see drawing).

Object. Play is divided into throwing and catching. Points can be made by either team in both series; however, points can be made most rapidly in the catching series by the point-catching team. Game is to 25 points.

Play. The first throw or choice of court is determined by coin (or Frisbee) toss.

   Throwing Series. Play begins with a throw from behind the serving line. Use any throwing technique, but saucer must remain in less than a vertical plane while in receiver's court. A good throw must be within boundary poles; if skipped, it must hit within skip center. In the receiver's court it must be within receiver's reach. If receiver touches a high throw, it must be considered a good throw. Receiving player must make one-handed catches (no trapping of Frisbee against body or any other object). Receiver has three seconds to release a return throw to the opponent's side. Play continues back and forth until one side fails to make a good catch. If a bad throw occurs during a throwing series, a point is awarded to the would-be catching team. Catcher then returns to serving line and continues the throwing series. If a player fails to make a good catch, one point is awarded to the thrower, and the catching series begins.

   One additional point is scored for each deflection before final catch.

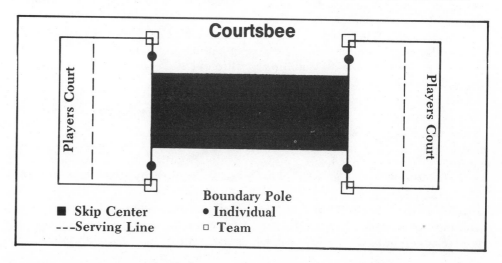

Courtsbee

Players Court   Players Court

■ Skip Center   Boundary Pole
---Serving Line   ● Individual
                       □ Team

Strategy. A hard thrower, as in Guts, can change Courtsbee into a Guts game and make points on his throwing. In such cases the skip center zone can be lengthened to 60 or even 90 feet. Courtsbee should be a catching game. The three-second-return rule keeps play active and demands a variety of catching and throwing styles. A premium is placed on trick catching as in the Millersville game, and in team play, where coordination between team members in various styles of deflections (tipping) enables them to rapidly increase their point total.

Keenest strategy of all, as in tennis, is to place the Frisbee into the areas of the court where your opponent has the most difficulty not only in catching but also in returning an accurate throw within the three-second time minimum.

Catching Series. The player or side who ended the throwing series (failed to make a good catch) now serves to the side designated as the point catcher(s). The point catcher can rapidly make points by making a variety of point catches. Catching series will end only when the point catcher fails to make a catch. During the catching series, a bad throw by either team gives the would-be catcher a point, and the catching series continues. If point catcher's opponent (the server) fails to make a catch during the catching series, a point is awarded to the point catcher and the catching series continues until the point catcher fails to make a catch

(regular or point). Throwing series begins again with a throw from behind the serving line by the former point catcher.

In team play, Courtsbee differs in these ways: the boundary poles are wider by 8 feet; either members of the team may make final catch; if saucer is uncaught, it is returned by the team member who last touched it (if neither touched the saucer in play, either may return throw).

Courts are changed when the cumulative score reaches 13 or multiples thereof.

Scoring. Regular scoring:

Bad throw—1 point to catcher.

Bad or no catch—1 point to thrower.

3-second violation—1 point to catcher.

Point-catcher scoring:

1 point: Behind-the-body catch, between- or under-the-leg catch.

3 points: Body spin (at least 270 degrees) plus 1 point catch by deflection (tip) plus any 1 point catch.

5 points: One deflection plus any spin plus any 1 point catch, or two different deflections plus a 1 point catch.

New Frisbee (Esalen Game)

New Frisbee is a game from the Esalen Sports Center Movement and was inspired by such people as George Leonard and Stewart Brand. It features a cooperation between thrower and catcher where each must play to his or her full potential.

Players. Two.

Equipment. A Frisbee and a place to run. There are no outer limits.

Object. Each player to realize his or her potential in throwing accurately and catching (and running) to the maximum. Failures to try in catching or to cooperate in throwing give points to opponent.

Play and Scoring. At the outset, each player designates which hand he or she will catch with and which hand he or she will throw with. Players take turns throwing and catching. Thrower tosses Frisbee in any direction. Catcher makes an all-out attempt to catch it. If uncatchable, including with a dive, catcher receives one point. Catchable but untouched flights reward thrower with one point. Touched (by any part of the catcher) but uncaught throws give thrower two points. Uncatchable throws gives catcher a point. Frisbees caught with wrong hand, or caught and cradled against the body, gives thrower two points. Frisbee must remain *under* a 45-degree angle to horizon throughout flight. If not, catcher gets one point. If course of throw brings a catcher within obstacle to a clean catch, the play is rethrown; two obstacled flights in a row gives catcher a point. Catcher calls *all* points including obstacles and angles; thrower may not protest.

Games are to 11 points (casual) or 21 (match). In match games, a knowledgeable observer should applaud good plays and calls to aid catchers in evaluating their physical limits.

Strategy. New Frisbee is less a test of saucer skill than a display of effort (catching) and cooperation (throwing). An ideal game should be a scoreless tie.

Adapted Games

Frisbee Golf, or "Folf"

At Wham-O in the early days of flying saucers, "Spud" Melin first adapted Frisbee to golf and George Sappenfield,[11] the park and recreation supervisor at Thousand Oaks, California, laid out the first permanent Folf course. Golf has not been the same since. The "holes" are usually shorter. They average, on most courses I've seen, between 60 and 100 yards. This very exciting sport was first a tournament event in 1969 at the IFA All Comers Meet. All the skills of Frisbee are called for in Folf: long-distance throws, accuracy (putting), curve shots, skips, even the rare running shot—the Frisbee rolling along the ground. On their Berkeley course, the Berkeley Frisbee Group has a stand of trees blocking the fairway. It is virtually impossible to throw around the trees or even over them, but an accurate roll will slip between the trunks.

Folf, unlike regular golf, can be played in any park, field, area, or campus using natural targets such as trees, road signs, and benches. I've used doors, garbage cans, library book drops, basketball goal poles, sun dials, flag poles, gates, and Civil War statues. The natural beauty and ecology is unaltered—golf cannot make that claim. One must account for the traffic of pedestrians. They have a shy aversion to our "discus plasticus," innocuous as it is. The complete folfer will carry a disc for distance, another for short accurate shots, and yet another for curve throws. In my folf bag I also carry a Pro Whiz Ring for rolls and a modified, heavy Fastback for strong head winds.

An unusual hazard on the Frisbee golf course at the Conejo Valley Community Park in California.

Hie yourself to your local park and lay out your own course, or appeal to the city park director to lay one out for all the Frisbee players in your area. Stick close to regular golf rules: 9 to 18 holes, fairways, and greens. Always include holes that require long, straight shots to challenge a player's distance ability, and holes for short, accurate throws with hole-in-one possibilities. For top-flight competition, toughen the target. On my Sacramento course (McKinley Park), number 7 hole is over the park pond. At times I use the corner of the pond, about 25 yards, but when I'm playing against a top competitor we throw the full width of the pond, over 50 yards. Needless to say, we have fished a few out of the water. The edge of the pond is lined with tall poplar trees and they snatch all but the truest drives. The course at Berkeley has several interesting holes. The running-throw hole, already mentioned, another around the light pole, another up a very steep hill. The finishing target is a narrow door on the side of a building—with a severe dogleg to the left.

Folf develops all your skills. It is an excellent way to polish and practice your game. If you are without a playing partner, play your backhand against your underhand or sidearm. Difficult pars and obstacles will call for all the possible throws in Frisbee

[11]He teaches a Frisbee course at Fresno State College, and started the first Frisbee Youth Camp in the summer of 1972 at Bass Lake, California.

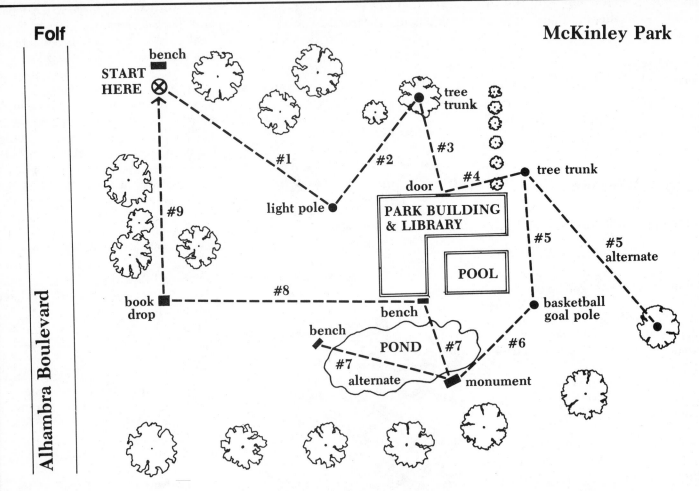

Folf — McKinley Park

START HERE ⊗

bench

#1 — light pole

#2 — #3 — tree trunk

#4 — door

#5 — tree trunk

#5 alternate

PARK BUILDING & LIBRARY

POOL

#9 — book drop

#8 — bench

#7 — POND — #6 — basketball goal pole

#7 alternate — bench

monument

Alhambra Boulevard

1. 90 yards, par 3, target—light pole.
2. 70 yards, par 3, target—tree trunk partially obstructed by two trees in front.
3. 60 yards, par 3, target—door to swimming pool.
4. 40 yards, par 2, target—palm tree trunk hidden behind front tree— requires curve throw. A possible hole-in-one.

5. 70 yards, par 3, target—basketball goal pole. Strong left-sided winds prevail here and tend to drop "drive" into swimming pool. Alternate 5 is 100 yards, par 3, target—tree trunk or barbecue grill.
6. 75 yards, a tough par 3, target— park monument at pond's edge. Approach shot has to be low and accurate.

7. 40 yards (25 yards over pond), par 2, target—park bench. Alternate 7 is 70 yards (50 yards over water), par 3, target—park bench.
8. 110 yards, par 3, target—library book drop.
9. 200 yards, par 4, target—park bench. Closing hole requires several good distance throws.

Par 26. Course record 23.

Frisbee Baseball (Basebee)

No sport is sacred to Frisbee improvement, even our alleged national sport. Prior to the 14th IFT, my oldest son, Chris, devised this adaptation. The difference between Frisbee baseball and regular baseball is the role of the batter. There is really nothing quite so ugly as hitting a Frisbee—so forget that. Instead the batter becomes the *plateman,* or slinger. He stands facing the pitcher, fifteen yards away. The batter's box is now the plateman's circle, six feet across. If the pitcher delivers the Frisbee across the circle, it's a strike; over the plateman's head, aground, or outside the circle—a ball. The plateman must first catch the Frisbee one-handed, and smoothly transform it into a throw, *all in a single motion.* This puts a premium on catching styles that can be converted into throws. This Frisbee skill is unique to basebee. Two-handed, stopped, and dropped catches count as strikes.

The plateman may sling for a homerun or place his hit, but he must throw the Frisbee within the foul lines. A special foul boundary, connecting first and third base and running through the pitcher's mound, prevents cheap bunting.[12] Best disc to use? Probably a Wham-O Pro, or if small children are playing, try the lighter weight Regular. For fun use CPI's giant saucer tosser—"the garbage can lid"!

Otherwise, basebee and baseball are identical: base runners, double plays, ground rules, fly outs, and

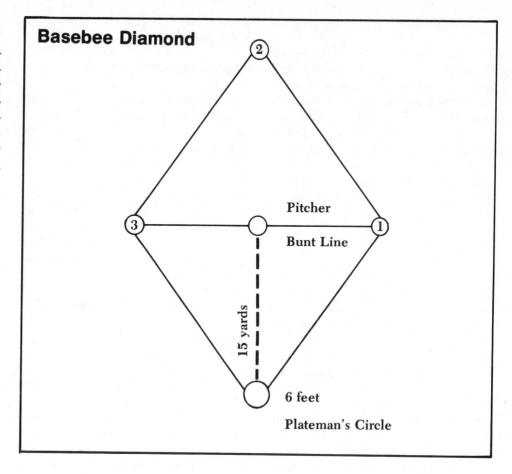

Basebee Diamond

Pitcher

Bunt Line

15 yards

6 feet

Plateman's Circle

all that. There is a version called Soakie in which base runners are out if hit with the Frisbee. Just throwing to the bases is a hassle because wind currents can spoil a seemingly perfect throw, but trying to hit a moving target with the disc is something else. There is probably nothing more frustrating in the whole pageantry of sports than playing first base and watching the base runner chugging in as you wait for an endless hover flight to settle into your hungry hands.

The pitcher should throw to the plateman's weaknesses. For example, a plateman with a weak left catching hand should find most of the pitches going to that side and low.

Novice players may find one-handed catches difficult. Two-handed catching could be allowed, not that this makes slinging any easier.

---

[12]An alternative: add extra infield players.

Frisbee Bowling

This game was suggested by Geoff Wong of Sacramento, California. Any size Frisbee is OK, but a heavier model such as the Master is probably best. Targets: ten mailing tubes, two to three feet in height, with clay in the bottom. Use same placement, alley length, and scoring as in regular bowling. Indoors, use the Mini or Horseshoe model and toilet-paper tubes.

Frisbee Football (Tiger)

Even football gives way to the Frisbee. The Frisbee adds a new dimension to passing and receiving—the arching throw—and makes the pass defender's job much more complex. He must be master of mid-course computations, e.g., spin, tilt, and wing direction. Otherwise, Frisbee football is played just like regular football, including tackling, but with the obvious exception that punts, extra points, and field goals are accomplished by throwing the Frisbee. Plays equally well as tackle or touch game.

Those who have played Frisbee football find it a fascinating variation of regular football. Pass receivers have told me that after playing Frisbee football and learning to catch the arching passes, they have become much more skilled in running *under* any missile. They become adept in twisting the body from one side to the other, even in midair.[13] Wham-O's Super Pro or CPI's All Star—superior

distance and curve discs—are top Tiger models.

Innertube Frisbee

The targets are inflated inner tubes about fifteen to twenty yards apart. Lay-upons count one point, inners two points. As in regular horseshoes, if your opponent lands on top of you, it cancels out your points. This game can be played in the water. On land I always lay the inner tube flat, but it could be secured between posts or propped up. This game will develop your curve shots.

Horseshoe (Wham-O) Frisbee

Wham-O marketed its first Frisbee game to keep pace with Eagle Rubber's Posey Pitch[14] and CPI's Flip-n-Fly. But Whiz Rings[15] are cheaper and just as good. Wham-O's Horseshoe Game has a hoop target on a stake and uses the Regular Frisbee.[16] Play like regular horseshoes, with these scoring rules:

Through the hoop counts 5 points.

Touching stake or leaning on stake counts 3 points.

Closest Frisbee to stake, measured by the measuring cord, counts 1 point.

If two yellow Frisbees are closer to the stake than the two red ones, both yellow Frisbees count one point each, and vice versa.

Frisbees landing outside the reach of the measuring cord do not

count.

Game is completed when first team reaches 21 points

Crossbee

Credit goes to the students at Haverford School near Philadelphia for

---

[13] I have heard of a football coach who drills his ends with Frisbees to develop just those skills.

[14] Game cost: $5.

[15] North Pacific Products, Bend, Oregon. Rings cost 50 cents to a dollar.

[16] Original game used a Horseshoe disc—a lighter, modified, speedy model.

this Frisbee adaptation of lacrosse.

Rules and strategies of lacrosse are followed.

Goal tenders use their crosses to protect against a score, but the Frisbee is hand-tossed about in the 30-yard-long field between the other three team members. If a player is tabbed by two hands, the Frisbee goes to the other side.

Indoor Games

Unless you're blessed with a warehouse for living space, you will find that flying saucers aren't much indoors except for these three: the Mini-Frisbee, the Mini-Whiz Ring, and Wham-O's extinct Speedy model (or its new and lighter version, the Horseshoe model).

The Styrofoam models can also be used, but are they really flying discs?

Hall Hockey (Friz-Banger)

This is a near-lethal game played in every college and prep school dorm hall. The best name I've heard for this mayhem is Hall Hockey.[17] The game is really indoor Guts, played in the hallway or "tube," usually one against one. Hitting the defender's wall, scores. In Friz-Banger a score consists of knocking over a bottle. Premium plays in both are floor,[18] wall, and ceiling skips.[19]

Hall Hockey is not loved by dorm managers; there's many a lighting fixture dangling because of it.

Indoors Frisbee Golf

This is my favorite indoors game and it's a world-beater, rainy-day pastime. The targets are limited only by your own imagination. I've used wash basins, umbrella stands, book shelves, shower stalls, baskets of all kinds, just about anything. Play same rules as in Folf.

Frisbee Lag

Pitching pennies, but with Frisbees.

Frisbee Basketball

Frisbees have not found their way to the basketball court readily. They dribble poorly. A version can be played indoors with Mini-Frisbees. Give several to a team sitting on throw rugs. They shoot at baskets on the floor or a shelf. With all the scooting and shooting, you don't miss the dribbling.

Mini-Guts

The big tournament game indoors! Mini-Frisbees are hard to catch—so try malt cups or such. To handicap a family, dole out different size cups.

A 10-by-12-foot rug with players sitting along the edge makes an ideal field.

Ringers

For a target, try an upside-down chair leg. Make ringers with a Mini-Whiz Ring.

Frisbee Hockey (Hockbee)

Hockey with a Frisbee—puck with stick or kick for action was suggested by John Oliveria and Steve Smeltz of Monterey Peninsula College. They played on a basketball court. Use a heavy Frisbee such as a Master.

---

[17]Submitted by Bruce Lennon of Davis, California.
[18]See Question Mark, skip of Pitt, page 64.
[19]For a good ceiling skip use the upside-down throw.

7. TOURNAMENTS

"We cannot all be masters."
—William Shakespeare,
Othello, Act I, Scene 1

The Oxford Universal dictionary defines tournament as "a contest in any game or skill in which a number of competitors play a series of selective games." Tournaments across the country have become the popular mode of competition among Frisbee players.

International Frisbee Tournament (IFT)

The first Frisbee tournament on record was the International Frisbee Tournament held in 1958 in Escanaba, Michigan. It is still held every Fourth of July weekend on the upper peninsula of Michigan. For years the legendary ball yard at Eagle Harbor near the shores of Lake Superior hosted the event. For several years

the tourney was held in a different city in order to find the best site. Cliff's Ridge Ski Lodge in Marquette, Michigan, may become the permanent location.

The IFT is the brain child of the Healy family: brothers Robert (Boots), John J. Jr. (Jake), Tim, and Peter.[1] What started as a family-and-friends frolic has grown into the premier Frisbee meet in all the world. The tournament is open to all Frisbee players,[2] and every year the field increases. Its out-of-the-wayness, however, has handicapped attendance;

---

[1]Tim and Peter died in a boating accident in 1969, saddening IFT players across the nation.

[2]Interested parties should contact Jon Davis, IFT Director, c/o Library Bar, Houghton, Michigan 49931.

Eagle Harbor, Michigan, the classic site of IFT, nestled around the crystalline waters of Lake Superior.

"Boots" Healy tossed out the first Frisbee of the 1968 IFT from the Memorial Pagoda roof.

still it is recognized as *the* tourney. (See Appendix for list of winners by years.)[3] Recently the IFT started a new tournament—the Guts Invitational—a $1,000-minimum-prize meet held each July.(See page 108 for full details.)

The Julius T. Nachazel Trophy A description of the IFT would be incomplete without mention of the trophy emblematic of Guts Frisbee mastership—the Julius T. Nachazel Cup. But who is Julius T. Nachazel? Professor Nachazel is a retired Michigan Tech University teacher of mathematics and civil engineering who lives in Houghton, Michigan. Mr. Nachazel was born March 26, 1893, in Traverse City, Michigan, and before college worked as a lumber-mill engineer and later became a second lieutenant in World War I. He also served as Mayor of Houghton from

1949 to 1951. During that time he lived near the Healy family and their four sons and regaled them with many stories about his military experiences and athletic interests. He showed them the trophy[4] created for the Third Ward Athletic Club of Houghton. The Healy boys obtained the cup "by some nefarious means," a phrase often used by Mr. Nachazel, and awarded it annually at the International Frisbee Tournament to the winning Guts team. The original cup was a forty-six-ounce tomato juice can standing on top of a smaller can with galvanized iron handles, and a can-lid base. It was highly polished and bore a World War I German scrolled emblem with an inscrutable inscription, "Parole Heimath," which has baffled cup experts for years.[5]

The first trophy contained a "rattle" in the smaller can, a built-in burglar alarm.

At the 1969 games, the original Nachazel trophy was presented to the Healy family, who had done so much to establish the tournament. In 1974 the Healys returned the trophy for its continued use. It is now enshrined at the Library Bar in Houghton, Michigan, and is a noncirculating trophy.

The Frisbee Tournament Trail

With five new major tournaments appearing in 1974, the Frisbee tournament trail was born. Short on money but long on enthusiasm, players can now travel the North American conti-

---

[3]Fires in the Pagoda Hall of Fame have scorched the record book; hence the incompleteness.

[4]It was awarded to the outstanding cook at the annual picnic, who was then elected president of the club for the next year.

[5]Legend holds that the piece came from "Kaiser Bill's" walking stick.

J.T. Nachazel and IFT director, Jon Davis, examine the original Nachazel Cup.

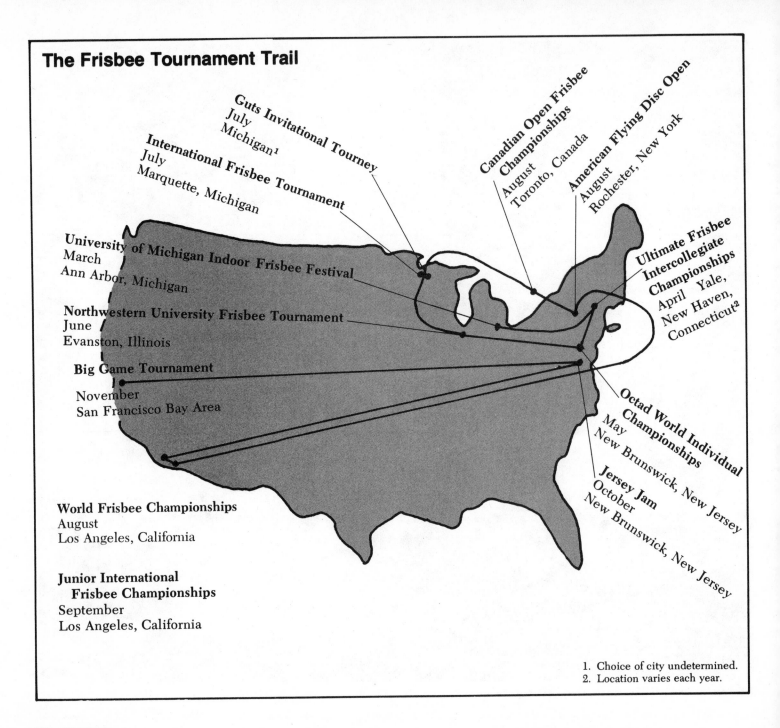

The Frisbee Tournament Trail

Guts Invitational Tourney
July
Michigan[1]

International Frisbee Tournament
July
Marquette, Michigan

Canadian Open Frisbee Championships
August
Toronto, Canada

American Flying Disc Open
August
Rochester, New York

University of Michigan Indoor Frisbee Festival
March
Ann Arbor, Michigan

Ultimate Frisbee Intercollegiate Championships
April Yale,
New Haven,
Connecticut[2]

Northwestern University Frisbee Tournament
June
Evanston, Illinois

Big Game Tournament
November
San Francisco Bay Area

Octad World Individual Championships
May
New Brunswick, New Jersey

Jersey Jam
October
New Brunswick, New Jersey

World Frisbee Championships
August
Los Angeles, California

Junior International Frisbee Championships
September
Los Angeles, California

1. Choice of city undetermined.
2. Location varies each year.

nent from March to November displaying their prowess. And with winter indoor meets soon to come, disc-sport will be a year-round thing. The following is an account of the trail, minus the IFT, which has just been described.

University of Michigan Indoor Frisbee Festival[6]

The first meet on the trail began in 1974, and it was the first indoor meet of its kind.[7] Festival directors emphasize fun rather than competition. The UMIFF is sponsored by the University of Michigan Frisbee Club, the Humbly Magnificent Champions of the World Disc Tribe, and the university's Intramural Department, which makes available the cavernous Intramural Building for the doings.

It features a three-man Guts contest, as well as accuracy, distance, and free-style events.

1974 winners:

Accuracy:	Joe Essman
Guts:	Library Bar (Bill Hodges, John Hodges, Bill Dwyer)
Distance:	Dave Johnson (figures not available)
All Tourney Team:	Joe Essman, John Hodges, Phil Roath

An indoors tournament should be an ideal showcase for accuracy and free style. The UMIFF sets an example of a format to come.

Intercollegiate Ultimate Frisbee Championships

Ultimate Frisbee boasts an intercollegiate league of twenty-three schools. The league is in the East, but plans for a Western conference are forming. The teams play a fall and a spring season. The first full season was in 1973.

In April 1975, the leading contingents—Tufts, Cornell, Clark, New Hampshire, Princeton, RPI, Yale, and perennial champion Rutgers[8]—met in a three-day single-elimination format to determine the Ultimate National Champion.

Although this is a "closed," tournament it represents the pinnacle of Ultimate play. Interested Frisbee enthusiasts will find plenty of disc action nonetheless.

Northwestern University Frisbee Tournament

This is another university intramural-sponsored meet open to all comers. A highlight of the 1974 games was the overall accuracy competition, which was won by Marie

---

[6]For details, contact Jo Cahow, 3196 Williamsburg, Ann Arbor, Michigan 48104.

[7]In truth the first indoors tourney was the short-lived Highland Avenue Aces Wilmette Guts Invitational, held December 8, 1973, in the Loyola High School gym in Wilmette, Illinois. At that meet Susie Kelly and Phil Roath of Ann Arbor and Bruce Koger and Jim Petersen of Chicago (Jim writes the *Playboy* Advisor column) won the Guts crown. On June 8, 1974, the Library Bar

---

Ultimate All-American Squad 1973–74

Andy Arrison	Tufts
Walter Belding	Clark
Stu Case	Rutgers
Jon Cohn	Cornell
Robert Evans	Princeton
Stan Hiemenga	Calvin
Steve Hannock	New Hampshire
Milt Haddicks	Rutgers
Irv Kalb	Rutgers
John Kirkland	MIT
Paul LaVigne	Holy Cross
Dave Leiwant	Yale
Ed Levy	Rensselaer Polytechnic Institute
Andy MacGruer	New Hampshire
James Pistrang	Tufts
Dan Roddick	Rutgers
William Scholtens	Calvin
Ed Summers	Tufts
Lance Taylor	American International College
Dave Uffelman	Princeton
Jim Welty	Rensselaer Institute of Technology

won Guts; John Connelly, distance—255 feet; John Hodges, MTA; and Bruce Koger, accuracy. The Aces' Tourney has not been held since.

[8]Rutgers' Ultimate Squad is a school-sponsored and financially endorsed activity!

Murphy, who also won Women's Distance.[9]

It will be an annual event on the Evanston, Illinois, campus each June.

1974 results:

Guts Three-Man: Triangle of Forces
(Bruce Koger,
Dave Bradshaw,
Steve Sewall)
Open Distance: Steve Sewall
243 feet
Women's
Distance:
Marie Murphy,
174 feet
Folf (par 54): Bruce Koger, 51
Accuracy: Marie Murphy

John Pickerhill is tournament director and Bruce Koger, who does the world's first Frisbee News on Chicago FM station WNIB on Thursday nights, ballyhoos this midsummer meet.

Octad

The World Invitational Flying Disc Championships, Octad, began in 1974 and seeks to be the greatest test of individual skills in Frisbee yet established. *Flying Disc World* and the Rutgers Frisbee Group sponsor this great event each May. The site is Rutgers University in New Brunswick, New Jersey.

Events and winners in 1974:

1. Frisbee Golf 1st Keith White,
(36 "holes," 127
par 132): 2nd
John Schaberg,
Dan Roddick—tie
2. Distance: 1st Dave Johnson
378 feet[10]
2nd
Vic Malafronte
375 feet
3. MTA: 1st John Kirkland,
10 seconds[11]
2nd Roger Barrett,
9.2 seconds
4. Accuracy: 1st Irv Kalb
2nd Scott Hyland
5. Trick-throw 1st Irv Kalb
accuracy: 2nd Dave Johnson
6. TRC: 1st John Kirkland
165 feet
2nd Phil Goetkin
161 feet
7. DDC 1st Vic Malafronte
2nd Irv Kalb
8. Trick catch: 1st Vic Malafronte
2nd John Kirkland
Overall Champion—John Kirkland

The 1975 Octad[12] was held over the Memorial Day weekend. Double Disc Court and Trick Catch were replaced with Discathon (see page 122) and free style competition.

Invitational Guts Frisbee Tournament[13]

This is strictly a Guts game tournament and the tournament with the big *prize:* $5,000 to the first-place team and $1,000 in other prizes. Participation is strictly by invitation.

In '73 and '74 the Invitational was an October event, but the 40-mph-plus winds of Michigan's Upper Peninsula wrecked meaningful Guts play, so the meet now follows the IFT in July—probably on the Keweenaw Peninsula near Hancock-Houghton, Michigan.

1973 results:

1st: C-R Losers (now called Diamond Mike's Team)
2nd: Bosch Hunt-Hers (now called the Library Bar Team)
3rd: Berkeley Frisbee Group

1974 results:

1st: Library Bar
2nd: Highland Avenue Aces
3rd: Diamond Mike's
Women's Winners: Humbley's
Magnificent
Champions of
the Universe

[9]Marie's toss was commendable, but the apparent woman distance champ is Monika Lou, who threw 234 feet at WFC. Other "heavies" are Jo Cahow, Inez Sam, Nina Wilds, Cole Fulweider, Margie Meiswick, and Kate May.
[10]This is the official world's distance record.
[11]This the official world's MTA record.
[12]For details, contact Flash Eberle, P.O. Box 101, R.C.M.H.C., Piscataway, N.J. 08854.
[13]Formerly known as Keystone Bay Autumn Guts Invitational (1973) and The Cliff's Ridge Guts Invitational (1974).

The Library Bar team of Houghton-Hancock, Michigan, reigning World's Champions of Guts Frisbee.

Canadian Open Frisbee Championships

This is the first non-U.S.A. tournament, and it began in 1972. It is part of the Canadian National Exhibition held each August in Toronto.[14]

1974 Events and Winners

Event	Winner
Guts Five-Man	Library Bar
Distance	Joe Essman, 280.5 feet
Accuracy	Doug Corea
MTA	John Kirkland, 8.9 seconds
Free Style	Ken Westerfield, Jim Kenner
Canine Free Form	Gunner (Labrador retriever)

Jeff Otis of the Canadian National Exhibition, John Mortimer, Jim Kenner, and Ken Westerfield are responsible for this fine tournament. They and other Canadian Frisbee players are part of the *great hope:* Frisbee in the 1976 Summer Olympics.

American Flying Disc Open

The Rochester Frisbee Club organized this major tourney in 1974, and although it had only two events—Frisbee Golf and Double-Disc Court—it is a major event on the tournament trail. It is held each August and is open to all comers.[15]

In the inaugural year, over sixty Frisbee buffs descended on the St. John Fisher College site in Rochester for the two-day meet. Thirty-six "holes" of Folf made up the first day, with the top forty surviving for the final eighteen-hole round.

1974 results:

Frisbee Golf (54 holes, par 210)	1st	Dan Roddick, 185
Double-Disc Court	1st	John Kirkland
Overall Champion		Dan Roddick
Prize: New Datsun B210		

The 1975 American Flying Disc Open will be held the first weekend in August. Plans are to add a free-style event and modify DDC into an indoor event more along the lines of Courtsbee, but with Double-Disc action. The American Flying Disc Open is an example of the kind of small tournament that will be appearing more often in the next few seasons.

World Frisbee Championships

After several years of inactivity, and coinciding with Ed Headrick's return to general managership, Wham-O sponsored the first World Championships of Frisbee in August 1974.[16]

At considerable expense to the company, players from all over the country were brought to the three-day meet in Pasadena's Rose Bowl.

Irv Lander, executive vice-director of the IFA, and co-hosts Ryan O'Neal and Tatum O'Neal greeted the more than seventy players from all over North America.

---

[14]For details, contact Ed Hirst, Irvin Toy Ltd., 43 Hanna Ave., Toronto, MGK 1X6, Canada.

[15]Contact Jim Palmeri of the Rochester Frisbee Club, 153 Susan Lane, Rochester, New York, 14616, for details.

[16]An earlier world's compionship was held in the spring of 1968 when the IFA held the first Master's qualification at the Rose Bowl and selected Jay Shelton as the Frisbee champion of the world on the basis of the greatest number of points achieved on the Master qualification tests. Then in the autumn of 1969, the IFA sponsored an All-Comers Meet in Brookside Park, Pasadena. The new distance champ that day was Bob May, with a toss of nearly 270 feet. Eleven-year-old Jeff Johnson set a junior record (under twelve) of 165 feet with a sidearm delivery. Jay Shelton retained his World Champion title with second in Distance, first in Accuracy, and a win in Folf, which made its tournament introduction that day.

WORLD FRISBEE *Rose Bowl* 1974 Invitational Flying Disc **CHAMPIONSHIPS** Sanctioned by the International Frisbee Association

World Class Master Proficiency Rating Form

Contestant: _____

Time In:	Out:	Time In:	Out:
Time In:	Out:	Time In:	Out:
Time In:	Out:	Time In:	Out:
Time In:	Out:	Time In:	Out:

Flight	Delivery	Sequence 1	Sequence 2	Sequence 3	Sequence 4	Sequence 5
Straight						
Straight						
Straight						
Hover						
Hover						
Hover						
Right Curve						
Right Curve						
Right Curve						
Left Curve						
Left Curve						
Left Curve						
Skip Flight						
Skip Flight						
Skip Flight						
Boomerang						
Distance						
Distance						
Distance						
Catches:						
Behind the Back*						
Between the Legs*						
Behind the Head						
Freestyle Tip						

*Feet must be off the ground.

3 out of 5 throws, or catches, required in one sequence. A total of 60 minutes allowed in actual competition.

®Frisbee is a registered T.M. of Wham-O Mfg. Co. for flying saucers used in sports games.

Certified By: _____   IFA _____

Schedule Of Events For The 1974 Invitational World Frisbee Flying Disc Championships

12:45 PM	Introduction of contestants, celebrities and dignitaries
1:00 PM	World Frisbee Championships Queen, Tatum O'Neal, tosses out the first Frisbee
1:05 PM	Women's "Worlds Guts Frisbee" Finals
1:30 PM	Men's "Worlds Guts Frisbee" Finals
2:00 PM	Demonstration of Frisbee flying disc catching by Ashley Whippet, member of IFA K-9 Corps
2:10 PM	Women's "World Distance Throw" Finals
2:30 PM	Men's "World Distance Throw" Finals
3:00 PM	Hula Hooping demonstration by former National Champions Sandra Gaylord, Melody Howe and Lori Lynn Ray
3:15 PM	Demonstration of trick Frisbee disc throws and catches
3:30 PM	World Finals of the new "Frisbee flying disc Game"
4:00 PM	Women's "Individual World Frisbee Championship" Finals
4:30 PM	Men's "Individual World Frisbee Championship" Finals
5:00 PM	Presentation of Awards

Tatum O'Neal–Academy Award Winner/ World Frisbee Championships Honorary Queen

Tournament Officials

Tournament Director: Irv Lander, I.F.A.

Supervising Staff: Ellis Biderson, Sally Hansen, Wayne Weaver, Ernie Wilkerson, Wham-O Mfg. Co.

Referees: Pasadena Department of Recreation Staff Members

Chief Referee: Bob Cook — Pasadena Supervisor of Sports Activities

Public Address Announcer: Shelley Morrison — Network Sportcaster — voice of "New York Sets" tennis team — Sportswriter

Filming & Rose Bowl Decoration: Sheila Heintz — Television Producer

Publicity & Press Relations: Goldy Norton, Tony Furman

Advisory Staff: Roger Barrett, Dern Blake, Dick Gillespie, John Calder, Steve Gottlieb, Ed Headrick, Irv Kalb, John Kirkland, Vic Malafronte, Dan Roddick, Larry Schindel, Spyder Wills

Guts match at 1974 World's Frisbee championships in the Rose Bowl.

World's Guts Champions receive winner's plaque from Jon Davis.

Jo Cahow, world's best woman player.

Events and Winners in 1974:

Guts	Library Bar, (Bob Hansen, John Hodges, Bill Dwyer, Bill Hodges, Bob Raade)
Men's Distance	John Kirkland, 271 feet
Women's Distance	Monika Lou, 234 feet
World's Men's Champion Runner-up	Vic Malafronte John Connally
World's Women's Champion Runner-up	Jo Cahow Nina Wilds

Nearly 15,000 spectators were also treated to a demonstration of Women's Guts Frisbee with Jo Cahow, Kate May, Nina Wilds, and Margie Meiswick, and an exhibition game of Wham-O's new *Frisbee Game*, won by the Aerobatic Coalition, captained by Dan Roddick. Ashley Whippet and Bismarck displayed their canine catching skills, and thirty-two players qualified for the new IFA rank of World Class Frisbee Master.

Wham-O promises to make the WFC an annual event![17] It may well become the premier meet of the season.

International Junior Frisbee Tournament

The International Junior Frisbee Tournament is sponsored by Wham-O and co-sponsored by park and recreation departments throughout the United States and Canada.[18] Since 1969 over a million and a half boys and girls, ages eight through fifteen,

[17]Interested parties should contact the IFA for details.
[18]The tournament went international in 1974, with the addition of Canadian youngsters. Contact your local Park and Recreation Department for information about entering the competition.

Junior Frisbee Tournament

Event	Throws or Catches	Possible Points Total
1. Backhand Right Curve into Circle	2	2
2. Backhand Left Curve into Circle	2	2
3. Sidearm or Underhand (must be specified) Right Curve into Circle	2	4
4. Sidearm or Underhand (must be specified) Left Curve into Circle	2	4
5. Backhand Skip Flight into Circle	2	4
6. Sidearm Skip Flight into Circle	2	4
7. Underhand Skip Flight into Circle	2	4
8. Behind-the-Back Catch with Left or Right Hand (must be specified)	2	4
9. Between-the-Legs Catch with either hand (hand must be specified)	2	4
10. Distance Throw: 30 yards or more, 1 point; 40 yards or more, 3 points; 60 yards or more, 5 points	3	3

Each contestant leads off one event. Events 1 through 7 are conducted over a 25-yard course with throws into 12-foot diameter circle.

Tie Breaker: The contestants involved will repeat Events 1, 6, 8, and 9. (Lefthanders substitute Event 2 for Event 1.)

Darrell Lewis receives Junior Frisbee Tournament prize in Madison Square Garden from Irv Lander of IFA.

The DYT·A·SIGHT DISTANCE award is present to
Pat Visser
for throwing a frisbee _90_
in the under nine division.

5th Annual International Tournament

on July 2, 1972
in Copper Harbor

Pat Visser of Kalamazoo, Michigan, a junior champion of IFT.

The International Junior Frisbee Tournament Winners from 1969 to 1974:

Year	Name	Age		Location of Tourn.
1969	Darrell Lewis, *Portland, Ore.*	16*	Winner	Madison Square Garden,
	Gary Knuth, *Normal, Ill.*	15	Runner-up	New York City
1970	Danny Sanders, *Oak Ridge, Tenna.*	15	Winner	International Hotel Convention Center,
	Gary Valenta, *Cedar Rapids, Ia.*	15	Runner-up	Las Vegas, Nev.
1971	Kenneth Schmidlein, *Waban, Mass.*	14	Winner	Las Vegas Hilton Hotel,
	Ezequiel Ochoa, *Denver, Colo.*	14	Runner-up	Las Vegas, Nev.
1972	Paul Wilson, *Charleston, W. Va.*	15	Winner	Las Vegas Hilton Hotel,
	Kevin Schmidlein, *Waban, Mass.*	15	Runner-up	Las Vegas, Nev.
1973	Kelly Forgét, *Las Vegas, Nev.*	15	Winner	Northern High School,
	Craig Hartman, *Cedar Rapids, Ia.*	11	Runner-up	Baltimore, Md.
1974	James Schmidlein, *Waban, Mass.*	13	Winner	Fenn Stadium, Boston, Mass.
	Danny Quinto, *Denver, Colo.*	15	Runner-up	

*Darrell was fifteen when he registered.

have competed each year through city, state, regional, and national finals to select the International Junior Champion of Frisbee.

The Junior Frisbee Tournament is now larger in numbers participating than the Punt, Pass, and Kick competition and the Soap Box Derby combined. The first-place award is a thousand-dollar Savings Bond to be used toward a college education.

Irv Lander of the IFA is the tournament director. The finals between the top two scorers are held on a major TV show.

Jersey Jam

This Folf and Free Style Meet closes the tournament for Eastern players unless they travel on to the Big Game tournament in November. The meet began in 1974 and featured a Folf target which the FDW, meet sponsor, suggests as a standard in Frisbee golf. This is a five-foot diameter ring with twelve-inch sides. Gary and Gina Seubert are tournament organizers, and plans for the 1975 Jam again call for a Columbus Day weekend meeting in Johnson Park, New Brunswick, New Jersey.

Winners of the 1974 tournament:

Folf	Kerry Kolmar, New York City
Free Style	Dan Roddick,
Overall Winner	Dan Roddick
Runner-up	John Kirkland

Big Game Tournament

Two great universities, Stanford and California,[19] annually square away in *the* traditional intercollegiate Frisbee Tournament, the "Big Game" meet.[20] Held first in 1969 during that special festive week in November at the Berkeley campus, California and the Berkeley Frisbee Group have never failed to win the event.

Winners:

1969 Records (N.A.)
1970 Distance: Bob May
    Accuracy: Rob Kalnitsky
    Medley Accuracy: Bob Sellers
    Guts: BFG (David Book,
        Vic Malafronte, Bob May,
        Chuck Pitt, Steve Sewall)
1971 Records (N.A.)
1972 Records (N.A.)
1973 Distance: John Kirkland
    Accuracy: Vic Malafronte
    Medley Accuracy:
        Steve Gottlieb
    Individual Guts:
        (Rained Out)
1974 Tournament rained out.

Bad weather has foiled the last several Big Game meets. Organizers are considering indoors for 1975.[21]

Other Tournaments and Activities

Expressing oneself in Frisbee is not limited to organized tournaments. Flying disc athletes have held underwater distance contests, juggled plates from unicycles, tossed saucers from speeding motorboats and while skydiving. Disc showmen have demonstrated at professional sport halftimes, the Indianapolis 500 race, and the Calgary Stampede. Frisbee teachers have taught at summer camps, high schools, prisons, free universities, and in front of the cameras of numerous major TV shows. Saucer enthusiasts have thrown for incredible distances from mountaintops such as Whitney, and sacrificed discs into volcanoes and canyons such as Kilimanjaro and the Grand. They have made shots on the floor of Death Valley, in front of Red Square, under the shadow of the Eiffel Tower, in the Casbah, across the International Date Line, and around both North and South Poles. A spectacular boomerang shot once circumnavigated four states.[22]

Marathon Frisbee throwing is the new campus craze. Yale holds the present record with 374 hours 15 minutes. Visiting dignitaries such as Russian cosmonauts and Chinese Ping-Pong champions are fascinated by the Western flying disc and can't resist tossing a few.

From all over the world come reports of meets, contests, and events held or planned. The following is an incomplete but representative list from universities and colleges including Southern Alabama, Brigham Young, Cornell, Duke, University of California at Davis, Indiana, North Carolina, San Diego State, Wesleyan, and Washington State, plus American River College, Marin College, College of Wooster, and Mount Union College; also Golden West College and College of Canyons in California and two Pennsylvania schools, Millersville State and Lafayette College.

San Francisco, Seattle, and Birmingham hold city-wide meets while Austin, Texas, has a special contest for its senior citizens. Urbana, Illinois, has a fall Frisbee fling in its parks and the State Fair of California held a contest on fair opening day.

Germany and South Africa have junior and senior championships country-wide. The German junior champs participated at the 1974 IFA junior meet in Baltimore. There's always a Frisbee in the air somewhere in the world!

Tournament Events

The IFT has set the traditional tournament events as three—distance, accuracy, and Guts.

The Distance Event

The distance contest is the most exciting individual event of any tournament. I am often asked what is the

---

[19]In 1973 Sacramento State College somehow elbowed in to make it a *three*-way meet.
[20]The "Big Game" is football.
[21]For details, contact The Californians-Oski Dolls Organization, c/o Associated Students of California, University Office, University of California, Berkeley.
[22]At the four-corner spot of New Mexico, Arizona, Utah, and Colorado.

Summary Of Events In Major Frisbee Tournaments

Tournament	IFA Proficiency Tests	Distance	Accuracy	Medley Accuracy	Trick-Throw Accuracy	Bull's Eye Accuracy	Free Style	MTA	TRC	DDC	Folf	Guts	The Frisbee Game	Ultimate	Trick Catch	Courtsbee	Canine	Discathon
University of Michigan Indoor Frisbee Festival March—Ann Arbor, Mich.	NO	YES	YES	NO	NO	NO	YES	NO	NO	NO	NO	YES[3]	NO	NO	NO	NO	NO	NO
Eastern Intercollegiate Ultimate Frisbee Championships April—Yale, New Haven, Conn.[6]	NO	NO	NO	NO	NO	NO	NO	NO	NO	NO	NO	NO	NO	YES	NO	NO	NO	NO
Octad—Rutgers University May—New Brunswick, N.J.	NO	YES	YES	NO	YES	NO	YES	YES	YES	NO[2]	YES	NO	NO	NO	NO[2]	NO	NO	YES
Northwestern University Frisbee Tournament June—Evanston, Ill.	NO	YES[4]	NO	NO	NO	NO	NO	NO	NO	NO	YES	YES[3]	NO	NO	NO	NO	NO	NO
International Frisbee Tournament July—Marquette, Mich.	NO	YES[4]	YES[5]	NO	NO	NO	NO	YES	NO	NO	YES	YES	NO	NO	YES[1]	NO	NO	NO
Cliff's Ridge Invitational October—Marquette, Mich.	NO	NO	NO	NO	NO	NO	NO	NO	NO	NO	YES	NO	NO	NO	NO	NO	NO	NO
Canadian Open Frisbee Championships August—Toronto, Can.	NO	YES	YES	NO	NO	NO	YES	YES	NO	NO	YES	NO	NO	NO	NO	NO	YES	NO
American Flying Disc Open August—Rochester, N.Y.	NO	NO	NO	NO	NO	NO[8]	NO	NO	NO	YES	YES	NO	NO	NO	NO	NO	NO	NO
World Frisbee Championship August—Pasadena, Calif.	YES	YES[4]	YES[9]	YES[9]	NO	NO	YES[9]	NO	NO	NO	NO	YES	YES	NO	YES[9]	NO	YES	NO
International Junior Frisbee Championships[6] September—Los Angeles, Calif.	YES	YES[9]	YES[9]	YES[9]	NO	NO	YES[9]	NO	NO	NO	NO	NO	NO	NO	YES[9]	NO	NO	NO
Jersey Jam October—New Brunswick, N.J.	NO	NO	NO	NO	NO	NO	YES	NO	NO	NO	YES	NO	NO	NO	NO	NO	NO	NO
Big Game Tournament November—Berkeley or Stanford[6a]	NO	YES	YES	YES	NO	NO	NO	NO	NO	NO	NO	YES[7]	NO	NO	NO	NO	NO	NO

Legend

1. Demonstration only
2. 1974 only
3. Three-Man Guts
4. Women's Contest Separate
5. Junior and Children's Division Held
6. Closed Tournament
6a. Invitations to participate can be arranged
7. One-on-One Guts
8. Beginning 1975
9. As described in the IFA Proficiency Tests

An impromptu Distance Event.

ground markers, every five or ten yards, help the thrower and the spectator follow the competition. Always throw with the wind. A distance record should be allowed only if the prevailing wind is less than 6 mph.[25]

The Wind. Cornering winds[26] are a problem. They are an advantage to throwers whose spin direction is the same as the wind. For example, the right-handed, backhand delivery—the most popular with distance throwers—is helped by a left cornering wind. Orient the field in the general mean wind direction and let the Frisbees fall where they may.

Put wind flags at the throwing spot, halfway downfield, and at the field's end. The flag heights should be: throwing spot, three or four feet; midfield, forty to fifty yards—the same height as the apogee of flight, or about ninety feet (if you are using a football field, flags two-thirds up the light poles should be about right); at the end of the field, fifteen or twenty

longest throw on record. The most spectacular I have seen was in the 1970 IFT at Calumet, Michigan. Bob May of Berkeley, California, delivered a 93-yard winning toss in the distance final. But several hours earlier May and I were throwing in warmups, and I was privileged to see on a windless field his practice toss travel from goal line to goal line on Aggisiz Field,[23] a perfect 100-yard throw.[24] At the time of the throw, he was at the pinnacle of his playing condition with perfect coordination and release. The current long throwers are making the 100-yard throw almost commonplace in recent tournaments. John Kirkland won the distance event at the 1974 World Fris-

bee Championships, outdistancing all contenders. But the longest recorded throw in a tournament was by Dave Johnson of Boston—378 feet (126 yards)—at the 1974 Octad. Other outstanding distance throwers: Vic Malafronte, Joe Essman, John Connelly, Roger Hedge, Jim Walker, and Joseph Robinson.

The Field. The football field has an ideal set of markings for a distance event, but the wind may not cooperate. Good results can be had on any large area of at least 100 yards. The 90-degree rule is best, i.e., throw from the apex of the 90-degree angle (the throw must fall within the angle lines extended). Distance stakes and

---

[23]Aggisiz Field has seen heroics before: George Gipp, Notre Dame football immortal, played high school football there.

[24]At the 1973 IFT, John Connelly, Dave Johnson, and John Kirkland of Boston exceeded May's throw, but the distance course had a nasty downfield slope of at least 5 degrees. Any distance record must be made over flat ground.

[25]The handheld Dywer wind meter is accurate enough and costs under seven dollars. Available in nautical shops or write: Dywer Instruments, Inc., Michigan City, Indiana 46360.

[26]A cornering wind blows across the left or right shoulder, and downfield at a 45-degree angle.

feet. Wind flags help the thrower judge wind direction and speed. If he finds a swirling wind, he can often use it to advantage. For example, a right-handed backhand thrower (clockwise spin) is helped by a left cornering wind at the beginning; but a right cornering wind would help his left warp curl at the finish. So he checks his wind flags, notes the desired breeze over his left shoulder, while midfield flags point straight down field. The finish flags indicate swirl to the right as the wind deflects off trees downfield. *Voilà!*

The Thrower. The complete distance thrower should have a competitive clockwise and counterclockwise effort. Most throwers will stick to one style they have mastered in timing and coordination. Few will change deliveries in midwind, so to speak. One outstanding exception is Tom Bodá. Tom has an excellent right-handed backhand delivery that stands him in good stead with the greats. But his specialty—and he's probably the best in the world—is a right-handed overhand wrist fling, a counterclockwise spinner. He feels equally adept with each and shows no hesitation to shift with the wind. He is the switch-hitting Mickey Mantle of Frisbee. Others should follow his lead.

Timing of the throw is as important as the wind condition. It takes several throws for a thrower to work into his "groove." Five to ten is a must.

The last element in distance

throwing is the approach leading to release. A few years back at the IFT there was an attempt to set a six-yard limit within a shot-put-like ring. Many people found this to be a handicap because they like a long run to pick up speed and momentum. There's not much advantage in a long run, but it seems to make them feel more comfortable. I recommend no limit.

Recommendations for Improving Event. If there are a large number of competitors, I recommend an elimination round. The qualifying distance should be dictated by the quality of the field (average 50 to 60 yards). Each thrower should have ten throws, especially in the finals. He should be allowed all the time he needs to find his particular wind conditions, otherwise competition is not meaningful. In one tournament I attended, throwers were allowed only three throws and were required to throw *within a one-minute time limit!* A simple method of keeping track of the best throws in small meets: the top three contenders stand by their best throw in the field. This obviates the need of markers and adds the psychological thrill of watching your competitor's Frisbee sail toward you. Otherwise use numbered field stakes.

The distance mark must be at the *point of impact*. The run should never count. I had the misfortune of viewing another tournament where the run was taken into account. Inferior players were conjuring up distances of eighty yards, half of which

was run![27] At the 14th International Frisbee Tournament, a novel but, to my mind, not successful modification was tried. A downhill street marked with a center line was the distance course. If your throw was seventy-five yards downfield but twelve yards off the line, your revised distance was sixty-three yards. Thus, distance became more a measure of accuracy.

Height of Release[28]. Probably the most important reason why the backhand, the sidearm, and the overhand wrist fling deliveries outdistance the underarm is the difference in the height of release. The former throws are accomplished at shoulder height; the latter, one and a half to two and a half feet lower. This leads to tailskating (see page 65) in strong withwinds for the underhand and nosegliding for the backhand and overhand wrist fling.

Nose Gliding (Toejam Power). A distance thrower always likes a modest wind at his back favoring his spin, and if he can get a mild gale-like blow behind him, he can boost his total distance considerably with nose gliding. With a high height of re-

---

[27]The run in Frisbee is seldom important. It is used in Frisbee golf to avoid obstacles and in Goal Line to drive an opponent downfield.

[28]Frisbee physicists may cringe over these simplistic explanations. See Jay Shelton's "Frisbee Physics" in the Appendix for a scientific exposition.

An accuracy contest at a Boy Scout camp called Frisbeeville.

but comes straight through from set to release.

Instead of sighting each throw, many accuracy throwers try to develop a rhythm or beat. Once into this, they will complete their throws very quickly.

There are several super-accuracy players. One is "Steady Ed" Headrick, captain of the 1968 and 1969 California Masters Championship Guts teams. Another is Robert (Boots) Healy, one of the bulwarks of the North Central Michigan team and a co-founder of the IFT. Noteworthy others: Jim Stowe of Birmingham, Alabama; Joe Essman of Wellston, Ohio; Ken Linna and Doug Hovey of Michigan; Irv Kalb of New Jersey; Jim Gabbard of San Francisco; Geoff Wong of Sacramento, California; Marie Murphy of Northwestern University; and Jay Shelton, World Frisbee Champion from 1968 to 1974.

The Guts Event

Guts Frisbee has always been *the* paramount event at the IFT. It is played with five-man teams, and the winners are proclaimed the World Champion team. Three-man guts competition is becoming quite popular, particularly in early spring tournaments such as the University of Michigan indoor.

In other places, especially California, Guts is often played individu-

lease, he must get the nose to drop in late waft, before wane, then the wind will force the plate along, using Toejam's recess as a plastic sail. Nose gliding is the secret strength of accomplished distance throwers.

The Accuracy Competition

Frisbees, despite their inherent tendency to soar and shift with the inconstant winds, can be thrown with great accuracy up to fifteen yards at least. A marksman can deliver his Frisbee to a catcher or target within a yard or so, eight or nine times out of ten at that distance.

Accuracy is best tested by throwing through a round target[29]. It should really be conducted indoors. The optimum distance to the target is fifteen to twenty yards. Give the thrower at least five to ten throws to develop his rhythm and groove.

Most accuracy throwers stand facing the target as in darts. I have yet to see a good accuracy thrower who used a running approach, even a short one.

There is a parallel between Frisbee accuracy and free-throw shooting in basketball. The player should use the style of delivery that is most comfortable, one he can reproduce over and over again with the least expenditure of strength. I prefer a straight armswing, backhand throw. The Frisbee does not traverse an arc

---

[29]The traditional target at the IFT is a rubber tire; 3 points for going through and 1 point for a rim touch.

The ball yard at Eagle Harbor filled with Guts teams battling for the Nachazel Cup.

al style, one-on-one. The competitors must then defend a goal line six feet in diameter. (For all the rules of team Guts, see Chapter 6.)

Special Tournament Events

The following special tournament events test the complete skill of a Frisbee player.

Maximum Time Aloft (MTA)

Maximum time aloft began with the BFG at Berkeley. It can be done as a group contest or timed with a stopwatch. The former is more exciting but requires excellent judges. With no more than five throwers, a count of three is made, then the discs are released in boomerang style. The contest is to keep the Frisbee in the air longest and to catch it. Catching a long boomerang is a challenge, but angling it in the air for the longest possible time and still catching it is a real test of skill. This event is most popular on the West Coast. In group fashion, no effort is made to keep times. The longest flight I have seen is 11.2 seconds. [30] I am certain longer flights are possible. MTA was introduced in 1973 at the IFT. In tournament play, John Kirkland set the record of 10.1 seconds at Octad in 1974.

Frisbee Golf

This is an excellent event combining accuracy, distance, and smaller skills such as the run. (See Chapter 6 for a description of Frisbee golf.)

Bull's-Eye Accuracy

This is an untried event but should be a fine addition. The thrower should be on a rise to view about forty yards downfield. The target would be laid out on the ground in concentric circles, like a large dartboard. There should be at least four circles: bull's eye (100), 50, 25 and 10 point areas. The total diameter should be fourteen feet, with each circle about two feet. The purpose of the event is to make the most points. This contest requires skill in mastering the roll of the Frisbee. The best throws would be curves, since straight throws would sail over; hovers would be good too. The warp curl would be important to consider.

Throw, Run, Catch (TRC)

The contestant throws in any direction he chooses and catches his own throw. The longest caught throw wins. Three to five throws per contestant. This event should test the ability to gauge wind and make a curving boomerang throw. Distances of forty to fifty yards are possible. In Ultimate games, leadoff throwers have caught their own toss (sixty yards) using a Master model. In tournament competition, John Kirkland holds the current record of 165 feet at Octad in 1974.

Free Style

Style in catching and throwing would be hard to judge. One way would pair contestants and award difficulty points for complicated deliveries and catches. For example, a B-T-B spin catch would be worth 5 points; a regular B-T-B catch, 3 points; and the legs catch, 1 point. The free style is rapidly becoming the favorite among noncompetition players.

Medley Accuracy

This event was introduced in 1969 at the Berkeley Big Game tournament. The ten-throw medley is right curve, left curve, and skip—three each—and one free choice. Same target as in regular accuracy. Curves must go around midcourse poles standing eight feet apart. Best score of ten throws wins. Medley accuracy rounds out a full test of accuracy skills.

Trick-Throw Accuracy (TTA)

This is the Octad's version of Medley Accuracy. Thrower begins at ten yards from the target—a five-foot diameter ring—and makes five different deliveries (e.g., overhand wrist fling, thumb, etc.), then moves out five yards at a time up to forty-five yards. Each "through" counts one point. TTA is a tough test of accuracy skills.

Discathon

A new tournament event first tried at

_____

[30]Steve Sewell, IFT qualifying rounds, 1973.

the Octad in 1975, Discathon combines distance, accuracy, and *stamina*. It's cross-country with a disc!

The contestant runs a two-mile course along a chalk-line course, trying to keep his throws as close to the line as possible to minimize his run.

Courtsbee

Courtsbee is untested as a tournament event so far. It is similar to trick catch but would test a player's agility and defense skills better (see page 95).

Double-Disc Court

DDC can be a fine tournament event and a test of a player's accuracy, overall catching ability, and agility. (See page 85 for a full description.)

The Frisbee Tournament (the Duodecathalon)

The Frisbee tournament has yet to be held,[31] but the BFG in their intrasquad meets have come close. They once held a tournament lasting nine successive weekends. The distance competition alone stretched over three weekends. There were sixteen different kinds of throws and ways of throwing, including: with opposite hand, between the legs, upside down (the Frisbee), and with a modified Frisbee.

A tournament with the following twelve events would be the absolute test of individual skill. The overall winner could be crowned World Champion of Frisbee without doubt. See Appendix for a suggested system of scoring.

1. Distance
2. Maximum Time aloft
3. Throw, Run, and Catch
4. Accuracy
5. Medley Accuracy, or Trick-Throw Catch
6. Bull's-Eye Accuracy
7. Folf
8. Guts, Individual
9. Courtsbee, Individual
10. Free Style
11. Discathon
12. Double-Disc Court.

[31]The proper location would seem to be Frisbee, Mo., in the southeast corner of the state. In my preliminary check, all I found was cotton fields, cotton gins, and railroad tracks. Too bad, not enough room for a tournament.

THE HARVEY J. KUKUK GOLDEN FRISBEE AWARD
Conferred This Day On Skylab 3 Astronauts

GERALD P. CARR
EDWARD G. GIBSON
WILLIAM R. POGUE

IN GRATEFUL RECOGNITION OF THEIR INTREPID, GALLANT, UNIQUE
AND NOTEWORTHY CONTRIBUTION TO MAN'S PROGRESS IN FLIGHT.

December 17, 1973

8. FRISBEE ORGANIZATIONS

"The best laid schemes o'mice and men gang aft a'gley an' leae us nought but grief and pain for promised joy."
Robert Burns, "To a Mouse"

Playing Frisbee is a crowd and sharing thing. Players love to pass around their techniques, accomplishments, and aspirations. Yet none of the several national, or even international, organizations speak completely to all these interests. The IFA does the best. Player organized groups much along the lines of the original IFA—now IF (see page 134) have been suggested.[1] Director of the IFA, Harvey J. Kukuk, works untiringly banding together all Frisbee followers.

One group cuts across the present lines of differences by rallying all to a common purpose—the inclusion of Frisbee in the Olympic games.

International Frisbee Association (IFA)

The International Frisbee Association began in the fall of 1967 and is now the largest Frisbee structure in the world, with nearly 70,000 members.

The IFA functions as a clearing house for Frisbee information and publishes quarterly the *IFA News*,[2] a four-page glossy, newsy sheet with photographs and gossipy items about the highest, the lowest, the most, and the least in Frisbee.[3] Harvey J. Kukuk is executive overseer of this chatty rag.

The IFA newsletter has improved greatly with Goldy Norton's editorship. It still falls short for serious players. More attention to basics and less to the bizarre is needed. Subscription is $3.00 a year for four issues ($4.00 for foreign subscribers).

IFA membership costs $2.00 for novice membership ($3.00 for foreign applicants). Through the qualification tests, detailed in the IFA pamphlet and reprinted below, one rises to the ranks of amateur, expert, master, and, highest of all, world class master.

Harvey J. Kukuk has been executive director[4] of the IFA since 1969, ably assisted by executive assistant director Irv Lander. Kukuk had earlier served eleven years as the tour-

---

[1] For information regarding such a proposed group write James Palmeri of Rochester, New York, Frisbee Club, 153 Susan Lane, Rochester 14616.
[2] Their mailing address is IFA, P.O. Box 4578, North Hollywood, Calif. 91607.
[3] If you've ever wondered who IFA Number One is—it's "Steady" Ed Headrick, captain of the legendary California Masters.
[4] Robert O. Werden was the first director, serving from 1967 to 1969. Klaus Albrecht of Speil Sport Fritzeiten, Munich, Germany, Wham-O's German licensee, is head of the European branch of the IFA.

nament director and chairman of the International Frisbee Tournament. A legendary figure in his own time, Kukuk's past exploits are so numerous that it would be impossible to recount them here. Suffice it to say, Kukuk was for years a key sports figure in the Upper Peninsula of Michigan, and served on many committees for the advancement not only of Frisbee, but also of all serious sports in the region. He has been described as a gentleman of shy and retiring nature, but competitively fierce and manly in his ways. His years in Frisbee have taken him to virtually every part of the globe to promote the sport. At many a meet, spectators and contestants alike hope to spy his features; few do. He is editing his notes for an expanded version of his book, *Frisbee as a Way of Life*.

With their kind permission, the official IFA proficiency manual is reproduced here.

In 1974 the IFA opened a new class of Frisbee supremacy—the World Class Frisbee Master.[5] So far only the thirty-two players who qualified at the 1974 Rose Bowl World Championships have earned this title. The rigors are described below.

OFFICIAL IFA PROFICIENCY MANUAL

---

[5] World Class Master qualification will be conducted only at the Wham-O World Frisbee Championships each August or specially designed IFA tournaments.

FOREWORD

The sport of FRISBEE has provided millions of people with great enjoyment and satisfaction. For many, the desire to obtain expertise with the FRISBEE has led them to search for new challenges in throwing, catching and developing new skills with the FRISBEE. It is for those individuals, who aspire to predominance in FRISBEE that the IFA Board of Governors commissioned the development of the FRISBEE Proficiency Rating Program.

By participating in the IFA Proficiency Rating Program, an individual is able to display, by means of classification certification, his achievements and skill off, as well as on, the playing field.

The purpose of the IFA Proficiency Rating Program is to foster the following ideals and to ensure the maximum recreational and competitive values from all FRISBEE activities.
The aims are:

1. To set up standards of proficiency, accomplishment and excellence in the use of the FRISBEE and provide a method by which every IFA member may judge his skill and versatility in the light of accepted standards of the IFA membership.

2. To encourage individual achievement by putting a premium upon individual skills and thus enhance the player's value in competitive play.

3. To acknowledge progress and to give recognition to accomplishment, to improve techniques and to increase the total proficiency in the use of the FRISBEE by each IFA member.

— 1 —

IFA PROFICIENCY RATING SYSTEM

The IFA Board of Governors has established the following degrees of individual proficiency, as determined by accomplishment of the IFA Proficiency Rating Standards:

NOVICE
A Novice is anyone who enjoys a FRISBEE, owns a FRISBEE, and is a member in good standing of IFA.

AMATEUR
An Amateur is an IFA member in good standing who has passed the Amateur Proficiency Test, which must be attested to by one IFA member in good standing.*

EXPERT
An Expert is an IFA member in good standing who has passed the Expert Proficiency Test, which must be attested to by two IFA members in good standing.*

MASTER
A Master is an IFA member in good standing who has passed the Master Proficiency Test, which must be attested to by three IFA members in good standing.*

Upon successful completion of the entire Master Proficiency Test, which is to be attested to by the judges on the candidate's proficiency rating card, the card and certification fee is sent to IFA headquarters for official sanction. The member will then receive certification as a FRISBEE.Master and be issued a special membership card and certificate.

Only members in good standing may hold and compete in the above classifications. A lifetime membership payment for any member to be in good standing is $2.00. Authenticated proficiency test scores, listed on the proficiency rating card, must be submitted to the IFA Board of Governors along with certification fee for advance in rating. NOTE: A member is not required to progress through each classification in order to become a candidate for a higher rating. Write IFA Headquarters for Expert and Master proficiency rating cards.

While IFA proficiency certification is predicated on the honor system, any member may be challenged by another IFA member of equal or higher rating to demonstrate his proficiency within his classification.

If IFA members are used as judges, IFA membership card numbers must accompany their signatures.

*If not available by a like number of permanent residents of your community who are professionally engaged in recreation, sports and/or physical education.

— 2 —

AMATEUR PROFICIENCY QUALIFICATION REQUIREMENTS

CONDITIONS AND TEST AREA

A 12-foot diameter circle should be drawn on the ground. Measuring from the center of the circle, at 15 yards distance, a "foul line" is drawn on the ground. The candidate must deliver his flights from behind the "foul line".

The catcher is free to move anywhere within the 12-foot diameter circle but is prohibited from stepping outside of it during the accuracy test. The candidate may elect to take any or all of the proficiency test within the 30-minute maximum time period allowed in each 24-hour day.

ACCURACY REQUIREMENTS

Within each of the following groups, the flights must be completed consecutively, with the method of delivery the candidate's choice. If the flight is properly executed, and the catcher fails, it will be judged to be a completed flight.

The candidate may schedule the following seven flight groups in any order he wishes.

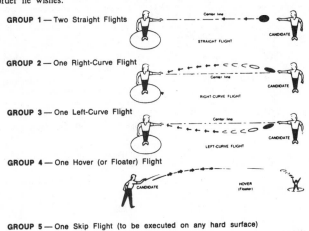

GROUP 1 — Two Straight Flights

STRAIGHT FLIGHT

GROUP 2 — One Right-Curve Flight

RIGHT-CURVE FLIGHT

GROUP 3 — One Left-Curve Flight

LEFT-CURVE FLIGHT

GROUP 4 — One Hover (or Floater) Flight

HOVER (Floater)

GROUP 5 — One Skip Flight (to be executed on any hard surface)

SKIP FLIGHT

— 3 —

GROUP 6 — Distance Flight whereby the candidate must obtain an average distance, in four flights, two up-wind and two down-wind, of not less than 20 yards.

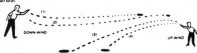

GROUP 7 — Repeat any two flights in the above Groups 1 through 5 using opposite method of delivery, i.e. if backhand was used, throw underhand.

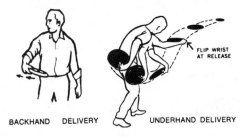

FLIP WRIST AT RELEASE

BACKHAND DELIVERY   UNDERHAND DELIVERY

CATCHING REQUIREMENTS

The candidate must be capable of catching two consecutive flights of any type using only the right hand, and two consecutive flights of any type using only the left hand, thrown from a distance of 15 to 20 yards. Note: These catches should be done consecutively, however, consideration will be allowed if the flights are not properly executed.

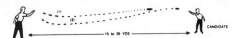

Upon successful completion of the entire Amateur Proficiency Test, which is to be attested to by the judges on the candidate's proficiency rating card, the card and certification fee of $1.00 is sent to IFA headquarters for official sanction. The member will then receive certification as a FRISBEE* Amateur and be issued a new membership card, expert proficiency rating card and special certificate.

— 4 —

EXPERT PROFICIENCY QUALIFICATION REQUIREMENTS

CONDITIONS AND TEST AREA

A 12-foot diameter circle should be drawn on the ground. Measuring from the center of the circle, at 25 yards distance, a "foul line" is drawn on the ground. The candidate must deliver his flights from behind the "foul line".

The catcher is free to move anywhere within the 12-foot diameter circle but is prohibited from stepping outside of it during the accuracy test. The candidate may elect to take any or all of the proficiency test within the 30-minute maximum time period allowed in each 24-hour day.

ACCURACY REQUIREMENTS

Within each of the following groups, the flights must be completed consecutively, with the method of delivery the candidate's choice. If the flight is properly executed, and the catcher fails, it will be judged to be a completed flight.

The candidate may schedule the following eight flight groups in any order he wishes.

GROUP 1 — Four Straight Flights

STRAIGHT FLIGHT

GROUP 2 — Two Right-Curve Flights

RIGHT CURVE FLIGHT

GROUP 3 — Two Left-Curve Flights

LEFT-CURVE FLIGHT

GROUP 4 — Two Hover (or Floater) Flights

HOVER (Floater)

GROUP 5 — Two Skip Flights (to be executed on any hard surface)

SKIP FLIGHT

GROUP 6 — Distance Flight whereby the candidate must obtain an average distance, in four flights, two up-wind and two down-wind, of not less than 30 yards.

DOWN-WIND   UP-WIND

— 5 —

GROUP 7 — Repeat any two flights in the above Groups 1 through 5 using opposite method of delivery, i.e. if backhand was used, throw underhand.

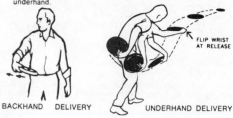

FLIP WRIST AT RELEASE

BACKHAND DELIVERY   UNDERHAND DELIVERY

GROUP 8 — One Boomerang Flight with the flight made from within a 10-foot square area. The candidate must throw the FRISBEE out of the 10-foot square area a minimum distance of 20 feet and have the FRISBEE return and be caught within the 10-foot square area. The FRISBEE may be thrown at any angle as dictated by the wind conditions.

"BOOMERANG FLIGHT

CATCHING REQUIREMENTS

The candidate must be capable of catching two consecutive flights of any type using only the right hand and two consecutive flights of any type using only the left hand, made from a distance of 25 yards. He must also be able to complete one behind-the-back catch using either the right hand or left hand. Note: These catches should be done consecutively, however, consideration will be allowed if the flights are not properly executed.

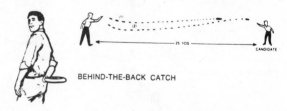

BEHIND-THE-BACK CATCH

Upon successful completion of the entire Expert Proficiency Test, which is to be attested to by the judges on the candidate's proficiency rating card, the card and certification fee is sent to IFA headquarters for official sanction. The member will then receive certification as a FRISBEE*Expert and be issued a new membership card, certificate, Master proficiency rating card.

— 6 —

MASTER PROFICIENCY QUALIFICATION REQUIREMENTS

CONDITIONS AND TEST AREA

A 12-foot diameter circle should be drawn on the ground. Measuring from the center of the circle, at 30 yards distance, a "foul line" is drawn on the ground. The candidate must deliver his flights from behind the "foul line".

The catcher is free to move anywhere within the 12-foot diameter circle but is prohibited from stepping outside of it during the accuracy test. The candidate may elect to take any or all of the proficiency test within the 60-minute maximum time period allowed in each 24-hour day.

ACCURACY REQUIREMENTS

Within each of the following groups, the flights must be completed consecutively, with the method of delivery the candidate's choice. If the flight is properly executed, and the catcher fails, it will be judged to be a completed flight.

The candidate may schedule the following ten flight groups in any order he wishes.

GROUP 1 — Four Straight Flights

GROUP 2 — Four Right-Curve Flights

GROUP 3 — Four Left-Curve Flights

GROUP 4 — Four Hover (or Floater) Flights

GROUP 5 — Four Skip Flights (to be executed on any hard surface)

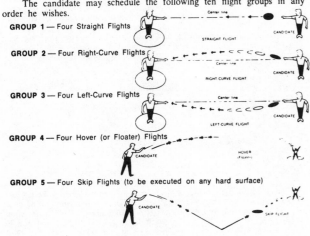

— 7 —

GROUP 6 — Distance Flight whereby the candidate must obtain an average distance, in four flights, two up-wind and two down-wind, of not less than 40 yards*.

NOTE: Group 6 may be waived upon acceptable letter of explanation.

GROUP 7 — Two Boomerang Flights with the flight made from within a 10-foot square area. The candidate must throw the FRISBEE out of the 10-foot square area a minimum distance of 20 feet and have the FRISBEE return and be caught within the 10-foot square area. The FRISBEE may be thrown at any angle as dictated by the wind conditions.

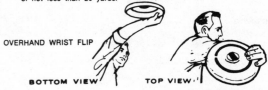

BOOMERANG FLIGHT

GROUP 8 — One accurate Overhand Wrist-Flip of any flight at a distance of of not less than 20 yards.

OVERHAND WRIST FLIP

BOTTOM VIEW   TOP VIEW

GROUP 9 — One accurate Side-Arm throw of any flight at a distance of not less than 30 yards.

CLOSE UP OF THROW

— 8 —

GROUP 10 — Repeat any two flights in the above Groups 1 through 5 using opposite method of delivery, i.e. if backhand was used, throw underhand.

FLIP WRIST
AT RELEASE

BACKHAND   DELIVERY   UNDERHAND DELIVERY

CATCHING REQUIREMENTS

The candidate must be capable of catching four consecutive flights of any type using only the right hand and four consecutive flights of any type using only the left hand, thrown from a distance in excess of 30 yards. He must also complete the following:

SPECIAL CATCHES

1. Two, not consecutive, behind-the-back catches using either the right or left hand only.
2. Two, not consecutive, between-the-legs catches using either the right or left hand only.

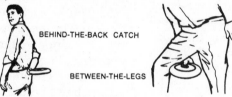

BEHIND-THE-BACK CATCH

BETWEEN-THE-LEGS

3. Two, not consecutive, index finger catches using either the right or left hand only.

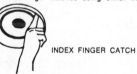

INDEX FINGER CATCH

IFA
AMATEUR PROFICIENCY RATING CARD

NAME _____
IFA No. _____
ADDRESS _____
CITY _____ STATE _____
ZIP _____

INTERNATIONAL FRISBEE® ASSOCIATION
P.O. Box 4578, No. Hollywood, Ca. 91607

AMATEUR PROFICIENCY
RATING QUALIFICATION
(See Proficiency Manual for Details)

ACCURACY (at 15 yards)		
GROUP 1	Up-wind _____ yds.	
Two Straight Flights _____	Down-wind _____ yds.	
GROUP 2	Down-wind _____ yds.	
Right-Curve Flight _____	Average _____ yds.	
GROUP 3	(20 yards average to qualify) _____	
Left-Curve Flight _____	**GROUP 7**	
GROUP 4	Two Underhand OR	
Hover (or Floater) Flight _____	Backhand Deliveries	
GROUP 5	Group _____ & _____	
Skip Flight _____	**CATCHING** (15 to 20 yards)	
GROUP 6		
DISTANCE	Two catches, right hand _____	
Up-wind _____ yds.	Two catches, left hand _____	

NOTE: Examiner please initial each group as completed.

Requirements for World Class Frisbee Master

General Requirements:

1. All required throws and catches must be completed within one hour (elapsed time).
2. Failure to complete any one requirement in five attempts at that requirement results in disqualification.

Throwing Flights. (30 yards to catcher in 12-foot diameter circle) Thrower must accomplish each of the following throws three times in five attempts, using each of three different deliveries (i.e., backhand, sidearm, underhand, thumb flip, etc.):

a. Straight Flight
b. Hover Flight
c. Right Curve
d. Left Curve
e. Skip Flight

Catching Flights. (30 yards within 12-foot diameter circle) Catcher must execute each of the following catches three times in five attempts. Bad throws will not count as attempts.

a. Behind-the-back catch, feet off the ground
b. Between-the-legs catch, feet off the ground
c. Behind-the-head catch
d. Free style tip catch

Boomerang Throw. Candidate must successfully execute three boomerang throws and catches in five attempts from a 12-foot diameter circle, with each throw going out at least 20 yards from the circle.

Distance Requirement. Candidate must successfully execute this requirement on three throws in five attempts using each of three different deliveries.

A successful throw must land in a 15-yard-wide zone which begins 50 yards away from the thrower.

All throws may be made with the wind.

NOTE: In all throwing requirements where the phrase "using each of three different deliveries" is used, this means that the player must, for example, make three out of five right curves using the backhand, three out of five right curves using the sidearm, and three out of five right curves using the overhand wrist flip. Similarly, in distance he must make three out of five successful throws into the 15-yard zone using, for example, the backhand, three out of five using the underhand, and three out of five using the sidearm.

The International Frisbee Tournament (IFT)

The International Frisbee Tournament is the oldest organization in Frisbee, dating back to the first meet in 1958. The Healy family, particularly brothers John J. and Robert H., are responsible for its development.

The Board of Governors of the IFT are elected for life terms and have served admirably in maintaining the tournament at the highest level of amateurism.[6] Many people have commented that Frisbee as performed at the International Frisbee tournament approaches the true meaning of amateurism to a degree virtually extinct in the sports world today. The week preceding the IFT is filled with gala activities as incoming teams from all over the country arrive. There is a parade with floats, a tournament queen, and all the sundry events associated with such extravaganzas.

The meet is held every year on the weekend closest to the Fourth of July. The Healys passed the director's reins to James Boggio in 1969, and then to Jon Davis of Houghton, Michigan,[7] in 1970.

The years have seen six different sites in the Upper Peninsula for the IFT. Copper Harbor, host in 1971 and 1972, hopes to be selected as the permanent site and has plans for a total Frisbee stadium with twenty Guts fields, a distance field of 150 yards, a wind-protected accuracy area, and a special field for Ultimate Frisbee; however, Marquette, the current site, and Hancock-Houghton, Michigan,

---

[6] There is an uncertain rumor that Avery Brundage asked to be on the IFT board and was turned down—not strong enough in his amateur ideals, the board felt.

[7] Mr. Davis is also well known in his city as the proprietor of the Library Bar, a public house frequented by students from Michigan Tech. University.

are also hot in the running for the permanent IFT site.

Old-timers still yearn for the legendary Eagle Harbor ballyard site[8] of the IFT from 1959 through 1969. In those days, Fletcher's Motel and Café of Eagle Harbor was the Frisbee capital of the world.

IFT plans for a Frisbee Hall of Fame are still unsettled, but as early as 1966 a proposal for an International Frisbee Pavilion was submitted to Mr. Kukuk[9] in the following letter from a prominent American architect.

Dear Mr. Kukuk,

Today we have forwarded to you by insured parcel post our proposal for The International Frisbee Pavilion. Before I describe the highlights of the proposal to you, I would like to take this opportunity to congratulate you and your fine organization. The great strides you have made in promoting international brotherhood and understanding through Frisbee competition, I'm sure, has few parallels in the Frisbee world today. Keep up the good work, and fight the hard fight.

At first glance, our proposal may appear to be nothing more than a giant Frisbee rising from the earth, but I would like to call your attention to the large carillon (or bell tower as we in the industry call it). The tower rises majestically against the background of the pavilion to a height of 350 feet. The tower is not without purpose, for it houses the bells (in the shape of Frisbees) which will call the competitors from Frisbee Freedom Village to the pavilion for competition. Naturally the bells will be cast of a copper alloy native to the fabulous copper country area. The drawings for Frisbee Freedom Village are incomplete at this time, but I assure you they are being executed in accordance with your instructions, and will be forwarded shortly.

The pavilion itself is an inverted concrete saucer 1208 feet 2 inches in diameter. The reason it looks like a Frisbee is because it is an inverted concrete saucer. It seemingly floats above its reflecting pool because of an ingenious device concealed in its dome. There you will find a rather large electromagnet of a

like charge and power to the one in the pavilion floor. The magnets of course repel each other, thereby supporting the saucer. Because the magnets are run on alternating current, the electric circuits in the dome will receive their current by induction—they need not be connected to any power supply, thus eliminating the need for conduit ruining the floating effect.

Housed in a hall near the magnet room at the top of the dome is the International Frisbee Hall of Fame. Enshrined there will be the unforgettables of your great competition. I would like to point out that the diameter of the dome is exactly equal to your world record Frisbee throw, thus assuring that competition may safely be held inside.

I believe most of the other items illustrated—the pagoda, winding moving sidewalks, gardens, 8-level parking garage below the dome, dining room, cafeterias, and stadium hung from above—are self-explanatory.

I hope you are pleased with the presentation, and that the funds come through soon.
Sincerely,
HENRY FLOYD WHITE,
Architect

P.S. I don't want to cast any doubts on our scheme, but we are going to have to find a substitute for the reinforcing steel in the dome. The magnets, you know.

At present there is *the* George Gipp[10] Memorial Pagoda and Frisbee Hall of Fame,[11] located on the famous Eagle Harbor, Michigan, ball yard. Its tiny size prevents display, even storage, of all the Frisbee memorabilia. At present they have:

1. "Thor" Anderson's victory cape.
2. Pictures of all the winning Guts teams.
3. A plaster cast of "Fling" Hyzer's right hand (the one with the extra finger).
4. A replica of the original Julius T. Nachazel Trophy.

5. Jon Davis' IFT Director Tripping Robe, awarded to him by the Nat Love Nine team of Boston at the 13th IFT.
6. Original manuscript of Harvey J. Kukuk's book, *Frisbee as a Way of Life.*

Olympic Frisbee Federation (OFF)[12]

This is a federation of the six principal Frisbee organizations—IFA, IFT, IFF, IF, WFA, and UKFA—plus selected individuals of established Frisbee renown gathered together for the purpose of furthering the cause of making Frisbee a part of the Olympic Games.

There is no current executive director, but this author has agreed to serve as acting executive secretary until the post can be filled.

Proposals, petitions, and com-

---

[8] The IFT might still be in Eagle Harbor except for the crowds—over 4,000 spectators at the 12th IFT. The quiet hamlet of Eagle Harbor couldn't take it any longer.

[9] There is a controversy about the correct spelling of his name: Kukuk on the West Coast, and Kuckuk in the Midwest.

Note in this letter he is referred to as the *Director* of the *International Frisbee Association.* Nearly two years before IFA originated (1968), there was a loosely organized Midwest IFA, and Harvey J. was the director. This same group continues today (still loosely) as the IF.

[10] The "Gipper" was born and reared in nearby Laurium, Michigan.

[11] IFT officials have tried to buy the pagoda for enshrinement on the permanent field. Contributions would be welcome. Send to George Gipp Memorial Pagoda Fund, c/o Jon Davis, Library Bar, Houghton, Mich. 49931.

[12] Organized May 27, 1967.

Frisbee sails past the George Gipp Memorial Pagoda on Eagle Harbor ball yard.

ments from players are welcomed.[13] If Frisbee is ever to be accepted as an Olympic sport, it will take a grass-roots movement to convince the Olympic establishment. (See petition form in Appendix.)

International Frisbeers (IF)

The IF is inactive today. It evolved from the original IFA organized several years before the current IFA by the early players at the International Frisbee Tournament. They were most active in 1969 to 1970 under the directorship of James Boggio[14] of Eagle Harbor.

The IF organized in opposition to the presbyopic practices of the IFA. They early recognized that a truly representative Frisbee organization must be free of affiliation with any Frisbee-making concern. Although quiescent, largely because of insufficient national notice, the IF is still enthusiastic in its advocacy of amateurism and noncommercialism in Frisbee.

The United Kingdom Frisbee Association

This is the main organization for flying-disc fellows in Great Britain, where discsport is rapidly catching on. For more information, contact Mr.

---

[13] For information, write Olympic Frisbee Federation, c/o Stancil Johnson, M.D., Acting Executive Secretary, 178 Central Ave., Pacific Grove, Calif. 93950.

[14] An early member of the famed North Central Champion Guts team.

Martin Coops, Secretary, 15 Jeffry's Place, London, N.W., England.

The World Frisbee Association (WFA)

This is a new group located in Arizona and headed by George Davis of Tucson. They hold their championship games at Mt. Lemmon—the Southern Arizona High Altitude Championships—and award the Willard Friedkin Memorial Trophy to the winning Guts team.

International Frisbee Federation (IFF)

This group, originally known as the Pacific Coast Frisbee Association (PCFA), held its first championships in August 1961 at Stanford University, then in 1962 at Berkeley, California. In 1963 and since then, they have had a summer meet called the World Frisbee Championships in Panama City.

The IFF tournament is distance and accuracy, no form of the Guts game at all. Accuracy is tested over a 75-foot course; distance is tested with and against the wind.

Al Clark, who co-developed the Clark-Shelton modified common grip, was the early champion of their meets. The *Frisbee News* is the official news organ of the group.[15]

Flying Disc World (FDW)

Really a periodical, and the only independent Frisbee news organ in print, the *FDW* is for serious and advanced players. It began in February 1974, the brainchild of Dan Roddick and Bob "Flash" Eberle. Subscriptions are $3.00 a year for six issues.[16]

FDW annually awards the Dispo to individuals and groups for outstanding service in disc sports. Jim Palmeri[17] of Rochester, New York, and Wham-O Manufacturing Company won the first Dispos in 1974—Jim for organizing the American Flying Disc Open, and Wham-O for sponsoring the Rose Bowl World Frisbee championships.

The Harvey J. Club

This is the most exclusive organization in Frisbee. Membership is by invitation only, professional and commercial players are not allowed, and only one member a year may be added. Formed in 1960, it is dedicated to advancing Frisbee in sport, and sport in life.

The club conducts a fund-raising drive each year, called the Fling of Quarters.

Local Clubs and Groups

In sharp contrast to the large international and national organizations are the local club and team groups. They form the true nucleus of Frisbee playing throughout the world.

Space does not permit a complete listing. A few of the outstanding ones are described.

The Berkeley Frisbee Group (BFG)

This is the stellar Frisbee club on the Berkeley campus. Although loosely organized, it holds squad tournaments and annually squares away against Stanford players in the Big Game Tournament. It may have the greatest collection of Frisbee talent anywhere. Many of its players have been described already in this book.

The BFG has the most unusual Frisbee field in Lower Sproul Plaza[18] on the Berkeley campus of the University of California. The plaza is a concrete space behind the Cal Student Union surrounded by tall buildings. The field is cluttered with huge planters holding full-size trees. These natural and unnatural barriers would seem to detract from play, yet every day and especially on weekends Lower Sproul is filled with aspirants. It is the center of Frisbee activity at the university. The distance course runs from the cafeteria to the student publications building —seventy-three yards. Many reach

---

[15] For further information, write Allen B. Jones, Director, International Frisbee Federation, Autodrome Panama, Apartado 8928, Panama 5, R.P.

[16] Mail to *Flying Disc World*, P.O. Box 101, RCHMC, Piscataway, N.J. 08854.

[17] Jim also started the world's first Frisbee store, The Flying Disc and Chess Shop, located at 102 Commercial West, E. Rochester, N.Y.

[18] Of late, the BFG has abandoned Sproul for nearby Willard Park (Everyone calls it the Ho Chi Minh Park).

[19] University officials tried to ban playing in Sproul once, and several hundred students protested successfully.

this distance, so the quest now is how high up the building one can hit. There are unpredictable swirls and counter winds here, and strange paradoxical flights occur. I don't consider Sproul a classic competitive field, but the Berkeley people love it.[19] I would prefer a grass field and more natural winds.

Library Bar

Jon Davis' Library Bar team currently reigns over the world in Guts Frisbee. For the last several seasons, they have been unbeatable. They have the best thumb thrower in the world in Bob Hansen, whose forehand firebrand has been unofficially timed at 90 plus mph! Even more important, they have the best scrambling Guts team in history. The Nachazel Cup left the Upper Peninsula of Michigan in 1968, when the California Masters up-ended Healy's North Central Quintet. The Library boys have brought it back and appear able to keep it there for a long time to come.

Highland Avenue Aces

This three-time world champion Guts team from Wilmette, Illinois—composed of John Connelly, David Bradshaw, Allen Blake, Tom Cleworth, and Steve Korth—grew up playing Frisbee on the street of their club's name.

Teamwork and cool determination are their trademarks. John Connelly is their best all-around player. He placed second in the World Fris-

Highland Avenue Aces clutch after falling Guts toss.

"Sky King" Richardson braces for Guts catch aided by Hugh Barry Anderson, while other Foul Fivers look on.

bee Championships, behind Vic Malafronte.

Foul Five (FF)

This group, captained by George "Thor" Anderson of Gary, Indiana, is the loosest, least practicing, and oldest (mean age of thirty-five) serious Frisbee group around today. Still, they've managed to win the Nachazel Guts title twice.

They are the best senior group in Frisbee and are valued for their experience. Some people feel that a part of the success of the FF comes from the hypnotic trance woven by the haunting melodies of their official bagpiper, Mel Visser of Kalamazoo, Michigan.

Humbley Magnificent Champions of the Universe (HMCU)

This modestly named tribe of several dozen from Ann Arbor-Detroit, Michigan, is one of the hardest practicing, most dedicated in Frisbee. They have played well in past IFT's and are always a threat for team titles. They also always have the best women's team at the IFT and have a fine tradition of sportsmanship. Their Jo Cahow won the World Champion Female title in 1974 at the Rose Bowl meet.

Other Groups

Other groups that deserve mention: North Central, once perennial host team of the IFT; Indiana Guts Masters; BFD of Santa Monica, California; Lee Street Co-op of California; Millersville Gang; Mahle's team of Wellston, Ohio; Diamond Mike's; the Half-Way Bar; Schreiber's Frisbee Association; Rochester Frisbee Club; Columbia High School (Maplewood, N.J.) Varsity Frisbee Team; and the WABX team.

9. THE DOG AND FRISBEE

"But thinks, admitted to that equal sky
His faithful dog shall bear him company."
—Alexander Pope, "An Epistle on Man"

Twenty-one inches and twenty-five pounds of World's Champion streaks down the gridiron. Out of the corner of his eye he studies the wafting flight of the shiny plastic disc. He notes the air speed, checks the angles of Hyzer and Mung, and computes his course to intercept the disc's, then suddenly he springs nine feet into the air and delicately captures the plastic bird in his jaws. Jaws? Yes, jaws. For this is Ashley Whippet, the World's Champion of canine Frisbee. The football crowd roars its approval and all across the nation men glued to the TV set yell into the kitchen for their wives to "drop the dishes, here's your dog. The Frisbee dog!" Ashley is everybody's favorite, the Olga Korbut of Frisbee and with that same verve and play-to-the-crowd instinct. And, Ashley, like Olga, hasn't an unnecessary ounce on his streamlined frame.

Ashley has appeared on the Mike Douglas and Johnny Carson shows. Douglas won two hundred dollars from Bobby Riggs when he bet Riggs his next guest could catch a Frisbee by mouth better than Riggs could. The Mouth of Tennis was no match for the Mouth of Frisbee. Ashley's biggest appearances have been as the star half-time performer at NFL football games, where he has stolen the show from such greats as O. J. Simpson.

Ashley has defeated all comers so far in muzzle-to-muzzle contests, although he was hard pressed by Bismark, a San Diego German shepherd owned by John Rhodes, at the World's Frisbee Championships in August 1974. Ashley and Bismarck collided running onto the field at introduction time. The stunned, smaller Ashley did not perform with his customary crispness. Bismarck was awarded the distance-catch award and Ashley the altitude-catching title. Gunner, a Labrador golden retriever and Canadian champion, owned by John W. Rae, was a stern test but no match for a healthier Ashley when they met several months later at half-time during the NFL playoff game of the Rams and Redskins. A Bismarck-Ashley rematch is needed, but knowledgeable canine Frisbee followers await the match-up of Ashley and Hyper Hank, winner of the Fullerton Fido Fetching Fracas.

Canine Frisbee is not really

new. As early as 1966 the following letter was received by Harvey J. Kukuk, then director of the International Frisbee Tournament.

Emanuel Evangelical Lutheran Church
7787 South 40th Street
Curtistown, Kentucky
May 27, 1966

Mr. Harvey J. Kukuk
Eagle Harbor, Michigan
Chairman of the Frisbee Tournament

Someone sent me a clipping about your great Frisbee Tourney. I wish I had known that since 1958 you had such a tourney.

I have a silvertip collie that I trained to fetch a Frisbee and for the last five years he has been pretty good at it.

By proxy (by way of a movie) I would like to enter him as a contestant for catching the Frisbee. I'm sorry that teaching engagements make it impossible for me to come in person. If you care to show the movie I am sending it along and the champions can review his status. If you do not have a contest for dogs, why not encourage young Americans to train theirs for a future contest.

Sincerely,
REV. H. A. CURTIS, Pastor

P.S. I am enclosing postage and insurance. You are welcome to use the film in any available time you have. Will you please mail the film back to me. I'd be very happy to hear some comments.

Here is Mr. Kukuk's reply:

July 13, 1966

Rev. H. A. Curtis, Pastor
Emanuel Evangelical Lutheran Church
7787 South 40th Street
Curtistown, Kentucky

Your film was mailed yesterday and, hopefully, should have arrived before this letter. The Ninth Annual International Frisbee Tournament was a great success and your film was scheduled as one of the highlights of the post-tournament awards ceremony. Unfortu-nately, the projector was a new automatic model and our projectionist was not too familiar with its operation. As a result, we had great difficulty feeding the film and getting it to roll properly and finally, about halfway through the reel, it snapped. I have had the film spliced and completely examined and have been assured that it is in excellent condition. Although this regrettable experience tarnished our awards ceremony, it in no way detracts from our most sincere appreciation of your interest in the Frisbee Tournament and your generosity in lending the film. I am sure that both you and your dog would have enjoyed the tournament; certainly all the Frisbee fans in attendance would have enjoyed watching the dog make a few catches. The International Frisbee Tournament is held in Eagle Harbor each year during the week of the Fourth of July. We hope that you and your collie can arrange to be on hand in 1967.

Incidentally, I have been in Minneapolis-St. Paul for the past few days investigating a claim that the local zoo has a monkey which makes accurate Frisbee throws of up to 75 feet. Since the weather has been exceedingly hot this week, the monkey's trainer has not been able to induce the little fellow to flip the Frisbee more than five or ten feet. He prefers to sit in the shade. If we could team your collie with the Frisbee-throwing monkey, wouldn't we have a wonderful halftime exhibition for 1967's tournament!

Reverend Curtis, thanks once again for the use of your film. I am confident that it will arrive in excellent condition, but don't hesitate to let me know if it appears damaged in any way. We're looking forward to seeing you and your collie at next year's tournament.

Yours truly,
HARVEY J. KUKUK, Director
International Frisbee Tournament
Box 185
Houghton, Michigan 49931

Director Kukuk, as usual, was ahead of his time. The seventies have seen a lot of canine Frisbee activity; every Frisbee player with a dog is eager to press Rover into play.

The Right Disc for Your Dog

Your dog should have his own disc. So far no manufacturer has made a special dog disc, so current stock will have to do. The ideal dog disc should be soft and chewy, but should not puncture as polyethylene saucers do. A reinforced nylon plate would help; and some beef flavoring[1] in the plastic would be a nice touch. The dog disc should have good distance and hover qualities (see Performance Table in the Appendix and a high pro-

---

[1]Suggested by Margaret Ryan of Pebble Beach, Calif., after weeks of difficult training with Debbie, her ten-year-old Boxer. Frisbee training may have started a bit late for Debbie; she prefers to watch Margaret run after the plate.

Near-perfect canine form in a low-level aerial snag.

file (see Measurement Table—Height, in Appendix).

The table below suggests a few discs for your dog based on its size:

Dog Size	Disc
Small	
Up to 12" at shoulder	Mini-Frisbee Horseshoe Keds
Medium	
12" to 20" at shoulder	Regular Frisbee Flinger II Super Saucer Tosserino CPI-Saucer Tosser Cossom
Large	
20" to 28" at shoulder	Pro Frisbee CPI All Star Swing Poletten All American Tee Birds*
Huge	
Over 28" at at shoulder	Master Frisbee Y Tournament Model CPI Giant Saucer Tosser Tournament Tee Bird* Gyrospin Gee Whizzer*

* All Tee Birds have the under handle; some dogs will like catching on the handle and some won't.

Once you've given a Frisbee over to dog play, that's it. It will never be good for anything else. We're speaking of the soft polyethylene models. The hard rigid plates like the German Big Prof Disc or the Remco Catch-It might seem to be a solution, but dogs don't like them and neither will you once you've heard that awful crunching sound of canine jaws on rock-hard saucer. No, you'll just have to sacrifice a few plates to your best friend. A highly trained dog could be taught to take the saucer tenderly in his mouth, but it would soil his zest for the sport.

Training the Dog for Frisbee

After years of playing fetch with sticks and other flightless things, the dog is fascinated by the sailing Frisbee. "Now this makes sense," he grins as he hauls in the "flying stick" and returns it to you. Many dogs will take to Frisbee like aardvarks to ants, but some will not. I consulted with Ms. Jacky Hungerland,[2] the noted California dog psychologist, on this matter, and she said, "Even though their hearts may be in the right place—yearning to soar—many dogs will find it physically impossible to play the game with any great success. Certain snub-nosed breeds—for example, a Pekingese or an English bulldog—will experience particular difficulty in making aerial catches and in bearing up under the demands on breath control and physical exertion. Still others will lack the motivation required for training and carrying off a snappy contest. Jowly hounds like the basset and bloodhound will generally lack the enthusiasm to pursue the sport."

Here are a few training suggestions for your reluctant Rags;

1. Roll the Frisbee along the ground or floor slowly so he can get the sensation of it. With a little encouragement he will want to take it into his jaws and chew.

---

[2] Ms. Hungerland is also a nationally famous trainer and dog breeder. She is fascinated with training dogs for Frisbee play and is opening the first school for Frisbee dog training—the Monterey Institute of Frisbee Dog Studies. Interested parties should contact her at P.O. Box 483, Monterey, Calif. 93940.

An unidentified dog studies whelm and angle of Mung in preparation for catch.

Ashley Whippet, The Mouth of Frisbee, makes spectacular high altitude catch.

Bismarck sails at the Rose Bowl.

John Rae and Gunner are awarded the 1974 First Place Frisbee Dog Award by Jeff Otis, co-sponsor of the Canadian Open Frisbee Championships.

2. In difficult cases, it may be necessary for you to chew on the Frisbee to give him the idea.[3]
3. If he's still uninterested, use the Frisbee as his serving dish.
4. If your dog is particularly large and likes his vittles, a wise precaution would be to take along supplementary feedings when you go to the field. Method 3 dogs can get a bit tacky about the reward.
5. If all else fails try the dog-see, dog-do method. Show him other dogs fetching Frisbees.
6. If still no results, take him to the vet's. Maybe he's sick or maybe all along you've had a large, untidy cat.

DOG-BEE

Frisbee Game for Dog and Human. Now you and your best friend and his best friend (his Frisbee) are ready to play. You don't need instructions for that. But in case either one of you is competitive and the other one will put up with it, here's the world's first and only dog versus human game,[4] Dog-bee. It's really an adaption of the Esalen game (see page 96).

Players: Two—a human and a dog.
Equipment: A Frisbee suitable to both players.
A place to run—there are no outer limits.
Object: Human must deliver throws within dog's potential to catch; dog must catch all throws within his potential to run.

Play and Scoring: Human throws disc in any direction. Dog makes all-out effort to catch it. If uncatchable, dog receives one point. Touched but uncaught throws give human two points. Untouched, catchable flights give human one point. Disc must remain under a 45-degree angle to horizon throughout flight; if not, dog gets one point. If course of throw brings dog within obstacle, the play is rethrown; two obstacle flights in a row gives dog one point. Games are to 11 points.

In match play a qualified judge could call points or at least oversee play to encourage effort and equity. The dog would perhaps play better if he knew when a score was made; e.g. ring a bell for each score of his, a buzzer for each score of yours. An intelligent dog will discern this, and it will whet his competitive spirit.

Strategy. Dog-Bee played to perfection would end in a scoreless tie—an athletic anthem to beautiful cooperation between a human and a dog. Scoring will occur when either fails to perform well. The human can usually score by varying the nature of the disc flights, i.e., longer, higher, and especially curves and partial return flights. The dog will score when the human misthrows, as he will when he varies his flights in an attempt to score.

Double Dog-Bee would seem like a natural; don't try it. Two dogs chasing the same disc is too dangerous for the dogs.

Double Disc Dog-Bee should be possible and would be an incredible game. Two dogs would be trained to chase and catch different discs.[5] The human throws the different discs simultaneously. By varying the relative sizes of the two discs, and the grip of the pair, the human can alter the flight characteristics before and after separation of the discs. A master thrower can make one disc go high while the other curves left or right; and imagine, trying to score on two determined dogs at the same time!

Canine Tournaments

Ashley and other dogs have exhibited their skills at many crowd gatherings such as football and baseball games, TV shows, and whatever. The COFC and WFC human meets have held special events for dogs, but the first all-dog meet was held on November 13, 1974, at California State University at Fullerton: The Fearless Fido Fetching Fracas, sponsored by Al Lohman and Roger Barclay, Los An-

---

[3]With this method, you run the risk that your dog, especially if he is one of those bright kinds, may prefer to watch *you* chew the saucer.

[4]For that matter I can't think of any adversary games between man and *any* animal. There's polo, fox-hunting, falconry, and cormorant fishing. But they're partnerships. There's also alligator and bear wrestling and kangaroo boxing, but I never considered them games.

[5]There would be several ways to distinguish the discs. But don't try color, since dogs only see shades of gray. Try using one disc with holes in it. It will make a flight sound the dog will follow.

geles disc jockeys. Ashley was unfortunately unable to attend this tournament, but the entry list was well over a hundred. Each dog was given the chance to catch five throws tossed by his owner or handler. Judging was based on average distance for five catches plus overall artistry of catching.

Hyper Hank, an Australian sheep dog owned by Eldon McIntire of Los Angeles, was the overall winner, with close competition from Schatzie, owned by Ken and Karen Gordon. Hyper Hank is a trick dog who has appeared on television commercials. He amazed the spectators with his flawless performance. "He's so bright," said Irv Lander, IFA offi-cial and co-judge of the meet, "he figures out flight trajectories better than NASA Control, Houston. The Hyper Hank-Ashley match-up will make the Ali-Foreman tussle look like a dog fight." Irv developed the judging format for the tourney, shown below with sample scoring.

Sample Score Sheet for Dog Frisbee Tourney

Runs (in yards) for Successful Catches

1. 52 yards
2. 61 yards   TOTAL 238 yards
3. did not catch AVG. 47.6 yards
4. 58 yards   per throw
5. 67 yards

Artistry Points for Five Categories[6]
1-3 Fair 4-7 Good 8-10 Excellent

(run)	1	2	3	4	5	Total	Avg.
Sense of Direction	7	7	6	7	7	34	6.8
Depth Perception	8	7	3	8	8	39	6.8
Leaping Ability	6	7	8	6	6	33	6.6
Level of Enthusiasm	8	7	5	8	8	38	7.2
Level of Agility	6	7	6	6	6	31	6.2
Total							33.6

Tourney Score:

Yardage:	47.6
Artistry	33.6
TOTAL	**81.2**

Ashley kicks up his heels in San Francisco.

Frisbee Organization for Dogs

The IFA has a special division for its dog members—the K-9 Corps. IFA estimates that as many as 250 of its 70,000 members are dogs, and applications are increasing rapidly; the quarterly *IFA News* now has a special section devoted to Frisbee Dogdom. Advance plans for the August 1975 World Frisbee Championship call for a full-scale dog event.

A few of the outstanding dogs mentioned in Frisbee circles are Rufus, Moon, Snookie, Bogie, Toby, Attila, Jessie, Caspie, Alexis, Mimi, The Wonder Dog, Molly the Miracle Mutt, Sly, Gigi, Tam-O-Shanter, Candy, Gopa, Natasha, Samantha, and Che.

---

[6] Ms. Hungerland suggests a sixth category—style. A truly accomplished canine competitor should be able to perform in-flight tipping and even acrobatic catches.

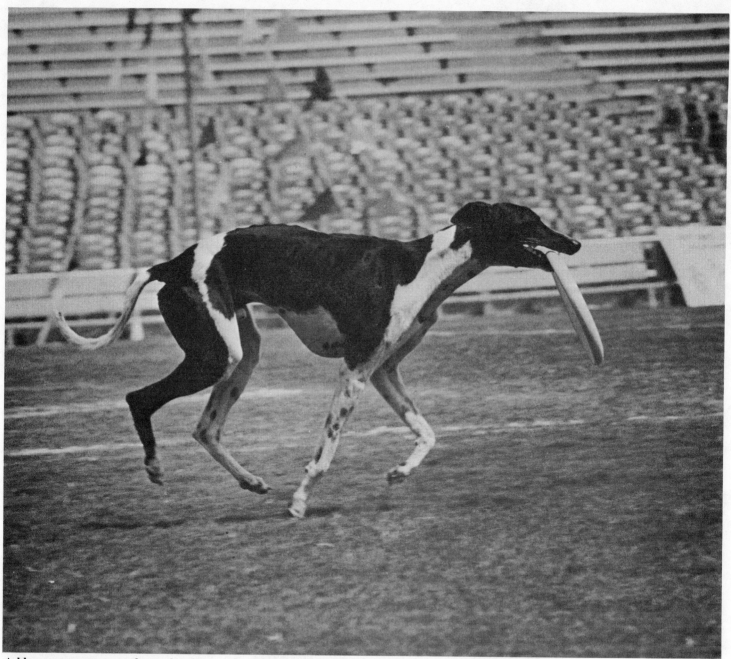

Ashley scampers to master for another throw.

Disc Bag emptied of contents.

10. CARE, REPAIR, AND TRANSPORT OF THE FRISBEE

"When the lion's skin will not reach
you must patch it out with the fox's."
—Plutarch's *Lives*

Frisbee is the least expensive sport in the world, or perhaps second to Hindustani Hopscotch.

A good Frisbee is a prized possession and deserves care. Certain models from certain molds are *priceless*—white Wham-O Pros, Olympic Ring label, mold number one, for example. In these days of vigilance against pollution, to avoid an avalanche of polyethylene, maintain your discus plasticus.

Care of the Frisbee

Cleaning. Soap and water are your Frisbee's best friends. So why not just take them into the shower with you? Caution: Avoid water too hot. And be careful about direct sunlight, especially in a closed car; it bleaches and brittles your beauties.

Marking. Always give your favorites an identifying mark. I recommend using a broad felt-tip pen[1] on the undersurface. Purists will want to add the accurate weight and performance characteristics.

The Scuff Problem. Skip shots scuff the saucer and leave strands of polyethylene waving in the breeze. Players call this stuff Frisbee hair. Steel wool will barber the problem, but the aerodynamic finish suffers. Spare your best from concrete.

Wellish's Malady. This is an incurable Frisbee disease. The fault is the factory's imperfectly tooled or dirty molds sticking to the plastic, a fault called flash. End result is a Frisbee *blister*. These are usually on the undersurface of the platter (Bernoulli's plate) and caused by the convex mold. The blisters should never be opened, else peeling results and Wellish's Malady begins. A Wellishing Frisbee peels more and more; there's no way to stop it. Balance is gone, skin drag is irregular, the Frisbee is terminal.

Artificial Surfaces. The search for a better surface continues. Polyethylene is decent enough, but for the purists, especially the "distance freaks," the perfect surface would reduce "skin drag" to the irreducible

---

[1] El Marko by Flair is my favorite.

minimum. Sprayed silicone has a drying problem with polyethylene. Some favor graphite gingerly sprinkled on just before throwing. Most tournament directors will not allow these alterations in distance contests.

The Damaged Frisbee. A torn or cracked Frisbee is a serious problem. Glues, cements, and adhesives are useless. Tape will last for a little while. There are two methods of successful repair, and the practical[2] one is:

The Malafronte Technique. Victor Malafronte of Berkeley, California, developed the following repair method. His tools are a soldering gun with a round tip, plastic from a broken Frisbee,[3] patience and much care. Any crack or tear can be repaired. Hybrids[4] can be grafted together. The method: the edges of the break are touched lightly with the hot soldering tip until they soften and fuse. Old Moonlighter plastic is then melted drop by drop into the break top and bottom side. The old and new plastic should be melted together for the best results. This is the tricky part, for the Frisbee may warp. For best cosmetic results, shave the excess plastic with a single-edged razor blade and polish with fine-grade sandpaper. Malfronte claims the repair is stronger than the original if done properly. He repaired one Frisbee seven times before the original crack reopened.

The Strain of San Gabriel. The site of the greatest stress in cupolar Frisbees is the ring of San Gabriel, where the thickness is less than one millimeter. The ring bears the greatest stress, for it connects the cupola with the flight plate at a more acute angle than any other Frisbee component. The elimination of the cupola in the All American and Fastback models solves this problem; but one wonders where the new stress point will be? Most Fastback breaks are showing in the Seldom Seen Space of Sewall.

The Misplaced Frisbee

It surely will happen, even to the best players, that your Frisbee will will afoul in a tree or on a neighbor's roof. Such fates have visited even the greatest, to wit: "Fling" Hyzer's great 1958 IFT out-of-bounds throw of 47.3 miles. Scooped up by a low-flying airplane it finally came to rest at the Escanaba, Michigan, airport.

Tree Rescues. There are two time-tested methods of retrieval: the aggressive and the passive.

The author is a long and strong advocate of the latter. Even the worst lie and besmirch may improve overnight with the aid of a fortunate wind or a curious bird. However, there will come a time when the aggressive technique is called for. First, let caution be your companion. There's many an expert or promising player untimely infirmed by an impulsive lean or uncareful craning for an errant Frisbee. Equipment is important (sneakers are always good). A simple barbed stick or an extra long plumber's friend are desirable tools.[5] A truly sad plight is the erstwhile chap who insists on freeing his Frisbee with yet another, only to be two up and away, as it were. The old adage that a Frisbee in the hand is worth two in the bush bears remembering. A tree that will keep one disc will keep two.[6] However, it is a pernicious tree that holds three Frisbees more than twenty-four hours.

Failing with the usual rocks, sticks, and wombats, I recommend a sure-fire, somewhat hazardous, yet-to-fail method—a shot put. The tree that can resist a shot put's furious frisking is yet to be met.

The last resort: call the Fire Department. When they arrive, point to the culprit tree and direct their attention to a cat you've just thrown into the branches. In their diligent duty-doing, firemen will never refuse a side request of, "Oh, and while you're there. . . ."

Roof Rescues. Roofs are, of course, another matter. Roof climbing is a wonderful way to meet your neigh-

---

[2] An unfeasible but highly effective method involves the expensive process of *electron welding*, which must be done in a vacuum.

[3] Moonlighter plastic flows more smoothly and evenly. It is the highest grade.

[4] Sometimes called Frankenstein Frisbees. Malafronte has one monster made of seven donor discs.

[5] I also recommend a slingshot, which mystically, brings us full circle to Wham-O's *first* toy!

[6] This appears to be a variant of the Charlie Brown kite-in-the-tree phenomenon.

bors. I enthusiastically recommend it to bachelor players. All of this presumes getting to the roof from the inside, a simple matter, by the by. Outside roof work is the most dangerous of all Frisbee rescues. Efforts should start with a sturdy latter, rope, sneakers, a long pole, and a touch of acromania.

The Lost Frisbee. All things considered, the Frisbee is never really lost (I like to think of them as "borrowed," although in one sense, I did lose one off the north rim of the Grand Canyon last summer), as may be the fate of, say, the golf ball, the shuttlecock, and the street puck. Wham-O Master models come with a serial number and guaranteed postage to facilitate return to rightful owner.

Transport of the Frisbee

The Disc Bag. The complete Frisbee player should have a container to carry his disc and other equipment necessary for the sport. My disc bag comfortably holds twenty saucers. It has a chamber in the bottom which will hold ten to fifteen plates snugly and a top section for my special Folf discs. Why twenty saucers? I like to have ten good discs for distance or accuracy practice and some special ones for Folf shots, plus a few for trading purposes.

For example, in sleeve one I have a mold 50 138.3-gram Super Pro for distance; in sleeve two a mold 2

117-gram All Star.[7] In sleeve three I like to carry a good curving saucer. I have a 1968 mold 10 Pro, 106.4 grams. I'd prefer a Pro Split Digit mold 16, vintage 1970; it holds a curve better, but I can't find one.

In sleeve four I have a 1974 yellow mold 15 Pro, 119.2 grams—the already famous Rose Bowl Pro made especially for the first World Frisbee Championships. I use it very sparingly, on grass only, and never in cold weather. It's great for curves against the wind and long-distance throws.

In sleeve five I carry a 167.7-gram mold 2 black Master, and in sleeve six a 117-gram Moonlighter mold 14. I might use my Super Pro in sleeve one for accuracy shots, but I

also like this heavy Master for mid-range putts for some psychological reason. And the Moonlighter is good, too. I also have a 61.5-gram Pro Whiz Ring in sleeve six. The ring comes in handy in high overhead throws, as in throwing over a tree.

In my bag I also carry:

1. Dwyer Wind Meter
2. Micrometer
3. Magnifying lens
4. Steel wool
5. Fine-grade sandpaper

---

[7] There appears to be only two CPI All Star molds. CPI does not use mold numbers, but number 2's have a concentric tooling mark on the outer periphery of Nachazel's ring. Number 1's are clean and may be a touch better in distance.

Author's Disc Bag with favorite flying discs in top chamber.

6. Rangematic distance finder
7. 15 feet of nylon rope
8. Canister of ethyl chloride
9. Roll of Johnson & Johnson Dermicel tape
10. Slingshot
11. Dry cloth
12. Plastic ruler
13. Gram weighing scale
14. Pen and paper
15. Broad felt-tip pen
16. Sea net
17. Vial of graphite
18. Chalk
19. Fingernail snippers
20. 100-foot roll of twine
21. Stopwatch

Nos. 1, 6, and 17 are for distance throwing and measuring, as well as sizing up Folf shots.

Nos. 2, 3, 12, and 13 are for measuring and examining discs in the field. You never know when someone will walk up with a Twirl-a-Boom in hand and want to swap.

Nos. 4, 5, 11, and 15 are for disc repairs and maintenance.

Nos. 8, 9, and 19 are for disc players' repairs and maintenance.

Nos. 7, 10, 16, and 20 are for disc rescues.

No. 14 is handy for Folf and exchanging data with fellow players.

No. 18 is for marking boundaries in games like Circle, Double Disc Court, etc.

No. 21 is for timing winds and Maximum Time Aloft.

I use rocks in the field for the slingshot and sticks as markers for distance.

The sea net (no. 16) needs an explanation. One of my Pacific Grove Folf courses[8] is along the ocean, and before I devised my net I lost some prize plates to the waves. The net now brings most of them back. It's a piece of old badminton net with tiny fishing sinkers tied at the corners. I slingshot the whole works onto the floating disc[9] and pull net and disc in by the twine (no. 20).

[8] Lover's Point—nine holes.
[9] Most discs will float for a while, except Moonlighters.

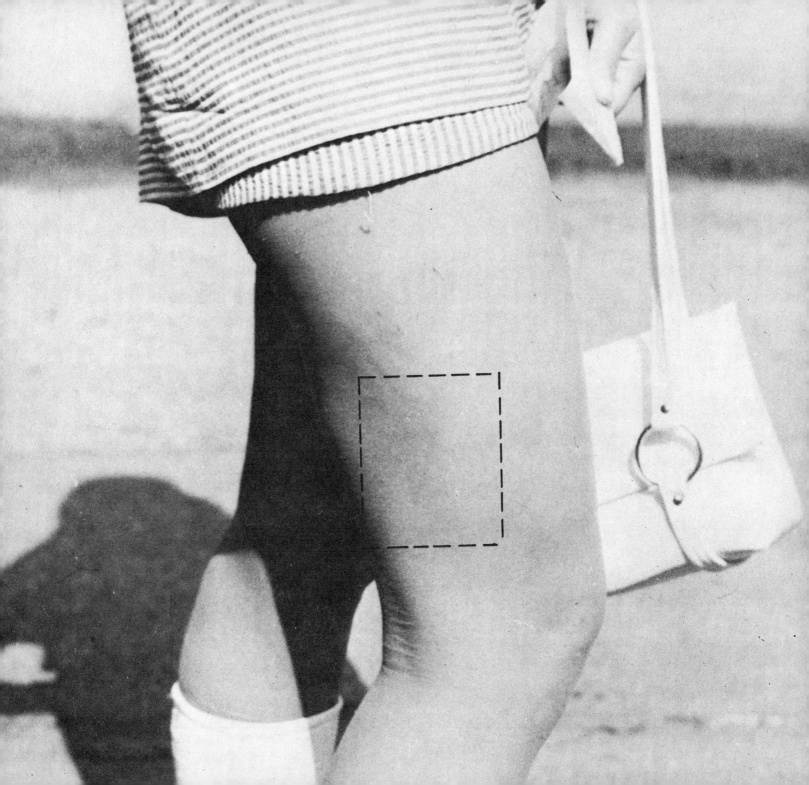

11. MEDICAL ASPECTS OF FRISBEE

by Roger Woods, M.D.

"Thanks be to God, since my leaving drinking
of wine, I do find myself much better, and do mind
my business better, and do spend less money, and
less time lost in idle company."
—Samuel Pepys' *Diary,* January 26, 1662

What Constitutes a Sports Injury?

Case 1: Judy H., a 26-year-old housewife whose health was excellent, was attending a garden party and amiably chatting with a group of guests seated on a patio. She was unaware of several other people participating in a friendly toss of Frisbee on a lawn adjacent to the patio. Suddenly a forceful, if errant, throw was unleashed and the Frisbee was beyond the reach of the intended recipient. It flew across the patio, striking the outer aspect of Judy's left thigh. Apparently more scared than hurt, she

Roger Woods is a practicing neurologist in Santa Monica, California. He is the medical director of the International Frisbee Tournament and the Institute of Frisbee Medicine in Santa Monica.

jumped from her seat, and a brief expression of distress and repeated apologies followed. She was able to enjoy the remainder of the reception and resume her social banter, and there was no impairment of gait or mobility. Careful inspection revealed a small area of redness at the site of impact with associated soft tissue tenderness to firm palpation. No swelling was apparent, and full range and strength of leg movement without discomfort were preserved. The redness slowly resolved within three to four days, during which time there was no functional limitation, and she has remained well since this incident.

Does Judy's misfortune represent a Frisbee injury? The inability to answer this question in simple fashion emphasizes some of the difficulties involved in calculating or reporting injuries associated with sports. No fatality or significant disability occurred, no legal or insurance action ensued, and she was not a participant in the game.

Competitive sports, both amateur and professional, enjoy great popularity in the United States. The dangers to which participants in these sports are exposed vary widely, but it is not possible to measure accurately the relative hazards because adequate data on the number of participants and the number injured in individual sports are lacking.[1]

[1] "Competitive Sports and Their Hazards," *Statist. Bull. Metrop. Life Insur. Co.*, 46:1-3 (Sept.), 1965.

Calculated risk is an assessment of the hazards in the sports being offered relative to the purported benefits. Subsequent conclusions underlie decisions affecting the participation of candidates. Calculated risk, unfortunately, is a much-bandied but poorly calibrated guideline. In the words of one epidemiologist, "We know far more, for example, concerning the short and long-term results of smoking or of maternal rubella than we do about the beneficial and injurious effects of the recreational activities that occupy the time of millions of adults and children."[2]

Decisions affecting participation involve the numerator (benefits) as well as the denominator (hazards) of the calculated-risk equation. It follows that equitable comparisons of hazards of various sports (and benefits when such can be quantitated) must calibrate all significant effects. Care must be taken that uniform understanding of criteria exists concerning, for example, the severity of an effect (was the sprain a mild tear or a complete rupture of the ligament?), its consequence (was disability judged for athletic performance or functional daily living?), and its significance (what was the long-term prognosis?).[3] In regard to Frisbee, the data is simply lacking. Careful review of medical literature fails to reveal a single instance of reported injury associated with Frisbee. Does this mean that no injury has ever occurred in relation to this sport? Certainly not, for we all have heard of someone sustaining an injuury as a result of Frisbee play, although these reports are usually secondhand and not verified by observers, and, furthermore, are always quite anecdotal. Probably what one can conclude is that while injuries do occur, they are minor in degree and few in number.

The only fatality I have ever heard of occurred in 1963 when a young Sherpa guide in Nepal leaned too far to catcher's left for a rapidly fading, left-handed counterclockwise throw with a nasty turnover. He plunged down a 9,000-foot snowbank and disappeared into a monster drift. Yet he never waned in his catch and snagged the Frisbee 300 feet from his final resting place.[4] Correspondence with the National Safety Council and major insurance companies has failed to reveal any instances of fatality or even injury associated with Frisbee. That this is so is because scientific methods of data gathering have not been applied, and reports of sports injuries are infrequent, incomplete, and lacking in uniform criteria.

Frisbee Injuries—A Semantic Problem

With respect to any particular sport, one must distinguish between the injuries that are incidental and relatively avoidable from injuries that are casual. In Frisbee, the former far outnumber the latter, although comparative statistics are slim.

Case 2: Chuck G. is a 32-year-old businessman whose prior health was unquestionably good. Early one morning, while engaging in a casual game of catch Frisbee, he ran after a poor throw. Unfortunately he was playing, rather recklessly, on a grassy glade, moist from the morning dew. A sudden change in the wind caused the Frisbee to fly off its predicted course and Chuck, in a mood of high spirit, suddenly lurched to one side. His footing slipped on the ground surface, poorly chosen, and in the fall that resulted the left ankle was sprained. Play continued and medical attention was postponed until the following day. His ankle was moderately swollen with considerable pain, particularly on weight bearing, and examination revealed joint structures to be intact but strained. Restriction of activity, use of elastic support stocking, and one week of hydrotherapy and other simple physical therapy techniques accomplished rapid resolution of pain and swelling, and Chuck was able to walk about normally within ten days and to resume Frisbee practice one week later.

This case is useful in illustrating the distinction that must be made between Frisbee injuries which are directly or casually incurred and those that are incidental to the sport. Clear-

[2] W. Haddon, Jr., "Principles in Research on the Effects of Sports on Health," in *Proceedings of the Seventh National Conference on the Medical Aspects of Sports* (Chicago: American Medical Assn., 1966).

[3] Kenneth S. Clarke, "Calculated Risk of Sport Fatilities," *Journal of the American Medical Association*, 197: 894 (Sept. 12, 1966).

[4] Decency dictated it: reports are that a Posthumous Master's medallion was tacked to the boot of his trailing ski.

ly, Chuck sustained injury in Frisbee participation. However, the chief factors responsible for his misfortune were improper use of footwear (rubber soles are advisable) and poor selection of gaming area. Under these circumstances, it is likely that similar injury would have resulted had he been running after an unleashed pet, abandoned lunch pail, or an overdue appointment. Frisbee, although a key factor, was obviously not of paramount importance in this case history, in that the risk of accident could have been significantly reduced by greater care (common sense) in selection of field and accessories. Could not one reasonably anticipate untoward results from playing tennis on a plowed field or hiking barefooted?

Certainly the more frequent and serious injuries, like Chuck's, are best judged as incidental to Frisbee participation. Isolated instances of players running against fixed hazards such as bleachers, sprinkler heads, trees, etc., are rumored, though poorly documented. Unannounced cliffs are a clear danger, as indicated above. Group participation necessarily creates the risk of two or more players colliding in the passion of pursuit; this risk can be minimized by players cooperating in the use of verbal expressions and/or behavioral gestures indicating their hell-bent intent to get that particular throw, much as do outfielders in baseball.

Minor cuts and bruises are not frequent and almost never directly inflicted. Another such incidental and usually inconsequential risk to which players may be susceptible is overexposure to sun or other elements. Playing in rain, gale-force winds, and blizzard conditions is not unheard of, particularly among zealous Frisbee enthusiasts.

A special comment is in order regarding insects,[5] at least those with a proclivity toward human flesh. This hazard is clearly geographic and seasonal. Just when climatic conditions are optimal for Frisbee play, the population of insects and instances of bites therefrom are at their peak, or so it seems. Mosquitoes and deer flies and other winged creatures have been all too much in evidence on the Lake Superior shores of the Keweenaw Peninsula on those July Fourth holidays, at which place and time the International Tournaments have always been held. Fortunately, no cases of malaria, other parasitic, or infectious illnesses are known to have resulted. Although fewer in number, the dreaded black fly has been the cause of most morbidity. This is a particularly sturdy and vicious predator. Measuring only ten to fifteen millimeters in overall length, these creatures attack with a fury and inflict a bite which is serious disproportionate to their size. Though their bites are less painful than those of, for example, deer flies, the black-fly bite tends to bleed excessively, causing the prey to discover clots in scalp hair only some time after having been struck by a swarm. So plentiful in number and annoying were they at the Fourteenth Tournament on July 4, 1971, at Copper Harbor, Michigan, that they came to be nicknamed the Frisbee Fly. Though distressing at least, these Frisbee Flies do not cause systematic illness, though some reactive inflammation and enlargement of regional lymph glands often occur, being mildly painful and tender for several days to one week. It is important to recognize that it is the human organism to which they are attracted and not the Frisbee. The most serious case of Frisbee Fly bite was that of a young girl who was accompanying her parents on an automobile ride to the tournament grounds; a swarm of flies entered their car and attacked this young innocent prey with a ferocity well-nigh unimaginable; before her father could stop the vehicle and come to her assistance, dozens of bites had been inflicted and her face and scalp bore the clear insignia of the dreaded black fly. Even surviving this assault, however, after application of cleansing lotions and steps to prevent recurrence, she was able to enjoy her afternoon as a spectator at the exciting games to which she and her family had traveled. Anyone who has been subject to an assault such as this is well aware that these flies are not easily dissuaded by waving the hand or shaking the head, nor are

---

[5] A minor though not any less offensive, occurrence is reported by Kristin E. Johnson nee Peterson of Pacific Grove, who in her zealous pursuit of an errant Frisbee ingested a covey of flying insects! This affliction is known as Kristin's Gag.

they easily brushed off or crushed; the only effective protection is the abundant use of insect repellent.

Two further complications, as it were, of Frisbee play should be mentioned; these constitute the neuropsychiatric hazards, both being quite incidental to Frisbee *per se* but occurring in many sports, particularly at convocations or organized events where spirits run high and competition is keen. The first of these is acute alcoholic intoxication of the nervous system. While not infrequent, this has almost uniformly been of mild to moderate degree, quite transitory, and not disabling. Although it is possible that it might lead to impaired judgment and diminished restraint over one's behavior and consequent verbal and physical assault, these things have never materialized at any of the International Frisbee Tournaments. This is true in spite of the use of considerable amounts of alcohol, albeit beer and malt liquor. These beverages have always been readily available at the tournament, properly so it would seem because of its widespread and quite appropriate use to relax tensions associated with the contest; beer has also proved useful in managing some Frisbee injuries (see below) because of its soothing effect. That major argument or physical confrontation has been absent at tournament time in spite of widespread usage of alcoholic beverage attests to the high degree of sportsmanship among Frisbee enthusiasts. As mentioned, with rare exception, the instances of acute alcoholic intoxication, though numerous, have been mild and have led at most to conviviality and quite socially acceptable name-calling.

Rare indeed has been severe alcoholic intoxication with depression of level of consciousness and short-lived incapacitation, generally resulting in collapse on or near the playing field. Prompt medical attention includes removing the body from the area of competition, removal of dentures or other artifices which might interfere with swallowing or respiration, and, if the patient is able to cooperate, administration of large doses of coffee by mouth. Generally, rather prompt improvement can be expected; on only a few occasions has confinement to bed been required.

The other neuropsychiatric condition which has been in evidence is the disappointment associated with defeat. Though common among participants in competition, this is scarcely an illness but rather a perfectly normal response to obvious psychological trauma, has never reached disabling or psychotic proportion, is always transitory, and has never required medical attention, though individuals have tended to treat themselves with therapeutic, usually modest doses of alcohol.

Frisbee Injuries—a Somatic Problem

We now turn our attention to injuries, always small in number and more potential than real, directly resulting from Frisbee participation. These may be categorized as secondary to direct trauma.

Frisbee Finger. Although not peculiar to Frisbee, this is unquestionably the most common injury. It constitutes damage to the fingernail and associated structures as a result of the impact of a Frisbee on the tip of the finger. Like other injuries within this group, Frisbee Finger appears more common among the relatively inexperienced player, and there is a direct relationship between risk of injury and weight of the particular Frisbee used; that is to say, it occurs more commonly with use of the 150-gram-Master model than with the Professional or Standard models, weighing respectively 108 grams and 85 grams; it is unheard of with the mini-Frisbee.

All degrees of seriousness of Frisbee Finger are possible, and may be graded as follows: Grade I constitutes minor degrees of onycholysis, or separation of the nail from underlying pulp. This is minor indeed, momentarily painful, but otherwise not serious, and generally does not require medical attention or interfere with continued play. Grade II consists of a more severe degree of nail separation associated with subungual hematoma, or blood clot, beneath the nail surface. This is generally more painful than Grade I but, again, rarely interferes with continuation of play and usually resolves with time without medical intervention. Some have advocated immersing the injured fingertip in cold beer to achieve pain relief and limit the amount of hematoma formation. Occasionally, when the blood clot is sizable and associated pain extreme, drainage is indicated and easily accomplished by flaming the tip of a paper clip with a match and using the paper clip to create a hole through the nail, permitting drainage of the clot and release of pressure; this technique, though simple, is best employed by someone with medical training or experience. Grade III is obviously the most severe type of Frisbee Finger and consists of avulsion, or complete separation, of the nail from the underlying bed. This is yet more painful and often precludes further activity for the next few days. Again, immersion of the affected fingertip in cold beer has been recommended, though it accomplishes nothing beyond temporary pain relief. Recovery generally occurs with time and no medical intervention is necessary. Swathing the exposed nail bed with a light Band-Aid is advisable. Fortunately, while the minor degree of Frisbee Finger is not terribly uncommon, complete separation of the nail is rare.

Ligamentous strain of the finger. Like Frisbee Finger, this is due to sudden and forceful impact of the Frisbee on the fingertip and consists of strain of the ligaments of the finger due to sudden stress. There may be associated swelling and the pain is usually exaggerated by use or movement of the finger, and of such intensity to prevent further participation for several days. Application of cold

and immobilization of the finger—rarely is splinting necessary—are generally adequate measures; if pain and swelling persist, more formal physical therapy and radiographic examination are indicated. While dislocation and fracture are conceivable, these have not been reported.

Bruises. These are self-explanatory and generally minor, require no medical attention, and do not limit activity. They result from direct impact of the Frisbee on the body surface. If the bridge of the nose should be struck in such fashion, epistaxis (nose bleed) may ensue; this usually subsides promptly with sitting or lying down, application of a cold pack across the nose, and compression of the nose with the fingers. Should bleeding persist, further evaluation is necessary to rule out more serious, underlying conditions such as high blood pressure or bleeding tendency.

Chronic Frisbee Abrasions (Frisbee Nodules). These are friction abrasions of the fingers secondary to repeated throwing. They can be prevented by judicious preparation, tincture of Benzoin, or light tape.

The hardened tumorous nodule of the seasoned player belies his favorite delivery.

Eye Injury. While this is the most serious injury that may result from direct impact, it is fortunately extremely rare. Generally when the orbit is struck, only the eyelids are injured, with resultant swelling and

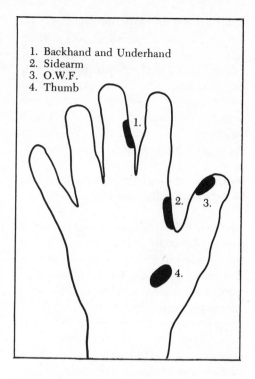

1. Backhand and Underhand
2. Sidearm
3. O.W.F.
4. Thumb

bruising (black eye). However, other possibilities include the following:

1. Corneal abrasion.
2. Hyphema or accumulation of blood within the anterior chamber of the eye, between the cornea and lens.
3. *Commotio retinae frisbee,* or retinal edema as a result of direct blow by the Frisbee to the globe. If the impact is severe, actual separation of the retina from underlying structures (retinal detachment) may or may not be associated with commotion.

These eye injuries are always serious because of associated visual distortion or loss, transitory or permanent, and all constitute medical emergencies and require immediate, expert attention. Their rarity cannot be overemphasized; only one eye injury has been encountered in recent years at the International Tournament and that was quite minor in fact.

Injuries not due to direct trauma, but to repeated joint action.

Frisbee Elbow (*epicondylitis: radio-humeral bursitis*). This is a syndrome of chronic pain in the elbow, particularly over the radio-humeral articulation, i.e., outer aspect. Swelling is rarely present and range of motion of the elbow joint is retained. Whereas the actual cause is unknown, it is common in individuals whose occupations require frequent rotatory motion of the forearms, such as tennis players, pipe fitters, and carpenters. Presumably, the causative factor(s) is cumulative, for the onset is gradual, quite in contrast to those injuries noted above that are the result of direct trauma. Although not actually reported as a consequence of Frisbee play, this is a potential slight risk were someone to repetitively throw with considerable and sufficient frequency and duration.

Shoulder Injury. It has been theorized that inflammatory disease about the shoulder, similar to Frisbee elbow, might constitute a risk of sustained Frisbee play. The author has had occasion to study and de-

scribe an early but serious case[6] of Frisbee shoulder in a 41-year-old sidearm stylist with nearly fifteen years of serious Frisbee activity, the last six years in frequent competition. The right shoulder is infirmed with tendinitis. Continued competition is doubtful. Rest and a switch to southpaw tossing is prescribed.

Comments

Earlier in this chapter, reference was made to the "calculated risk equation." Most of the foregoing material has dealt with the denominator, or hazards under consideration here. For completeness, I chose to list the complications that might occur as a result of Frisbee play, recognizing that many of those, including the more serious ones, exist more potentially than in fact.

It is only appropriate, however, to emphasize the safety of the sport, judging from the millions of Frisbees in use and the small number of risks and reports of injuries on file at the Institute of Frisbee Medicine.[7] In addition to what has been previously mentioned, it is worthwhile to note that Frisbees are apparently nonallergenic; and there would appear to exist no possibility of the ingestion[8] of Frisbees by young children or pets, quite in contrast with marbles, for example, or other accidentally self-inflicted injuries such as those involving darts, firearms, etc.

The advantages and benefits of Frisbee far outnumber the hazards.

Frisbee is good for the soul. It refreshes the spirit and is a ready means of escape, however brief, from those stresses and pressures which are part of everyday existence. Even the fatigue that follows vigorous play feels good. In the words of one prominent recreational therapist, "People are more themselves at play."

The game of Frisbee is an excellent source of exercise, suitable for all ages, which can be gauged to the individual's own taste, endurance, and/ or physical limitations. Strength and coordination are improved and reflexes are quickened. As is true with some other outdoor sports, regular participation tones the musculo-skeletal system.

An associated feature of such exercise is guaranteed caloric expenditure. The table indicates the influence of muscular activity on the degree of caloric expenditure. It has been estimated that Frisbee participants may expend from 180 to 500 calories per hour, the actual amount being directly proportionate to the exertion involved. Most such data are somewhat

---

[6]Johnson-Woods Syndrome—an early, serious case of Frisbee Shoulder (unpublished).

[7]Dr. Woods is too modest to describe this institute since it was his sole efforts that established it in 1970. The Institute of Frisbee Medicine has already established Frisbee as the best medically studied sport. It is located on Medical Square Suite 730, 2021 Santa Monica Blvd., Santa Monica, California 90404.

[8]Dr. John Tatomer of Burlingame, Calif., cautions the use of Frisbee as a teether for tads. His son, Nick, gummed a Moonlighter so voraciously that he now glows in the dark!

inexact and based on indirect calorimetry. At the Institute, plans are in preparation for a direct calorimeter chamber of sufficient size to permit Frisbee activities within; the enormous dimensions and attendant expense have impeded development, however.

Inasmuch as the first law of thermodynamics is obeyed by living organisms, the balance that is derived from caloric intake and energy expenditure is the prime factor, under normal circumstances, which determines whether weight gain or loss occurs over a period of time. Frisbee play can thereby prove to be an invaluable adjunct to weight-reduction schemes; as with other forms of muscular exertion, it is most valuable when coupled with restriction of caloric intake (i.e., dieting). Fat Frisbee fanatics are significantly rare.

It is scarcely possible to imagine another sport that is so beneficial in all aspects, healthful and safe, fun, and easily available and learned.

Approximate Calorie Expenditure of Man as Affected by Muscular Activity

Type of Muscular Activity	Calories per Hour
Sleeping	65
Awake, lying still	77
Awake, sitting up, at rest	100
Reading aloud	105
Standing relaxed	105
Standing at attention	115
Light muscular exercise	170
Moderately active muscular exercise	290
Severe muscular exercise	450
Very severe muscular exercise	600

Source: A. White, P. Handler, E. Smith, and D. Stetten, *Principles of Biochemistry*, 2nd ed. (New York, 1959), p. 311.

12. FRISBEE CLINIC

"It is better to learn late than never."
—Publilius Syrus, Maxim 869

Questions and Answers

How can I make my Frisbee go straight?

Point and think the Frisbee into the target. Develop a smooth delivery with an easy and quick wrist snap. Add power later.

Why does my Frisbee turn over?

Turning over is usually a Hyzer-angle problem with beginners, i.e., the wing's angle with the ground is too acute. Beginners release their Frisbee too flat (under Hyzer), so that in flight the Frisbee turns over. Also, an out-of-balance flying disc—a cheap, bad design, poor lip, or one with nicks—will turn over, especially in a long flight.

How can I skip my Frisbee?

The underarm delivery is the easiest to skip, but any throw can do it. Aim about eight to twelve feet in front of you and release with the nose down (hypo-Mung angle). If the bounce is too high, aim further out; if too low or no bounce, move the skip closer to you.

What is a curve skip and how do I do it?

Instead of the nose, the wing is the bounce part. Throw just like a curve but with a negative Mung angle. In curve skips, multiple skips are possible—as many as four or even six!

How can I throw a curve?

A curve is really a straight throw tilted on its side and underthrown. At the apogee of the flight, gravity overcomes momentum and the downward curve results.

Can you make a Frisbee come back to you?

Yes. It's called a boomerang or, better, a return throw. It is really an exaggerated hover, thrown into the wind. The greater the wind, the less the Mung angle necessary. It requires near-perfect release, timing, and judgment of the wind speed.

What is the best way to throw a Frisbee?

Whichever way is best for you. Today the most popular delivery is the backhand, both for distance and accuracy. Develop as many throws as you can. This will increase your overall enjoyment, and add to your proficiency in such games as Frisbee Baseball and Frisbee Golf.

How can I make my distance throws longer?

There are many factors in distance throwing: timing, coordination, body control, plus knowledge and use of the prevailing air currents. Most of today's great long-distance throwers use the backhand. They practice several hours a day during tournament season to develop and maintain their timing and coordination.

What is the most accurate way to throw?

There is much controversy here. I have always felt, taking a page from darts, that the delivery with the fewest number of body movements should be the most accurate. I use a modified backhand delivery. The arm-swing eliminates the arc, the Frisbee comes straight through from set to release. I recommend a stance sideways to the target point and "think" the Frisbee into the target. Remember, always aim for the *center* of the target.

What is the best flying disc?

Best for what? Perhaps the Wham-O Moonlighter, Split digit mold number 14. For houseplay? The Wham-O Mini and Speedy (nowadays called the Horseshoe model), plus Whiz Rings and the Nerf Disc. For the beach? In strong winds, either a Master model or, if you find one, the heavier Y-tournament models. For distance? The CPI All Star is impressing many players. And the Super Pro is outstanding.

How can I repair my cracked Frisbee?

In truth, it will never be the same. But you can restore its integrity if not its ideal state. See the Malafronte Method, page 150.

My Frisbee wobbles in flight. What am I doing wrong?

Your release is wrong. The uncurling (wristing) must be smooth. It is the final complement to a strong arm-swing. Tennis players sometimes have difficulty in Frisbee. They tend to lock their wrist and produce a turn-over flight. Develop a smooth wrist snap. Sacrifice a little power for smoothness. You can add power later.

Do discs hurt? I am afraid to try to catch one.

Flying discs are the least dangerous of man's sport missiles, with the possible exception of the shuttlecock. In usual play, the only injury will be to your pride, not your person. You might start with the Whiz Ring or Nerf Disc.

How do you do the behind-the-back catch?

First, master the in-front catch, then turn around.

I am a right-handed backhand thrower. My throws always go to the right side of the target. Why?

Your release is too slow. And probably you are having a turn-over problem. Try moving your front foot further to your left; in baseball terms, close your stance. This will bring your Frisbee back into the target. If you have the opposite problem, you should open your stance a little.

What is the best way to throw into a strong wind?

With everything you've got. A few more degrees of Hyzer and a little less Mung will help. Power is not as important as it seems. Smoothness and coordination make the difference.

Can you do a boomerang throw in zero wind condition?

Yes, throw it straight up and it will fall straight down. Otherwise, no.

My Frisbee has scuff marks all over it, little pieces of plastic sticking out. Is there anything I can do?

This is called Frisbee hair. Use very light sandpaper carefully. Frisbee hair comes from throwing on hard surfaces, especially concrete. If you must throw on concrete, pick out several Frisbees you like least, and use them.

I have tried and tried to throw sidearm, but it keeps flopping over in a few yards. What is the trick?

There are three things you must do. (1) As your arm comes in sidearm style, the elbow must advance in front of the wrist. (2) The wrist must be hypersupinated; i.e., with your hand in front of you palm side up, twist the wrist so that the thumb goes down as far as it can (if your hand is palm down, you twisted the wrong way). (3) There is no follow through. The Frisbee pops out of the hand, like cracking the whip.

13. ENVOI

"A big book is a big nuisance."
—Callimachus, Fragmenta Incerta, Number 359

We set out to collect, describe, and understand the many features, peculiarities, and nuances of Frisbee and Frisbee play. Our efforts were somewhat hampered by the lack of previous study of the subject. There were no giant's shoulders. Let us not be judged too harshly for our beginning efforts. Hopefully, readers will contribute the missing details and material wanting, and the understanding needed, in the time to come. The author welcomes this.

Several important mysteries beg solution. Who made the Twirl-a-Boom flying disc? Where did the Y-models come from? And who created the Guts game?

Certain facts must be evident by now: Frisbee is not just a plastic toy flying saucer. A saucer-shaped missile, be it metal or plastic, has captured the interest of all ages for centuries; plastic appears to be the ideal saucer substance in terms of weight per mass and durability; flying discs lend themselves so well to other sports, even baseball and football; and, sadly, Frisbee players suffer because many manufacturers opt for a quick toy profit instead of an ideal discus plasticus. Competition is the best stimulus to improvement; Frisbee is no exception.

Frisbee is naturally designed for the human hand and is as much a curiosity to us as the hummingbird, the magnet, and the gyroscope, drawing our attention to it in wondrous disbelief.

APPENDICES

THE PHYSICS OF FRISBEE FLIGHT

"And now I see with eyes serene,
the very pulse of the machine."

William Wordsworth
She Was A Phantom of Delight

by Jay Shelton

Were it not for the presence of air, Frisbee flights would have no more variety of grace than those of rocks and shotputs. In a vacuum, even feathers and gold nuggets would soar with the same trajectories if launched with the same initial velocities. The reason is that without air, the only force acting on an object in free flight is that of gravity, and gravity has the same effect on all objects in the absence of other forces; namely, it increases their velocity toward the center of the earth by about 32 feet per second every second (the "acceleration of gravity"). Clearly the force of gravity is a contributing effect to the flight of a Frisbee, but all of the Frisbee's distinctive flight characteristics, such as its ability to hover and to curve left and right, must be due to forces

from the air, for this is the only other source of force on a Frisbee in free flight.

Ordinarily air friction is a familiar contribution. It retards all kinds of Frisbee motions; it slows a Frisbee's rate of spin, its forward motion, and its rate of fall. This latter effect is largely responsible for a Frisbee's apparent ability to "float" toward the end of a floater flight; if the Frisbee has no horizontal motion relative to the air, it is really just falling. It falls slowly because the air-friction forces resisting the broadside falling motion are relatively high. Negligible lift is obtained from spin alone without motion relative to the air.

But gravitational and frictional forces are not enough to account for the more distinctive features of Fris-

bee flight. A Frisbee can sail along a nearly horizontal path for long distances, which clearly is possible only if there is a lifting force on it to counteract the ever-present gravitational force. This lift is present when a Frisbee is moving relative to the air and when it is tipped upward slightly (so that it has a "positive angle of attack"—the angle between its overall motion and its orientation).

The resulting lift force is quite similar to that felt by your hand when you hold it outside the window of a

Jay Shelton received his Ph.D. in physics from the University of California, Berkeley, and now teaches physics at Williams College, Williamstown, Massachusetts. He is the former distance record holder, and from 1969 to 1974 was considered the world's champion Frisbee player.

moving car; your flattened hand can feel very strong forces acting either up or down, depending on which way it is angled (giving it a positive or negative angle of attack). This force is in addition to the "drag," or frictional force, which is the force you feel pushing your hand and arm back toward the rear of the car; or, in the case of a Frisbee, the force that causes a Frisbee's speed to decrease during most flights.

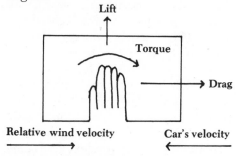

(Hand sticking out moving-car window, thumb on leading edge, leading edge tipped slightly up.)

This kind of lift is experienced by any approximately flat object moving relative to a fluid (such as air) with a slight, positive angle of attack. If air is deflected downward, the reaction on the object gives it lift. Thus, a Frisbee can also receive lift flying upside down as long as it is angled slightly above the direction in which it is moving, so as to deflect air down. The same is true for many airplanes. The details of the exact shapes of objects designed for lift are critical for the ratio of lift to drag forces. This ratio of lift to drag is what engineers try to optimize in airplane wings. In the case of a Frisbee, the leading and trailing edges of the "wing" are the same because of the symmetry and spin. This constraint makes it harder to achieve high lift-to-drag ratios.

The spinning of a Frisbee is what gives it orientational stability so that it may receive steady lift from the air throughout a flight. Without spin, a Frisbee tumbles, much like a leaf, its orientation constantly changing; hence, the direction of the lift force constantly changes and is never large because the velocity is never large. A nonspinning Frisbee (or leaf) tumbles as it falls because it receives twisting forces (torques) from the air. Again, when you hold your flattened hand outside the window of a moving car, in addition to the lift and drag forces, you can feel torque trying to twist your hand. If you orient your hand with a slight positive angle of attack, the wind acts to twist your hand toward the broadside orientation. An airplane can counteract this tendency with its horizontal tail surfaces. A Frisbee resists it largely with its spin.

A spinning Frisbee has what is called angular momentum by virtue of its spinning mass. The angular momentum of any object remains constant in time (both the rate of spin and the orientation of the spin axis) unless acted on by a torque. The larger an object's angular momentum, the more torque it takes (acting over a given time) to change the angular momentum by a given amount. Any Frisbee moving relative to a fluid is subject to torques whether or not the Frisbee is spinning. But a Frisbee that is spinning very slowly or not at all has very little angular momentum, and hence these torques can easily change the Frisbee's orientation, whereas a fast-spinning Frisbee has a large angular momentum and so the same torque is relatively ineffective in altering its orientation.

If you have ever held a spinning gyroscope in your hand, you have felt its resistance to having the orientation of its spin axis changed. Rockets and satellites are often given a rotational motion on purpose to aid the stability of their orientations. The tendency of a spinning object to hold the orientation of its spin axis is also at the heart of gyro compasses and many inertial navigation and guidance systems.

What it does for a Frisbee is to tend to hold the Frisbee in the same orientation with which it is launched. This enables a Frisbee to obtain a fairly steady lift throughout a flight by keeping it level in straight flights or banked at a constant angle in ordinary curved flights.

Now, of course, torques may be effective in changing the orientation of a Frisbee during its flight. Everyone knows a Frisbee is capable of much more intricate (or disastrous) flights than those wherein the orientation of its spin axis stays fixed. In some long floating flights and boomerang flights, the orientation of a Frisbee may oscillate once or twice as the Frisbee "rocks" back and forth while floating down. The spin axis of a Frisbee in many beginners' flights veers continuously from near vertical toward horizontal as the Frisbee slices down toward the ground. In other words, in almost all flights the spin axis changes at least slightly. The really remarkable thing is that a Frisbee is as stable as it is. Try throwing an assortment of other round, roughly flat objects (pie tins, some coffee-can lids, cardboard, Frisbees with a central circular cutout, Frisbees filled in with Styrofoam or covered with surgical rubber), giving them as much spin as you can, and you may be surprised at how fast the spin axis rotates about the direction of flight. In many cases the direction of rotation reverses midway in a flight as the object's speed decreases. The design of a normal Frisbee is quite special for minimizing torques and their effects.

The clearest example of a torque changing the spin axis of a Frisbee is the skip shot. A skip shot has nothing to do with the resilience of the plastic. If it did, a Frisbee would "bounce" off a smooth surface no matter what part of it contacted the ground. In fact, a skip only results if the outer edge (away from your body in an ordinary cross-body delivery) of the Frisbee makes contact. The Frisbee jumps up because the torque from the ground causes the Frisbee's rotational axis to tip back toward the thrower. The Frisbee's orientation then points above the horizontal, and it merely sails off in a new direction, riding up on the air.

Again, the physics of the skip shot is well illustrated by the behavior of a gyroscope. Orient a spinning gyroscope so that it spins in the same direction a Frisbee would just before skipping. Then, holding the gyro-

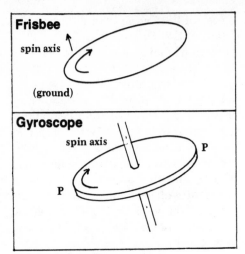

Hold loosely at points P; tweak clockwise. Axis will tip back towards you.

scope loosely, give it a little twist or tweak clockwise around the direction in which the Frisbee as a whole is moving, i.e., a twist about the forward-pointing horizontal direction. With some practice you will notice that the gyroscope's spin axis tips back toward you, not sideways in the direction you were twisting it. (To easily see this effect you must hold the gyroscope in such a manner and loosely enough so that it *can* rotate backward.)

Exactly the same thing happens to a Frisbee when it contacts the ground in a skip shot. A slight impulse of torque is imparted to the Frisbee from the ground, and it recoils the way any spinning object does—by changing its spin axis in the manner described.

One can get some intuitive understanding of this behavior by considering the motion of the part of the rim that actually touches the ground. Just before contact, this part of the rim has an instantaneous velocity in the forward and slightly downward direction. Note that the velocity direction and the radius line of the Frisbee out to this point on the rim together define the plane of rotation. When this part of the rim hits the ground, it receives an upward impulse. This changes its velocity to slightly above straightforward. The new velocity coupled with the radius line defines the new plane of rotation, which is now slanted upward. The Frisbee then goes up because of its tendency to move in its plane of orientation. This analysis is somewhat of an oversimplification since we have only focused on the motion of one part of the rim, ignoring the effects of and on the rest of the Frisbee. But it may nonetheless give some insight into why an object spinning about one axis, upon receiving a tweak about a perpendicular axis, responds by rotating its spin axis about the third perpendicular direction.

Keeping in mind the explanation of the manner in which torques change the spin axis of a rotating Frisbee, we are in a better position to look at the subtler aspects of a Frisbee's stability. The angular momentum contributes enormously, as discussed previously, but despite this stabilizing effect, the orientations of spin axes change, especially when Frisbees are thrown tipped vertically or upside down. Also, Frisbees with modified shapes (e.g., with a central cutout or with the bottom covered with surgical rubber) twist quite violently about the direction of flight. In all these cases the aerodynamic torques are evidently enough to change the orientation of the spin axis despite the large angular momentum resulting from the spin.

In these cases of unstable flight there is a net torque about the horizontal axis perpendicular to the direction of flight; i.e., there is more (or less) lift on the front or leading half of the Frisbee than on the back or trailing half. Airplane wings are subject to the same kind of torque, and balance is achieved by the tail's exerting an equal and opposite torque. The response of a Frisbee is for its spin axis to tip left or right for an ordinary right-handed throw depending on whether the lift on the front or back of the Frisbee is greater. (Remember that the spin axis rotates about the third axis, the first two being the spin axis itself and the torque axis.)

One might think that the lift on the sides of a Frisbee would be different because of their different velocities with respect to the air, one side moving into the wind and the other away from the direction of travel. What would be the consequence of this? It would result in a torque about the straight-ahead horizontal axis. Again applying the same principles, the Frisbee's spin axis would respond by tipping backward or forward, depending on the sense of the torque. The Frisbee would then arc upward or nosedive downward. Since this kind of flight is not observed, such torques are evidently negligibly small.

The aerodynamic stability of the modern Frisbee is admirable and leaves little room for improvement. However, a Frisbee's drag is fairly high, as already mentioned. One practical application of the above considerations might be in modifying current designs to minimize drag without upsetting the vital and delicate relative positions of the center of pressure (analogous to the center of gravity, but for aerodynamic forces) and the center of gravity. Such a Frisbee would float just as well but could be thrown further.

Since any design is more stable when given more angular momentum, another obvious design consideration would be to have as much of the Frisbee's mass as possible toward the outside of the disc. Angular momentum depends both on mass distribution and rate of rotation, and for a given rotation rate, it is greater with more mass further away from the center. Of course, a limit is set by the strength of the material in the center of the Frisbee. Frisbees can easily be modified by laying additional weight inside the rim, enhancing stability. However, the increased mass means a greater gravitational force and hence less "float" in flights. The outward-biased mass distribution in an ordinary Frisbee contributes to the increased stability of a Frisbee in comparison to such objects as pie tins and coffee-can lids.

WEATHER AND THE FRISBEE

Big whirls have little whirls that feed upon their velocity, and little whirls have lesser whirls and so to viscosity.[1]

by Jack E. Kaitala

Meteorology and the Frisbee

The science of meteorology deals with the physical processes that occur in the gaseous envelope that surrounds our planet; namely, the atmosphere. Many and varied are the disciplines that enter into the study of the atmosphere; they encompass far more than the well-known problem of weather prediction. Of primary importance to us is the lowest layer, which extends from the surface to approximately 150 feet. It is called the atmospheric boundary layer, and in it the myriad of human activity takes place: we work and play, and go about the business of living.

The boundary layer comprises the omnipresent portion of our environment. The complexity of the air motion in this layer antagonizes our efforts to accurately predict such things as (1) the diffusion of air pollutants, (2) the evaporation of water from the oceans, lakes and rivers, or (3) the capriciousness of the wind that will affect objects that soar and glide.

This capricious nature of the air flow in the boundary layer of the atmosphere can be summed up in a single word—turbulence—a term of rather murky substance, there being no general agreement on its definition. The little verse which prefaces this chapter is one of the more profound statements on the nature of turbulence. It testifies to the inbreeding of the eddying swirls of which turbulent motion is composed—the small swirls arising from the larger ones. However imperfect or incomplete our understanding of turbulent air flow, some basic features have evolved in its study. A major purpose of this chapter is to pass some of this information on to you, for it is the turbulent nature of the wind that alters the flight of the Frisbee as it majestically courses through the lowest reaches of our atmosphere.

Jack E. Kaitala received his Ph.D. in meteorology from the University of Michigan. He is a member of the American Meteorological Society, the Society of Sigma Xi, and is currently affiliated with the Fleet Numerical Weather Central at Monterey, California. His principal interest is the adaptation of turbulent boundary layer theory to numerical weather prediction. He was formerly a member of the Foul Five Guts Frisbee team.

[1] *L. F. Richardson (1926), Atmospheric Diffusion Shown on a Distance-Neighbor Graph,* Proceedings of the Royal Society, A, 110, P. 709.

Some of the discussions that follow may tend toward textbookish treatise. The author begs your indulgence; he will try to minimize such goings-on where possible, and try to maintain balance between your entertainment and your information. We will begin with the large-scale weather features that you can deduce from a weather map; and then work our way down to the small-scale features of air flow in the surface layer that are crucial to the problem at hand. After you have read this, you will hopefully have not only an ever-increasing appreciation for the flight of your Frisbee, but a more enlightened understanding of your environment.

The Wind

If you want to Frisbee tomorrow, it would be nice to know what kind of weather to expect, especially the speed and direction of the winds. You can listen to a weather forecast that is sufficiently detailed to provide wind information; or, if you could have the opportunity to glean a forecast of tomorrow's weather map, you could make some judgments, above and beyond the forecast, as to whether you want to Frisbee or stay at home and read a book.

How to Estimate Wind Speed and Direction from a Surface Weather Map

Common experience has probably made you quite familiar with the basic information present on a surface

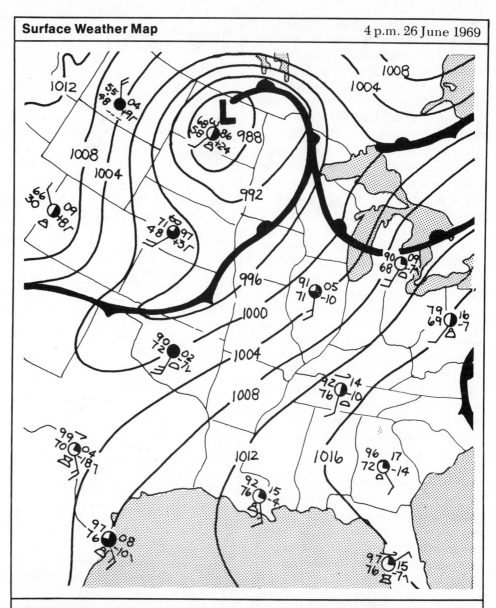

Surface Weather Map   4 p.m. 26 June 1969

FIG. 1. A surface weather map for the central United States. The map shows a low pressure center in North Dakota with an occluded front (⏣⏣⏣⏣, the cold air has overtaken the warm air) extending through Minnesota and Iowa, which becomes a cold front (▲▲▲▲) that extends into New Mexico. A warm front (⏜⏜⏜) extends through the Great Lakes region. The station models are explained in Fig. 2.

weather map. Your local newspapers and television weathercasters will always display information on such a map as a basis for detailing the weather of interest to the public. However, the map in Figure 1 contains more detail than the usual type that is displayed in newspapers. Weather information at the various reporting stations is encoded on the map. This is called a station model, and it is explained in Figure 2. Note especially the manner in which wind information is recorded.

The weather of the continental United States is predominated by the migratory highs and lows that travel from west to east. The daily weather map is simply an inventory of their position at a given time. Highs are generally thought of as being the harbingers of good weather, while lows are generally associated with bad weather (they are also called storm systems). Cold and warm fronts are associated with a low (the caption for Figure 1 describes the frontal structure associated with the low in North Dakota).

The solid black lines in Figure 1 give you a more detailed idea of the distribution of pressure (pressure that has been corrected to sea-level) over the midsection of the continental United States. Each line represents a value of constant pressure, and it is called an isobar. We commonly talk about pressure in units of inches of mercury, but the meteorologist prefers units of millibars (the metric system), and as a basis for conversion, 1013 millibars equals 29.92 inches of mercury.

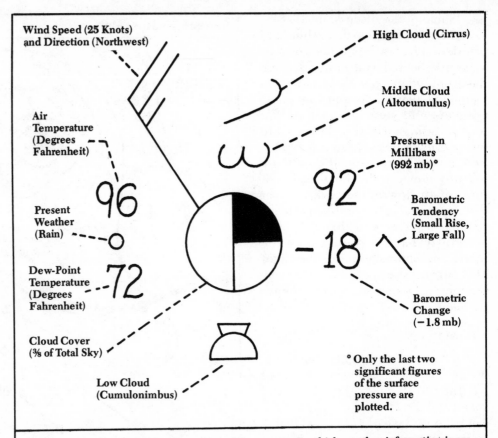

FIG. 2. A Station Model: an illustration of the manner in which weather information is encoded at a reporting station. Each entry is briefly explained in parentheses. The wind shaft indicates the direction from which the wind is blowing; each wind barb indicates the speed; a long barb = 10 knots, a short one = 5 knots.

Almost all barometers contain both scales. Note the closed isobar in North Dakota that surrounds the low; it is labeled with a value of 988 millibars. Anywhere inside this line, the pressure is smaller than this value; outside it, pressures increase from 988 millibars. There is a high pressure center out in the Atlantic, not shown on this map. You might have guessed its presence because of the increasing pressure as you move out over the ocean. Each line is drawn at a pressure interval of 4 millibars (the determination of the lines is called scalar, or contour, analysis). Thus you can get an idea of what the pressure is at any point on the map; and where the pressure is changing more rapidly, or slowly, by examining the packing (i.e., the spacing) between the isobars.

The spacing between the isobars is a measure of the pressure gradient. When the isobars are close together, the gradient is large; when they are further apart, the gradient is correspondingly weaker. This is important to the problem of estimating the wind speed and direction, for it is a well-known fact that air will move from high to low pressure. The stronger the pressure gradient, the faster the air will move in response to this gradient. In the language of the physicist: the air accelerates in response to the pressure gradient force.

The discussion of wind is hardly this simple, for there are other forces which become as important as the pressure gradient force in explaining the ultimate direction and speed in which air will travel in response to the forces exerted upon it. Suffice it to say that the pressure gradient force is crucial because it initiates the movement of the air. Once in motion, other forces (e.g., the deflecting force due to the earth's rotation, the centrifugal force, friction) become influential, but describing them involves the use of mathematics, and for our purposes, this is to be avoided.

We can note, in returning to the surface weather map, that the winds tend to blow in channels defined by the isobaric pattern. In the Northern Hemisphere, their forward direction of motion is such that lower pressure lies to the left, higher pressure to the right (the opposite is true in the Southern Hemisphere). If you look closely, you can also see that the winds reported by the stations tend to be deflected across the isobars toward low pressure; and thus, the winds blow into the center of a low and away from the center of a high. It is the frictional force that is responsible for this last bit of behavior of the winds at the surface. Thus we have counterclockwise circulation of air around a low, with the winds tending to be deflected in toward the center of the low; and clockwise circulation around a high, with the winds tending to be deflected out away from the center of the high.

You should also note that the wind speeds tend to be larger where the pressure gradient is stronger. As an example, note the reported speed in Montana (the tightly packed isobars in the colder air on the "back side of the low"), as opposed to the reported speeds on the station models down in Tennessee and Georgia (the more loosely packed isobars in the warm air streaming out of the Gulf of Mexico and the Atlantic). Please don't be misled by the larger wind speeds reported at Brownsville and New Orleans. These are undoubtedly due to the sea breeze effect. (It is produced by the cold air that is "drawn" in from the Gulf of Mexico due to the inland heating.) This is a local effect and should not be confused with the general principles that we are trying to establish here.

We can summarize by saying that winds are generally lighter in highs (which tend to have weaker pressure gradients) than in lows (which tend to have stronger pressure gradients).

Thus the pressure pattern on a weather map can tell you quite a bit about wind speed and direction, as well as about the weather in general. There is considerably more detail to the structure of the wind than that which can be extracted from a surface weather map, and in order to shed some light on this, we have to deal with the nature of wind turbulence. But first a word about the prediction of winds and weather prediction in general.

A Commercial for the People Who Forecast the Winds

I can't offer any *simple* rules of thumb that would enable an educated guess of tomorrow's weather, let alone tomorrow's winds. The atmosphere is too complex to be described by any simple rules of thumb or weather proverbs. The best source of weather information is your local branch of the National Meteorological Center (NMC). It provides estimates of the average winds not only for the next day, but for the next few days as well. Admittedly the forecasts are not yet perfect, but they are right most of the time, and they continue to get better as our knowledge of the atmosphere increases.

Weather information is readily provided to the public by the communications media (newspapers, television and radio). Some of these sources are better than others, so a little judgment is required in seeking the best source. Certain FM radio stations (e.g., Marine Weather Reports) broadcast continuous weather information. Some TV and radio weathercasters who happen to be professional meteorologists are also good at providing the kind of detail that would allow you to form a judgment about whether tomorrow's weather will be advantageous for the flight of the Frisbee. This is by no means an indictment of nonmeteorological weathercasters; some happen to be very good at conveying information without having to resort to the "show-biz schtick" that often masks the content of their message.

One- to five-day numerical forecasts are prepared in Washington, D.C., by the NMC. The NMC utilizes computers and the experience of professional forecasters of long-standing experience to deliver the best possible product to the public. Personnel at local branches of the NMC interpret the product, often hand-tailoring and modifying it, so that you the user have the best information available.

So much for the commercial. Now let's go on to the business of turbulence and the Frisbee.

Micrometeorology, Turbulence, and the Frisbee

The micrometeorologist, as the prefix micro implies, studies the small-scale, physical processes that occur in the boundary layer. Some examples of practical problems that are of interest to him include (1) heat and moisture exchange between the

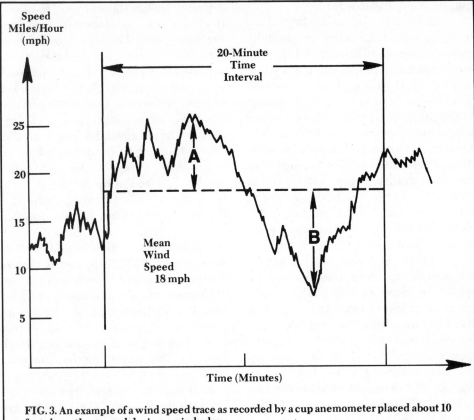

FIG. 3. An example of a wind speed trace as recorded by a cup anemometer placed about 10 feet above the ground during a windy day.

air and an irrigated field, (2) the effect of a shelter belt of trees on air flow, (3) loading of wind gusts on buildings and bridges, and (4) diffusion of an air pollutant. Solutions to the problems posed in each of these examples, and almost any other problem a micrometeorologist would be asked to investigate, would demand that he be able to specify, as is best possible, the turbulent character of the wind. The problem of the flight of the Frisbee is no exception.

The next two sections are intended to give you a quick introduction to atmospheric turbulence, with as little scientific jargon as possible.

A Few Words about Turbulence

If you were able to set a cup anemometer (a device that measures wind speed) about 10 feet above the ground and obtain a record of the wind speed (i.e., a wind speed trace), it would have the general appearance of Figure 3. The trace would be quite wiggly and irregular. You could estimate an average speed by simply drawing a dashed line through the middle of the trace, as has been done in the figure. By doing this, you would have obtained a 20-minute, average value of the wind speed. All the other blips and pulses in the trace, which depart from the average value, constitute the turbulent part of the wind. With reference to Figure 3, the turbulent gust at A represents an eddying component of the wind whose speed is approximately 7 miles per hour (mph) greater than the average value (18 mph) of the wind. The turbulent lull at B is about 10 mph less than the average; a calculation that our senses would reduce to "the winds have died down." In the context of the preceding statements, we have provided a strikingly succinct definition of turbulence: it is the departure of the wind from its average value. This seems arbitrarily simple, but I don't think that a better definition of turbulence has as yet been offered.

Turbulence in the air flow of the boundary layer depends chiefly on two factors: (1) the character of the surface over which the air passes ("surface roughness;" e.g., water, sand, grass, tall shrubs), and (2) the heating (or cooling) of the surface.

It is only logical to suspect that the presence of obstacles in an otherwise steady air stream would disturb the flow, causing the air to be deflected and altered in its course, in passing over and around these obstacles. The continued deflection of the air would produce a small-scale maelstrom of little whirls, colliding and bumping into one another; in short, turbulence. From wind tunnel studies it is known that increasing the roughness of the underlying surface increases the amount of turbulence in the overlying air flow. As a consequence, air flow over a smooth surface such as water is less turbulent than air flow over a grassy plain.

Common experience has probably introduced us already to the nature of the second factor—winds tend to be stronger during the day than at night. This observation is tied in with the manner in which heating and cooling take place in the boundary layer. In the discussion that follows, it must be remembered that the lower reaches of the atmosphere are by and large transparent to short-wave radiation. As an oversimplification, the air does *not* heat up in response to the sun's rays; the surface does. This heat is (1) almost immediately transferred back into the first few meters of air (a matter of minutes), (2) more sluggishly transferred into the remainder of the boundary layer (a matter of hours), and eventually through deeper layers of the atmosphere (a matter of days). At night under clear skies, the surface cools due to infrared (long-wave) radiation loss; and the heat is transferred to it from the overlying, warmer air. This process is very slow when compared to the daytime movement of heat. This is the stability (temperature inversion) of the surface air layer. The important point is this: the surface is where the action (heating) takes place, and the atmospheric heating follows behind (rapidly by day, slowly by night).

The rate at which the heat is transferred in the boundary layer is controlled by the turbulence mechanism. It plays a vital role in distributing the heat through an ever-deepening layer. As the daytime heating of the surface progresses, very large eddies spring into existence to transfer this heat to the cooler air layers aloft. At the same time, cold air is brought down from aloft as nature attempts, through the mechanism of convective turbulence, to wipe out the temperature gradient that is being generated. The sum-and-substance of this activity typically manifests itself in the strong, gusty winds that we so

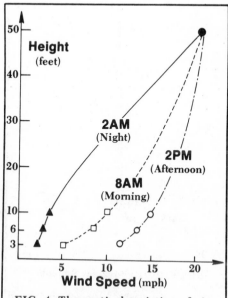

FIG. 4. The vertical variation of air temperature in the first 50 feet of atmosphere during a 12-hour period (cf. Fig. 5).

often observe on a hot day.

Figure 4 portrays an idealized course of the vertical variation of temperature (a temperature profile) in a 12-hour period. Note that almost all of the temperature change takes place in the first 10 feet of the boundary layer, the change becoming larger the closer you get to the surface. Temperatures at the 6-foot level are the ones we experience, since this is the height at which temperature measurements are generally made.

Temperatures decrease rapidly with height during the day. This type of temperature profile is called unstable—the sharper the decrease of temperature (i.e., a larger temperature

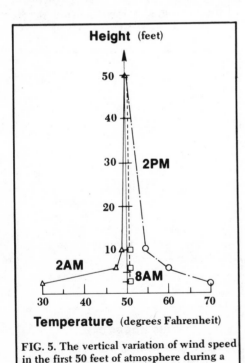

FIG. 5. The vertical variation of wind speed in the first 50 feet of atmosphere during a 12-hour period (cf. Fig. 4).

gradient), the larger the instability in the boundary layer and the more active the convective turbulence. Note that the temperature at 50 feet is relatively unaffected by the heating at the surface. There would be some warming at this level, but it would be less than 1°F. and thus not perceivable on the temperature scale in the figure.

A similar situation applies to the idealized course of the vertical profile of wind (Fig. 5). Most of the changes in wind speeds are observed near the surface, which can be seen by comparing average speeds at the 6-foot level. The wind at 50 feet, like the temperature, is relatively unaffected by the changes that are occurring near the surface. The gradient of wind speed is directed toward the surface proper, where the speed must approach zero because of friction. As a consequence, there is a continuous deficit of momentum in the surface layer, and nature attempts to minimize this gradient by transferring faster moving air down to the surface, where it is consumed by friction. So turbulence transfers momentum as well as heat. When the air is unstable, the turbulence is more efficient in transferring momentum down to the surface, and we experience an increase in wind speeds.

As night approaches, the surface cools by long-wave radiation; the cooling of the overlying air layer follows suit. This is the inversion condition, for the temperature now increases with height. This is a stable air layer, for the warm, lighter air is above the cold, heavier air. As a consequence,

the convective turbulence that was present by day has been shut off. Momentum cannot be transferred as effectively into the surface air layers and, as a consequence, wind speeds are observed to diminish at night. In addition, the turbulent fluctuations present in the stable layer near the surface get damped out, whereas the winds at greater heights above the surface (50 feet in our example) remain much the same as they did by day.

The important point is this: almost all of the daily changes in temperature and wind speed that we experience are confined to a very shallow layer of the atmosphere (50 feet in our examples), while the remainder of the atmosphere above this height "barely perceives" these relatively dramatic changes. However, there is a gradual response to the events at the surface (through the exchange of heat and moisture from the surface) which can eventually lead to changes in the large-scale synoptic patterns, but this is subtle and very hard to trace. In another perspective, the warm air rising over a heated corn field in Iowa on a sunny Sunday afternoon may trigger events in the air layer "upstairs" that could lead, after two or three days, to the development of a storm system over the East Coast. This concept is the cornerstone of how small-scale turbulence eventually affects the general circulation of the atmosphere. But this need not concern us here. Our interest is in the "character" of the surface-layer air turbulence, and so we will now move on to a discussion of some of the unsavory eddy currents that inhabit the boundary layer and what they could do to our Frisbee in flight.

Three Types of Turbulent Eddies

Now that you have developed a feeling for the character of turbulent air flow, especially regarding how it changes through the course of a day and night, we can proceed to some specific details which are more pertinent to the Frisbee in flight. If we consider a fair summer afternoon—a few light, fluffy clouds overhead, warm southerly winds that average around five miles per hour, and Frisbee in hand—the following types of turbulent eddies (ET's) will probably be present.

1. ET number 1: Very short, energetic, small-scale pulses of wind; usually lasting 5-10 seconds; these can come at you from all directions and tend to be random in character; these are the gusts of wind that rattle your windows, ripple the flag, and tug at madame's skirts (Let's hear it for the ET1's).
2. ET number 2: A larger-scale type of eddy that can last from 20 to 30 seconds; these eddies are more organized than the ET1's; they are tied in quite intimately with the vertical component, and are active in the transfer of momentum into the surface layer.
3. ET number 3: A very large eddy whose time span is about 2-3 min-

utes; these eddies are most often associated with a dramatic shift in the horizontal wind direction; turbulent motions of this type can be associated with the development of small cumulus clouds on a warm, summer afternoon.

Suffice it to say that you really cannot do much about the behavior of the ET1's on the flight of the Frisbee. These whimsical breezes will attack a Frisbee from any direction because of their random character. ET2's and ET3's have a characteristic type of behavior, and as will soon be pointed out, you can take advantage of them, especially with regard to a distance toss.

Moisture and Temperature

The density of air, which depends on moisture and temperature, is not as important as wind turbulence with regard to the flight of the Frisbee. Density can, however, make some difference, since it is directly proportionate to the amount of resistance encountered by the Frisbee as it passes through the air. As a consequence, the Frisbee should travel faster and farther when temperatures are warmer, since warmer air is less dense than cold air. Moist air is lighter than dry air (in comparing two equal volumes at the same temperature), so that an increase in humidity is coupled with a shift to atmospheric conditions more favorable for Frisbee.

Wind Turbulence; When to Throw

The most definitive statement that can be made in this context is that optimum Frisbee is associated with conditions of little or no wind. As a general rule, the winds associated with a warm front, or the winds near the center of high pressure system, tend to be light and go hand-in-hand with good weather, and thus good Frisbee.

It should be noted that the sequence of wind and temperature changes described in Figure 4 are representative of the day-night transitions associated with a high pressure system. These conditions generally occur with the warmer, balmy days of late spring, summer, or autumn for the continental United States. Early morning, late afternoon (dusk), and night are therefore the optimum times for Frisbee. Frisbee under the lights—why not?

We are, however, diurnal creatures, and would therefore be more prone to frolic and thus Frisbee at midday, when the sun is high. So, unfortunately, is the turbulence. Your course of action in these circumstances, should you wish to improve distance and accuracy, is described below.

What to Do When Wind Turbulence Is High

As the day progresses and the sun rises to its zenith, the three categories of eddying motions, previously described, spring into existence. At first only the ET1's are observed, but as the air in the boundary layer warms and the winds pick up, the ET2's and ET3's appear, and play a very active role in the transfer of heat (and also moisture) through an ever-deepening vertical layer. It is the ET2's and ET3's that concern us, for the ET1's, as previously stated, are impossible to predict—they will carry a Frisbee in just about any direction, at any moment. There is one thing that may be noted about the small, short-lived pulses of the ET1 category—they are more apt to occur when the winds have picked up. They are in all probability born within the larger-scale eddies of categories 2 and 3. Recall the little verse at the beginning of this chapter.

ET2's tend to be tied quite closely to the vertical component of the wind. Their existence seems to be directed toward the continual exchange of momentum between the faster moving air aloft (which does not feel the effects of surface friction) and the more slowly moving air closer to the surface. In fact, the air in the boundary layer is continually draining momentum from the faster moving air aloft, and dissipating it as friction. And therein lies the systematic aspect of the ET2's. When the winds begin to accelerate, we are probably receiving a new supply of momentum from aloft. As a consequence, increases in horizontal wind speed tend to be associated with downdrafts.

The forward moving component (horizontal component) of an ET2

tends to be about three times larger than the vertical one. If we assume that the average wind is approximately as large as the horizontal gust component, we can calculate an effective wind component on the back of the Frisbee as it begins to slow down. By slowing down, we mean the state of affairs that is reached after the energy imparted to the Frisbee in the toss has been expended in doing work against the gravity force, and the random buffeting by the ET1's (which hopefully would aid as much as hinder the flight of the Frisbee). The wind force would then become dominant, and the Frisbee would experience a small downward component (about one tenth that of the horizontal component), along with a following tail wind.

The key to identification of an ET2 lies in the fact that it tends to propagate in the mean-wind direction. So when they encounter you, from your backside, standing there awaiting the precious moment of truth for the big distance toss, you should sense the wind striking you directly from your back. Give it five seconds, so as to distinguish it from a grubby little ET1, but more crucially, to allow it to fill the "up-wind void" with a potentially beneficial tail wind.

Having now established the existence of an ET2 surging down the intended line of flight, you can perform your take-off maneuvers, and attempt to catch the benefit of an additional following wind—you probably have another ten seconds to release before this particular ET2 will have

died or otherwise gone away.

It is still not too bad to release, even slightly after ten seconds, for the gust-updraft. You may lose the benefit of an additional tail wind, but stand to gain an upward wind force from the ascending current that is so often associated with the sensation of winds "dying down."

Both the downdraft-gust/updraft-lull tend to be stages of the same eddy. However, experimental evidence seems to indicate that you will be most likely to encounter and recognize ET2's and, most important, utilize them in the order specified above.

ET2's are always present in what

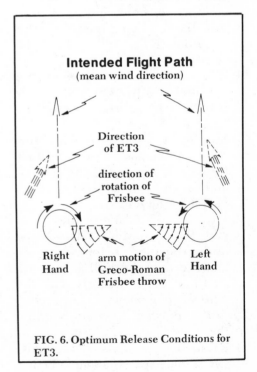

FIG. 6. Optimum Release Conditions for ET3.

we commonly call a gusty wind. Even with overcast skies, when most of the turbulence is ET1, we still find ET2's, and incidentally, no ET3's. It is interesting to note that with decreasing cloudiness (or increasing sunshine, as you may prefer), and thus increased heating of the surface, the time frame (the period of the ET2's) shifts back to larger and larger time scales. Thus, on a very warm and sunny day (i.e., clear sky), ET2's may be running around fifty to eighty seconds in duration.

We have thus far described ET2 turbulence, which tends to be confined to the horizontal and vertical directions. ET3's tend to be associated with the lateral, or crosswind, turbulent component of the wind. These eddies are identifiable as distinct shifts in the horizontal direction of the wind. In comparing with the ET2's, the requirements on timing the Frisbee release are less stringent for these gigantic swirls, for they tend to last from one to three minutes. As was the case for ET2's, the persistence of ET3's, as well as their time scales as you would perceive their period of existence, tends to increase with an increase in the warming of the air in the boundary layer.

The presence of an ET3 manifests itself in a decided shift in the wind azimuth, e.g., about thirty degrees from the mean wind direction that has predominated for most of the day. If you wait for about thirty to forty seconds, and the winds persist from either the right or left of center, you may reassess the intended flight path with a new mean wind direction; or, if

you utilize the Greco-Roman release, you may "opt" to take advantage of the new crosswind component, coupled with your original selection of intended flight path. With reference to Figure 6 you can gain additional Frisbee *rotational* speed, depending upon whether the wind is left or right of center, and whether you are right- or left-handed. Incidentally, ET3's show no real preference for right-handers or south paws—they are equal-opportunity eddies and are as apt to occur from the left as from the right of center.

I hate to bring a note of discord into this discussion, but most of the statements that have been made so far are overpoweringly subject to chance. In fact, turbulence is almost purely statistical in nature. As such, I can only hope to put the odds in your favor. Indeed, one of the most powerful physical statements that can be made about the nature of turbulence is bound up in the little verse at the beginning of this chapter. As a consequence, the ET3 could conceivably contain five or ten ET2's during its existence, so that you now have two time scales to decipher in making your preflight plans. Furthermore, as the ET2 surges downwind, now immersed in an ET3, those small-scale whirls of ET1 are liable to develop, especially in the air layer close to the ground. But this is the nature of turbulence as we now understand it.

A few final statements about ET3's. They tend to be associated with the development of little wooly clouds (the fair-weather cumulus).

Therefore, you may deduce their existence if you spot nicely organized rows of puffy little clouds cropping up and growing as the day progresses. The cloud lines will tend to move in much the same direction as that associated with the onset of an ET3.

I now say unto you, cast your eyes to the celestial dome, and look for the fair-weather cumulus clouds. Their direction of motion points the way to the path that may be most favorable to you. And if someone inquires as to your heavenly deliberations, inform him, "I seek the longitudinal roll vortices, for verily, they shall point the way." The surfer seeks the ideal wave...Frisbee players engage in SITE: seeking ideal turbulent eddies.

Frisbee at the Beach

Most of us are familiar with the lake breeze (or sea breeze) that develops and strengthens through the course of the day, generally peaking in the early afternoon and dissipating at dusk. I call attention to, as a possible hint to better Frisbee conditions, the vertical temperature structure of the air as it passes from the water onto the land. Since the water is cooler than the adjoining land surface (this is the motivating reason behind the lake breeze), the air layer adjacent to the water will be decidedly cooler as it comes onshore. Depending on how cold the water is, an inversion (i.e., a stable, low turbulence layer) may be present over the water, and would still be present right at the water's edge. As the air penetrates inland over the heated, sandy beaches, it will rapidly become unstable. But near the edge of the beach, or right in the water (if it is not too deep), the air should be considerably less turbulent than that over the beaches; and thus we have a good Frisbee court, with a constant onshore wind component at water's edge. This would be an excellent place to experiment with the effect of increased rotational spin due to a crosswind component—made all the more attractive by the presence of a stable, low turbulence wind flow.

Some Final Thoughts

All of the previously mentioned helpful hints regarding utilization of turbulent motion would demand that you make a careful and knowledgeable survey of wind conditions (i.e., the average wind speed and direction, and the turbulence, type and degree) prior to engaging in SITE. The best answer to this problem is to set up an array of fast response wind speed and direction sensors, with on-line analog-digital conversion; and with immediate availability of sufficient computing power, calculate the spectral and cospectral representation of the turbulent components of the wind. You could then discern the types of turbulence present (this is the usual fashion in which micrometeorologists gather and interpret wind data), and therefore make appropriate preflight plans. Clearly you will not, under normal circumstances, be able to do this. As a substitute, I offer the following.

Get a watch with a second hand, a scratch pad and pencil, a discerning eye, and the patience to wait about thirty minutes in order to gain a sample of what types of eddies are occurring. In order to catalog the ET1's, you could note the frequency of occurrence of strong, pulsing gusts; a rippling, snapping flag or the rapidly vibrating branches of a small tree serve as good indicators. For the ET2's, you could count the number of "dead spots" which are followed by a rapid acceleration of the wind, which sustains itself as an above-average wind speed for ten to twenty seconds—note that the total period of an ET2 includes both the pick-up and dying-down times. For ET3's, you would want to note how much (e.g., ten, twenty, thirty degrees). If you sample for a thirty-minute interval, you could calculate the *average period* of each of the ET's by the following equation:

$$\frac{\text{Period}}{\text{(Minutes)}} = \frac{\text{Sampling Interval (Minutes)}}{\begin{array}{c}\text{Number of occurrences}\\ \text{during the sampling}\\ \text{interval}\end{array}}$$

The more often you observe a particular type of eddy during the sampling interval, the greater your statistical confidence in your estimate of its average period.

Knowing the average periods of the ET's, you can now make appropriate adjustments to your preflight plans. As an example, I observed twenty ET2's during the last thirty minutes (period equals ninety seconds). Half of them occurred from the left of center (i.e., association with an ET3). Ten ET3's were observed (period equals three minutes, five left of center, five right of center). I stand here awaiting the moment of truth: I would suspect that I would encounter one ET3 from the left of center in the next six minutes, which should contain an ET2 with the favorable gust, full sequence over a ninety-second period. About halfway through the first forty-five seconds of the gust-downdraft phase of the ET2, now immersed in the ET3, I will release to take advantage of the following tail wind and increased rotational spin, for I am a right-handed Frisbee player.

Finally, in response to a request directed to me by the beloved Harvey Kukuk, I hereby specify the high country on the eastern slopes of the Rockies (e.g., Boulder or Denver, Colorado) during the winter time condition of a chinook (translation: snow-eater) as the most fascinating meteorological environment for distance Frisbee throwing. In this warm, dry wind, descending the eastern slopes of the Rockies, and sublimating the snow out from underneath it, I find a following wind of ideal character. It is strong, its air density is low (due to the high elevation), and it will be relatively stable owing to the dry adiabatic descent, with subsequent warming; and its passage over the cold snow surface. With the proper snap of the wrist and follow through, I just might be able to dislodge the left rear hub cap from the legendary Thor Anderson's gleaming pace car in Gary, Indiana.

GLOSSARY

Against Wind Wind blowing against throw.

Air Bounce of Spyder Wills See *Dip*.

Angle of Attack See *Mung Angle*.

Angle of Francioni See *Francioni Angle*.

Angle of Roll See Hyzer Angle

Arcuate Vanes Slightly raised and curved diagonal ribs on Frisbee.

Base-Bee Frisbee baseball.

Bead of Barrett Vestige of sprue, usually in navel.

Bernoulli Principle As air flows over the Frisbee's surface, the top-side flow is slowed over the curved area, producing lift.

Blisters Raised surface spots, usually on Bernoulli's plate; if opened leads to peeling and Wellish's Malady. Caused by dirty, sticky molds.

Brickbats Frisbee with extra firm flight plate. Outstanding for distance throwing. All from mold 15, 1968 to 1969.

Bubble Tops Flimsy flight plate, flaps in flight. Poor distance performers. Syn: Blight of Bradshaw, softness.

Bump of Boggio Circular raised line on cupola roof surrounding nipple of Pluto Platter, Speedy, and Horseshoe models.

Cheek Inside face of lip or rim. Runs from Ditch of Davis at top to

edge of bottom.

Circle of May Circle band on cupola floor between Malafronte's mound and nipple.
Syn: Montgomery's Ring.

Clark-Shelton Grip Modified common grip, for backhand throw.

Climb Same as *Well*.

Cornering Wind Comes 45 degrees over your shoulder; if wind and spin direction are the same, distance will be augmented.

Crown See *Cupola*.

Cuffing (the ear) Non-throwing hand holds Frisbee to increase power by heightening whelm.

Cupola Central raised structure of

Frisbee; also called: cabin, dome, and crown.

Curl Pre-yaw rotation prior to whelm. Curl directly proportional to spin.

Dip A pre-well flight variant peculiar to backhand throws. Disc flies slightly downwards then suddenly wells up into normal flight.
Syn: Air Bounce of Spyder Wills.

Ditch of Davis Area where Frisbee's cheek joins Bernoulli's plate. Syn.: Toejam's Recess.

Double Frisbee Throwing and catching two Frisbees together.

Drop Sudden waft failure.

Ear Lateral sides of Frisbee in flight.

Edge Bottom-most part of lip.

Flight Plate Top surface of Frisbee from lip to lip.

Flutterball Fling Hyzer's legendary throw. Records reveal it was a clockwise, backhand, very low throw with terminal wobble.

Folf Frisbee golf.

Francioni Angle A vital aerodynamic angle between Bernoulli's plate and cheek, i.e., the degree of toe-ing in of the rim.

Frankenstein Frisbee Frisbee made from pieces of other Frisbees.

Frisbee Finger A catching hazard, blunt trauma to finger tip.

Frisbee Hair Scuff tags of fractured polyethylene.

Frisbee Nodule Chronic abrasion bump(s) on finger(s) of release.

Frisbee Whelp Raised skin bruise secondary to direct trauma from flying disc.

Garbage Frisbee Opprobrious practice of playing Frisbee in a crowd. Syn.: showboating.

Gillespie's Groove Reversed Morrison Slope. First appeared on Fastback. Produces low-profile faster disc, but unstable and breakable.

Gollum The catch you almost made, the Frisbee fades away "as tho' sighted."

Groove An accuracy term. Best pattern of swing and release.

Headrick Lines Concentric raised rings on most Wham-O Frisbees, on Morrison's slope. Syn.: friction ridges, speed rings, flight rings.

Height of Release Point of whelm measured from ground. Important in nose gliding and tailskating.

Hellring's Rings Raised concentric lines on Bernoulli's plate found on Master, Tee Bird.

Hover Hyperspin, hyper-Mung throws that fall like a parachute with little or no warping.

Hyzer Angle Angle of roll, Frisbee's sideways tilt at whelm.

Knerr's Line or Ridge Raised circular rib, just outside color band.

Knock-off Toy industry term for imitation product.

Kukuk Ridge Raised circular rib between color and script band.

Lifts A mid-phase secondary climb. Syn.: rises.

Lip Outer part of Frisbee, from Seldom Seen Space of Sewall to edge. Also called rim.

Melin's Line or Ridge Raised circular rib between script band and Slope of Schultz.

Minute Mound of Malafronte Circular ridge or line on cupola floor separating Nachazel's Ring and Circle of May.

Morrison's Slope The outer third of most discs where the flight plate descends to form the lip.

Mung Angle Angle of pitch, the Frisbee's upwards tilt during first phase of flight. Syn.: pitch angle, attack angle.

Nachazel's Ring A cupola floor structure, a circular band, bordered by outer edge on San Gabriel Ring and on the inner edge by Minute Mound of Malafronte. Syn.: Doughnut.

Navel Indentation in center of cupola. Syn.: Gate.

Nortoning A descriptive term for the degree of hooking of the index finger over the lip in the common grip. The greater the hooking, the more the nortoning.

Nose Front of Frisbee in flight.

Nose Gliding Getting the nose down early in a strong favoring wind to lengthen distance. Syn.: Toejam power.

O'Clock System Method of measuring the amount of curl prior to whelm, based on yaw rotation around clock superimposed on Frisbee if holding hand is arbitrarily at 3 o'clock.

Occasional Ring of Oliveria A small raised ring running just below Toejam's Recess.

Overshot Injection molding term; means too much material placed in mold.

Paradox Throw A throw with opposite spin to what one would expect.

Parting Line See *Shelton's Line.*

Plate of Blake Also called centering ring; under surface structure supporting cupola or center area.

Plateman "Batter" in Frisbee baseball. Syn.: slinger.

Rim See *Lip.*

Run A post-Was event; downed Frisbee rolls like a wheel and runs along the ground.

Question Mark Skip of Pitt A special skip flight ending in a small curly-Q run of the Frisbee. Produced with underhand throw as disc skips off of Morrison's slope instead of lip.

San Gabriel's Ring Circular band connecting cupola floor to Bernoulli's plate; site of greatest stress in cupola models.

Scrambling Guts Frisbee term; team members back up primary catcher, playing for deflected catch. In controlled scrambling, players bat plate softly until best thrower can secure a catch.

Seldom Seen Space of Sewall The space between the first line of Headrick and the lip. Site of greatest stress and breaks in Fastback models.

Set Body position of thrower just before throw begins.

Shelton's Line Line bisecting lip, found in every Frisbee made by injection-mold method. Syn.: parting line, seam.

Sink Guts term for shot that drops at line to score. A thumb-throw feature.

Slope of Schultz A cupola feature on flight plate between wing and cupola roof.

Split When Frisbees separate in double Frisbee throw.

Sprue Remnant of Frisbee's "umbilical cord." Injection point from mold machine. See *Bead of Barrett.*

Stern Shots Deliveries made from behind the thrower.

Tail Trailing end of Frisbee in flight.

Tailskating Prolonged welling in phase one. Syn.: dragging your tail.

Trap A Guts term for illegal catch. Any catch other than a "clean" one-hander.

Thwart of Thor When Frisbee (primary) or hand holding Frisbee (secondary) strikes body during throw.

Tipping Striking bottom side of plate with hand, foot, etc., to produce artificial hover and easy catch.

Toejam Power See *Nose Gliding.*

Toejam's Recess See *Ditch of Davis.*

Turnover The bane of distance throwers and the primary fault of flight, Frisbee turns on lateral axis; usually caused by poor balance, inadequate lip mass, or incorrect Hyzer angle. Syn.: roll over, flop over.

Undershot Injection-molding term; too little material injected.

Waft Fifth flight period and longest in time and distance. The quintessence of a distance throw. If everything goes well, the waft shows it. Syn.: float.

Wane Sixth period of flight, characterized by first sign of float failure as power of throw declines.

Warp Eighth flight period, characterized by sideways turning, *warp-curl*, to the opposite direction of spin of Frisbee, which is now greatly reduced.

Was Ninth, last and shortest flight. The moment of contact with ground or other object. Syn.: Touch down.

Wasting Flight's seventh period, force declines rapidly and Frisbee falls, spin begins to slow.

Wax Fourth period of flight, Mung angle leveling out.

Wedge Second period of flight, brief, characterized by Mung angle. Syn.: insertion.

Well Third period of flight, exaggerated in high return (boomerang) flights; if overdone results in attenuated waft. Syn.: climb.

Wellish's Malady Fatal Frisbee illness caused by "flash" in the molding; *blisters* open, peeling occurs, large pieces of plastic lost; wellished, finished.

Whelm Flight's first period. The letting go of the Frisbee; the Hyzer angle is the prime feature of whelm. Syn.: release, hatch.

Wing Section of flight plate from lip to cupola.

With Wind Favoring wind for throwing.

Wristing Last element in throwing, wrist snaps quickly to produce spin of Frisbee. Syn.: Uncurling.

Yawing Spinning.

ABBREVIATIONS

The following abbreviations are approved by the Olympic Frisbee Federation.

AFDO —American Flying Disc Open

BFG —Berkeley Frisbee Group

BH —Backhand

BTB —Behind-the-Back

BTH —Behind-the-Head

BTL —Between-the-Legs

C —Clockwise

CC —Counterclockwise

COFC —Canadian Open Frisbee Championships

CPI —Concepts Products Incorporated

DDC —Double Disc Court

ET —Elbow Tip

FDW —Flying Disc World

FH —Forehand

GST —Giant Saucer Tosser

HAA —Highland Avenue Aces

HDT —Head Tip

HLT —Heel Tip

HMCU —Humbly Magnificent Champions of the Universe

HT —Hooked Thumb

IF —International Frisbeers

IFA —International Frisbee Association

IFF —International Frisbee Federation

IFM —Institute of Frisbee Medicine

IFT —International Frisbee Tournament

KT —Knee Tip

MIFDS —Monterey Institute of Frisbee Dog Studies

MTA —Maximum Time Aloft

OFF —Olympic Frisbee Federation

OWF —Overhand Wrist Fling

$ —Body Spin

S —Somersault

SA —Sidearm

SBTB	—Spinning Behind the Back	
SD	—Split Digit (mold number)	
SN	—Small Numeral (mold number)	
SSSS	—Seldom Seen Space of Sewall	
ST	—Saucer Tosser	
TD	—Thumbs Down	
TRC	—Throw, Run, and Catch	

TTH —Thumb Throw
TT —Toe Tip
TTA —Trick Throw Accuracy
TT,p —Thwart of Thor, primary
TT,s —Thwart of Thor, secondary
TU —Thumbs Up
UA —Underarm

UD —Upside down
UKFA —United Kingdom Frisbee Association
UMIFF —University of Michigan Indoor Frisbee Festival
WFA —World Frisbee Association
WFC —World Frisbee Championships

CHRONOLOGY OF FRISBEE

Circa 400 B.C. Myron sculpts Discobolus. Uses oversized Greek Frisbee in overhand wrist-fling grip.

202 B.C. Battle of Zama. Legend of Roman soldiers using razor-sharp, Frisbee-shaped shields to defeat Hannibal and Carthage. (legend)

A.D. 1827 Elihu Frisbie hurls collection plate in protest against Yale's compulsory chapel. (legend)

1860 Albert B. Fall constructs 84-pound Frisbee in Inverate, Mass. (legend)

1871 William Russell Frisbie moves from Bransford to Bridgeport, Conn., to manage new pie company. Shortly afterwards he buys it, renaming it, the Frisbie Pie Company.

March, 26, 1893 Julius T. Nachazel born in Traverse City, Michigan.

1903 W. R. Frisbie dies. Son, Joseph P., becomes head of Frisbie Pie Company.

1918 Nachazel captures the Kaiser's Walking Stick—emblem later used for original Nachazel Trophy.

1940 Joseph P. Frisbie dies. Widow Marian Rose manages company.

1940-45 Drivers for Frisbie Pie Company ambassador their prowess in tin sailing at WW II army camps.

1947 Morrison carves first plastic disc from block of solid tenite.

1948 The first molded plastic disc, the arcuate vane model, is manufactured. Rich Knerr and "Spud" Meline found Wham-O Company.

late 1948	The First Premium Flying Disc, the Arcuate Vane with Lil' Abner label, appears.
fall, 1949	Sachnoff Hypothesis (potato chip tin lid) origin.
1951	Morrison makes second disc, the Pluto Platter.
November 7, 1954	First Invitational Guts (Disc) Game. Blossom Brothers Five of Theta Delta Chi at Dartmouth defeat Tweedy Free Throwers from Montreal.
January 13, 1957	First Pluto Platter from Wham-O; the first commercial flying disc.
July 1958	First Invitational Frisbee Tournament held at Escanaba, Michigan.
September 30, 1958	Patent No. 183,626 awarded to Fred Morrison for his "Flying Saucer."
1958	Frisbie Pie Company of Bridgeport, Conn., shuts down.
May 26, 1959	Frisbee becomes registered trademark No. 679,186 for "Flying Saucers for Toss Games."
May 1, 1960	Peers Park Invitational Festival held. First tournament of the now defunct Pacific Coast Frisbee Association.
August 1961	First Pacific Coast Frisbee Association Championships held at Stanford University.
March 1962	Allen Jones sets individual marathon mark of 8,640 throws in twelve hours (wearing out six partners.)
April 1962	Second Pacific Coast Frisbee Association championships held at Berkeley, California.
October 1962	Nachazel Trophy insured for $750,000 with Lloyd's of London.
July 1963	International Frisbee Federation (formerly Pacific Coast Frisbee Association) holds its world Frisbee championship contest in Cali, Columbia. Contest still held annually, usually in summer in Panama City, Panama.
October 1964	Professional model Frisbee, introduced.
Summer, 1965	Street Frisbee Game devised.
Early 1966	Wham-O tools up second pro mold—ill-fated Number 4.
May 27, 1967	Olympic Frisbee Federation organized.
June 1967	H. R. "Fling" Hyzer leaves North Central Team for new Wisconsin team.
Summer, 1967	CPI introduces Saucer Tosser.
July 1967	North Central loses first Guts Crown to Foul Five in 9th IFT.
Fall, 1967	Joel Silver introduces Ultimate Frisbee to Columbia High School, Maplewood, New Jersey.
November 1967	Mini-Frisbees introduced.
November 9, 1967	International Frisbee Association organized. Headquarters in Los Angeles.
January 13, 1968	Toejam, Utah, diggings with Frisbee-shaped mud pies unearthed.

February 1968	International Frisbee Association *News* begins quarterly publication.
March 1968	Master Model Frisbee developed.
March 24, 1968	5:40 P.M. First recorded catch of three Frisbees by two people—Dave and Ken Roberts of Jacksonville, N.C.
April 27, 1968	First International Frisbee Association Master's Tournament at Rose Bowl.
July 1968	California Masters defeat North Central, long-time reigning champion and home team, in Guts at 11th IFT; bring Nachazel Cup to California for first time.
February 1, 1969	Marathon Frisbee throw at Millersville, Penn., lasts 217 hours, 46 minutes, 3 seconds.
Spring, 1969	First Ultimate Frisbee Game at Maplewood, New Jersey's Columbia High School The Columbian newspaper staff defeated the Student Council.
May 1969	First Pennsylvania State Championships at Millersville. Now held annually.
June 1969	U.S. Navy begins Frisbee research in hopes of developing a "self-suspended flare." Moonlighter Frisbee introduced.
July 1969	California Master's Team Guts winners second time at IFT. Fabled North Central Team makes last IFT appearance.
	Original Julius T. Nachazel Cup retired to Healy family.
September 1969	Harvey J. Kukuk becomes executive director of International Frisbee Association,
October 1969	First "Big Game Tournament" held at Berkeley, California.
Mid-December 1969	First National Junior Frisbee Tournament held at Madison Square Garden.
1970	First Frisbee thrown on top of Mt. Whitney, 14,000 ft., by Bill Massalsks and Bill Chaney.
February 1970	Frisbee declared the national sport of the Island of Yanuca in Fiji Archipelago. Columbia High School, Maplewood, N.J., Varsity Frisbee Squad organized.
Spring 1970	University of Oregon Frisbee course offered, first ever in college, no credit given, Ronald J. Lovinger, instructor.
April 1970	Dr. Roger Woods opens Institute of Frisbee Medicine in Santa Monica, Calif.
May 29, 1970	First Canadian Tournament held at Banff, Alberta, Canada.
June 1970	Jon Davis named director for the 13th Invitational Frisbee Tournament. Navy shelves Frisbee flare research after one year and $375,000.
July 1970	13th IFT moves to Calumet, Michigan. Foul Five team of Gary, Ind. wins *new* Julius T. Cup.
August 6, 1970	Jonny Hines scales 12,395 foot Mt. Fuji in Japan, and sails white Master

	Frisbee to symbolize international Frisbee friendship.
November 7, 1970	First interscholastic Ultimate Frisbee game won by C.H.S.V.F.T. over Milburn High School. Score: 43 to 10.
January 1971	All-American Frisbee model appears.
Spring 1971	New Jersey (Ultimate) Frisbee Conference formed with five teams.
May 1971	First Marin College Tournament.
Summer, 1971	WFA holds first tournament in Arizona.
July 1971	Highland Avenue Aces of Wilmette, Ill., wins Guts Championship over a field of forty two teams.
August 1971	Fastback Frisbee introduced.
September 1971	Sacramento State College offers Frisbee course. First in nation to award college credit. William Schneider, instructor.
Spring, 1972	CPI introduces All-Star model.
May 1972	Harvey J. Kukuk becomes director emeritus of IFA. Irv Landers assumes executive directorship.
June 1972	*Official Handbook of Frisbee* by Goldy Norton published.
July 1972	Highland Avenue Aces defend Guts Crown over BFG in the IFT at Copper Harbor, Mich. Riverside Demolay chapter sets marathon throwing mark of 280 hours and nineteen minutes.
August 30, 1972	First Canadian Open Frisbee Championship. Held at Canadian

	National Exhibition, Toronto, Ontario. C-R Losers of Michigan defeat Highland Avenue Aces.
November 6, 1972	Rutgers defeats Princeton 27-25 in first intercollegiate Ultimate Frisbee game. Played on same field and 103 years later to date of the first intercollegiate football game.
Fall, 1973	Wham-O introduces the Super Pro.
September 1, 1973	OFF circulates first petitions to include Frisbee in Olympics at 16th IFT. MTA becomes IFT event. C.H.S.V.F.T. demonstrates Ultimate Frisbee at 16th IFT.
September 2, 1973	Highland Avenue Aces capture third IFT Guts title defeating Bosh Hunt-Hers, 21-16.
October 13-14, 1973	First Annual Keystone Bay Guts Invitational (now Cliff's Ridge) with $1500 prize money.
December 8, 1973	First Wilmette (Ill.) Invitational Tournament.
February 1974	*Flying Disc World*, the independent Frisbee journal, begins.
March 16, 1974	First University of Michigan Indoor Frisbee Festival.
May 4-5, 1974	OCTAD, World Individual Flying Disc Championships, held for first time. Overall champion—John Kirkland (Rutgers Univ.)
June 1, 1974	First Northwestern University (Evanston, Ill.) Frisbee Tourney.
Summer, 1974	Yale students set new Frisbee marathon, record of 374 hours and 15 minutes.

July 7, 1974	Library Bar defeats Highland Avenue Aces at 17th IFT Guts and returns Nachazel Cup to Michigan Upper Harbor.
Late July 1974	Vic Malafronte and John Kirkland sign for Frisbee pre-game exhibition with Harlem Globetrotters.
August 2-3, 1974	First American Flying Disc Open in Rochester, N.Y.
August 23-25, 1974	World Championship Rose Bowl Tournament, Pasadena. Vic Malafronte declared overall men's champion; Jo Cahow overall women's champion. The Frisbee Game by Wham-O introduced.
October 12, 1974	First Jersey Jam Tournament.
October 12-13, 1974	Veteran Frisbee Flingers - Copper Harbor.
December 13, 1974	First Annual Dispo's awarded by *Flying Disc World* for outstanding service in disc sports. Individual award to Jim Palmeri; group award to Wham-O Manufacturing Co.
January 1975	Roger Barrett holds world's first Frisbee auction. Olympic ring mold number 1 sells for thirty dollars!

INTERNATIONAL FRISBEE TOURNAMENT RECORDS

The IFT is the oldest and most prestigious Frisbee tournament. Although meets such as the Wham-O-sponsored World Championships or the *Flying Disc World*–sponsored Octad may soon replace it in championship significance, a win at the IFT is still *the prize*.

The following are the winners of the seventeen meets held since 1958.

MEN'S

Guts

1958–1966	North Central
1967	Foul Five
1968	California Masters
1969	California Masters
1970	Foul Five
1971	Highland Avenue Aces
1972	Highland Avenue Aces
1973	Highland Avenue Aces
1974	Library Bar

Distance

1962–1966	Jake Healy
1967	Fritz Wall
1968	Jay Shelton
1969	Ken Headrick
1970	Bob May
1971	Dan Myers
1972	Bob May
1973	John Connelly, 309 ft., Tournament Record
1974	Bob May

Accuracy

1967	Robert Healy
1968	Robert Healy
1969	Ed Headrick
1970	Doug Hovey
1971	Ken Linna
1972	Jay Shelton
1973	Pete George
1974	Not held

MTA (Maximum Time Aloft)

1973	Roger Barrett, 9.3 seconds, tournament record
1974	Bruce Koger

WOMEN'S

Distance

1971	Mary McMahon
1972	Inez Sam
1973	Women's event combined with Men's
1974	Margie Meiswick

Accuracy

1970	Arlene Barron
1971	Jackie Harvey
1972	Inez Sam
1973	Women's event combined with Men's
1974	Not held

Guts

1971	Humbley Magnificent Champions of the Universe
1972	Same
1973	Same
1974	Same

JUNIORS
(6 through 12)

Guts

1971	Junior Librarians
1972	U.S.A. Jaguars
1973	Not Held
1974	Not Held

Distance

1970	Jeff Johnson
1971	Jeff Johnson
1972	Not Held
1973	Not Held
1974	Not Held

Accuracy

1971	Greg Davis
1972	Kurt Schaffer
1973	Not Held
1974	Not Held

CHILDREN
(0 through 6)

No Guts Competition

Distance

1971	Pat Visser
1972	Pat Visser
1973	Pat Visser
1974	Not Held

Accuracy

1969	Laura Anderson
1970	Mike Johnson
1971	Pat Visser
1972	Laura Anderson
1973	Pat Visser
1974	Not Held

MEASUREMENTS OF FLYING DISCS

All measurements are in the metric system except maximum lip thickness, cupola thickness, and mid-wing thickness, which were measured in thousandths of an inch by an Omega micrometer.

The Angle of Francioni, which describes the angle of the lip (cheek) and Bernoulli's Plate, was measured by the Francionimeter developed by Eric Peterson of Salt Lake City. Its range of reading is 70 to 100 degrees.

Cupola diameter is of the roof only. For double-cupola models, both measures are given. When there were significant differences between molds of the same model, the results were averaged. Weights were measured on a Torbal balance model PL-12, with assistance from Dennis Norrby of the Community Hospital of the Monterey Peninsula pharmacy.

Model	Outside diameter	Inside diameter	Cupola diameter	Cheek width	Weight	Height	Maximum Lip thickness	Mid-wing thickness	Cupola thickness	Angle of Francioni
Super Pro	25.1	23.9	—	1.75	138.0	3.4	233.6	NA	—	81.3
Pro Model	23.9	22.5	5.7	1.5	107.3	3.2	225	57	75	79
CPI All Star	24.0	22.9	5.8	1.7	117.0	3.0	203	67	70	80
Moonlighter	23.9	22.5	5.7	1.5	111.0	3.2	236	NA	NA	83.3
All American	23.7	22.5	—	1.5	102.2	2.6	230.3	42	45	82.3
Twirl-A-Boom	23.0	21.7	6.4	1.5	118.25	3.2	249	NA	—	78.0
Master	27.4	26.3	6.5	1.07	156.4	2.7	216.0	57	65	79.36
CPI ST	23.5	22.2	6.0/14.0	1.3	90.1	2.6	196.6	NA	NA	77.2

Model	Outside diameter	Inside diameter	Cupola diameter	Cheek width	Weight	Height	Maximum Lip thickness	Mid-wing thickness	Cupola thickness	Angle of Francioni
Tournament	28.6	26.9	7.5	2.0	178.2	3.7	261.0	56	64	81.6
Regular II	22.5	21.6	5.7	1.4	87.0	3.2	215	NA	NA	84.4
Regular I	22.7	21.6	5.9	1.4	87.1	3.1	212	NA	NA	77.9
Swing Poletten	22.1	21.0	7.0	1.3	106.3	3.1	232.6	NA	NA	77.6
Sailing Satellite	28.7	27.3	7.6	1.7	137.4	3.6	212.5	NA	NA	75.51
Pluto Platter	22.7	21.5	5.8	1.3	74.8	2.7	213.0	49	53	82.5
Tosserino	23.4	22.2	13.0	1.2	100.5	3.0	228.3	NA	NA	82.2
Flinger II	22.2	21.5	—	1.3	82.8	3.5	205	48	53	77.8
Sportcraft	23.3	22.1	1.6/5.8	1.2	92.7	2.6	180.0	NA	NA	78.0
Fast Back	23.8	22.8	13.5	1.4	106.2	2.8	204.6	NA	NA	78.5
Wiffle	22.4	21.6	5.6	1.1	84.9	2.2	200.3	NA	NA	77.4
Speedy	20.4	19.3	5.1	1.2	51.7	2.7	140	43	NA	80.33
Horseshoe	20.0	19.2	5.9	1.2	58.3	3.1	152.6	44	43	80.5
Zolar	23.3	22.2	6.0	1.5	93.0	2.7	176	NA	NA	75.1
Whirl-King	21.9	20.6	6.2	1.3	105.0	2.9	227	NA	—	94.5
Catch-It	22.0	20.8	14.0	1.4	85.8	3.7	193.0	47	47	83.0
Disneyland	23.3	22.3	—	1.4	86.2	2.2	186.6	NA	NA	77.5
CPI-GST	38.2	36.4	7.5	2.4	270.7	5.6	252	61	NA	77.0
Psychedelic Disc	23.3	22.8	—	1.1	116.3	2.7	190	NA	—	89.0
Tee-Bird Tournament	29.9	NA	NA	1.5	196.2	15.2	123	NA	NA	93
Gyrospin Gee-Whizzer	30.2	NA	—	1.5	202.7	15.4	124	NA	NA	93
Cox	28.0	26.7	8.6	1.6	170.0	6.3	228	NA	NA	88.3
Tee Bird	24.5	23.3	—	1.5	139.3	11.4	216.3	NA	NA	NA
Atlantis	22.2	21.1	8.0	1.0	87.0	3.2	190.0	NA	NA	NA
Belly Button	21.9	21.1	6.5	1.1	81.9	3.0	169.0	NA	NA	83.7
Flinger I	22.4	21.6	—	1.1	85.8	3.0	159	NA	—	77.1
Morrison	23.3	22.3	—	1.1	96.7	NA	213	NA	NA	NA
Disco	22.7	21.5	5.9	1.4	102.5	2.2	210.0	NA	NA	73.5

Model	Outside diameter	Inside diameter	Cupola diameter	Cheek width	Weight	Height	Maximum Lip thickness	Mid-wing thickness	Cupola thickness	Angle of Francioni
Hasbro-Glo	22.4	22.2	7.7	1.7	101.5	3.0	88.3	NA	NA	89.0
Herfy	22.6	219	—	1.2	88.4	2.4	163.3	NA	—	97.6
Pie Tin	24.7	NA	NA	NA	120.9	NA	NA	NA	NA	NA
Mini-I	9.8	9.0	2.4	0.6	13.2	1.5	155	NA	NA	NA
Whiz Ring	24.3	24.1	—	0.3	340	1.1	82.0	44.3	—	NA
Bottle Cap Lid	22.0	21.8	—	2.0	83.1	2.9	107.6	NA	—	92.8
Mini-Whiz Ring	15.6	15.4	—	0.2	9.0	0.6	38.0	38.6	—	NA
Nerf	22.8	22.8	—	—	20.0	2.4	—	2.4	—	—
Flap Jack	23.2	22.8	—	1.0	79.1	1.1	129.6	55	—	NA
Pro-Y	23.2	22.2	5.7	1.5	90.0	2.6	179	NA	NA	77.87
Kool-Aid	22.5	21.5	—	1.2	90.0	2.7	158.3	NA	—	82.2
Super Zinger	23.8	22.9	14/6	1.4	86.2	3.1	191	NA	NA	79.6
Disc-Voll	23.7	22.6	7.7	1.5	99.2	3.0	209.3	NA	NA	78.4
Big Prof-Disc	23.0	22.5	5.5	1.3	91.8	2.6	139.0	NA	NA	94.6
CPI-ST Single Cupola	23.9	22.3	12.7	1.3	100.6	2.7	191.3	NA	NA	77.5
Vercal Ring	23.9	23.8	—	0.85	31.4	1.1	59.3	34.3	—	NA
Gold Medal Winner	22.5	21.4	5.4	1.7	106.3	2.9	197.3	NA	NA	73
Whzzzzzz	23.5	22.5	—	1.4	106.0	3.1	176.6	NA	NA	23.0
Fly Star	22.0	21.5	—	1.0	85.1	2.5	148.3	NA	NA	NA
Speegul 2	23.6	22.5	3.7/7.5	1.5	101.1	2.7	224	NA	NA	75.5
Super Saucer	22.5	21.6	—	1.4	91.1	2.7	191.5	NA	NA	80.50
Keds	18.6	17.7	8.0	1.1	60.4	3.5	159.6	57	55	78.6
Aerodisc	27.3	26.2	6.6	1.7	166.5	3.3	206	NA	NA	87.37
Zing-Wing	21.5	20.5	—	1.4	89.1	2.8	191.6	NA	NA	83.5
Boom-A-Ring	24.1	24.8	—	0.6	34.4	1.2	73.6	45.6	—	NA
Fastback Premium	23.6	22.6	14.3	1.65	101.4	2.6	214	NA	NA	79
Trix Mini	9.7	8.9	2.6	0.8	11.7	1.8	151	NA	NA	NA
Whiz Bee	22.6	21.8	5.7	1.3	63.2	3.0	146.6	NA	NA	82.8

Model	Outside diameter	Inside diameter	Cupola diameter	Cheek width	Weight	Height	Maximum Lip thickness	Mid-wing thickness	Cupola thickness	Angle of Francioni
Psychedelic Comet	23.2	22.6	—	1.05	106.1	2.9	144	NA	—	NA
Brand X	22.4	21.5	—	1.5	98.5	2.6	151.3	NA	—	79.7
Wiffle Scaler	24.5	24.1	—	0.7	33.2	1.2	86.3	42.6	—	NA
Cossom II	23.3	22.4	$^{1.6}/_{5.9}$	1.2	97.5	2.8	180.3	NA	NA	81.8
Flying Whiz	21.0	20.9	—	0.4	31.1	1.3	64.3	43	—	NA
Mars Platter	22.3	20.7	5.9	1.6	82.3	2.9	188.6	NA	NA	<70
Best Ever	23.3	22.5	12.9	1.2	90.6	2.8	149.0	NA	NA	80.0

The world's only Francionimeter.

FLYING DISCS PERFORMANCE TABLE

The Performance Table is the result of hundreds of hours of testing most of the major flying discs and a few pretenders. When mold differences were significant (e.g., Wham-O Pro), the final score was averaged.

Discs were scored from 0 to 100 in ten categories of performance. Since the categories differ in their importance in disc play, each category was assigned an importance factor (e.g., throwing 1.4; bounce 0.7). The performance factor was then multiplied by the raw number score to give a weighted score. The two righthand columns give the raw total score. Highest score in each category appears in italics.

	Throwing 1.4	Catching 1.2	Accuracy 1.0	Velocity 1.0	Turnover 1.2	Curve 1.1	Bounce 0.7	Break 0.4	Hover 1.0	Run 0.5	Raw Score	Performance Score	Rank
Super-Pro Wham-O	94	69	89	86	92	90	88	89	86	92	877	828.0	1
Pro Wham-O	92	75	88	83	92	87	92	87	78	89	863	817.6	2
Moonlighter Pro Wham-O	94	71	88	88	90	86	89	88	76	93	863	814.3	3
All-Star CPI	93	71	86	80	92	87	91	94	79	90	863	812.8	4
All-American Wham-O	88	77	83	86	89	79	79	71	74	91	819	781.5	5
Twirl-A-Boom	87	67	81	80	86	81	90	89	71	86	818	768.1	6
Master Wham-O	85	51	85	72	86	78	89	77	85	95	803	751.8	7
Kool-Aid Amsum	84	74	78	72	65	76	81	87	74	74	765	720.5	8
Saucer Tosser CPI	81	73	79	73	76	73	81	67	69	76	748	715.0	9
Y-Model Tournament Size	79	48	77	64	81	79	79	70	90	92	759	712.6	10
Regular II Wham-O	79	73	69	70	81	72	67	73	68	72	724	693.7	11
Regular I Wham-O	78	73	69	70	81	71	67	70	68	72	719	690.0	12
Sailing Satellite Wham-O	69	63	76	70	78	68	79	64	76	84	727	685.5	13
Pluto Platter Wham-O	77	72	69	70	77	74	67	61	68	72	707	682.3	14
Swing Poletten	70	75	62	76	69	76	73	78	70	70	719	679.7	15
Tosserino North Pacific Products	82	69	70	69	56	73	77	75	49	75	695	654.5	16
Flinger II Skyway	68	74	69	71	59	51	77	79	66	59	673	631.9	17
Sportcraft Cossom	68	71	65	71	54	54	77	75	64	78	677	627.5	18
Fast Back Wham-O	69	41	66	91	50	70	87	35	47	81	637	595.2	19

	Throwing 1.4	Catching 1.2	Accuracy 1.0	Velocity 1.0	Turnover 1.2	Curve 1.1	Bounce 0.7	Break 0.4	Hover 1.0	Run 0.5	Raw Score	Performance Score	Rank
Wiffle Wiffle	51	52	45	70	63	49	64	52	61	65	572	537.4	20
Speedy Wham-O	46	51	63	51	67	62	59	50	53	58	618	531.5	21
Horseshoe Wham-O	42	45	61	54	66	60	65	67	51	51	562	521.8	22
Zolar Empire	44	54	60	70	51	48	62	54	54	63	560	520.9	23
Catch-It Remco	55	41	55	78	54	49	50	54	46	69	551	515.0	24
Giant Saucer Tosser CPI	39	28	54	65	77	58	25	36	*91*	50	523	511.3	25
Whirl-King Sock-It	47	42	49	72	51	41	60	70	70	55	557	511.0	26
Cox L.M. Cox	42	32	65	61	66	47	42	39	73	76	543	510.1	27
Disneyland Cameo	41	52	65	67	63	41	67	75	24	55	550	500.9	28
Tee Bird North Pacific Products	61	84	51	64	25	21	12	76	69	11	474	488.3	29
Belly Button Barrett	40	59	42	66	50	54	53	50	50	54	518	488.3	29
Tee Bird Tournament Allentown	63	86	54	60	29	36	10	56	68	07	469	480.7	30
Tee Bird Whizzer Allentown	63	86	54	60	29	36	10	56	68	05	467	479.7	31
Atlantis	47	35	54	71	42	38	60	55	56	62	520	476.0	32
Flyin' Saucer Morrison (soft) Pipco	49	52	52	47	43	56	48	75	42	50	520	473.8	33
Psychedelic Disc Eagle	42	41	43	76	53	39	66	80	33	57	530	473.2	34
Flinger I Skyway	31	54	43	73	42	37	60	49	64	64	517	472.9	35
Disco (Hong Kong)	54	37	49	70	51	40	41	41	40	61	484	459.8	36

	Throwing 1.4	Catching 1.2	Accuracy 1.0	Velocity 1.0	Turnover 1.2	Curve 1.1	Bounce 0.7	Break 0.4	Hover 1.0	Run 0.5	Raw Score	Performance Score	Rank
Hasbro-Glo Hasbro	28	42	54	58	52	40	31	67	33	15	420	397.0	37
Flyin' Saucer Morrison (hard) Pipco	44	31	49	49	39	56	51	01	42	24	386	395.3	38
Herfy Republic	37	43	41	56	40	41	37	55	41	20	411	392.4	39
Mini-II Wham-O	35	20	24	50	71	38	35	65	21	42	401	366.5	40
Frisbie Pie Tin	32	15	50	68	39	20	02	90	48	40	404	355.2	41
Mini-I Wham-O	33	20	24	50	71	32	35	59	21	42	387	354.7	42
Whiz-Ring North Pacific Products	45	92	45	28	29	37	22	29	07	07	341	334.2	43
Bottle Cap Lids	32	42	44	60	32	30	31	34	31	12	348	333.3	44
Mini- Whiz-Ring North Pacific Products	31	80	35	30	23	21	13	31	04	04	272	282.6	45
Nerf Parker	24	91	12	10	12	14	00	10	10	00	183	208.6	46
Bozo Fun Flyer	21	80	12	18	01	15	00	10	08	00	165	171.1	47
Flap Jack Fun Stuff	11	18	04	21	01	08	00	10	00	00	73	76	48

TABLE OF WHAM-O PRO MOLDS

Mold Number	Origin	Production Years	Features	Faults	Fate
1	Retooled from Pluto Platter[1]	1964→Present	Oldest Mold	After 1969, retooled mold had numeral backwards Ɩ[2]	Available only from foreign licensee
4	NM	1966→1969	Rarest Pro Mold	Lightest	Unknown
10	NM[4]	1968→1970	Very Stable	Very Sluggish Bouncer	Retooled to become All-American model
14 SD	NM	1968→Present	Moonlighters in '68 weighed 129 grams! HEAVIEST!	Very few—can't buy them in U.S.A.	Available only in Canada
14 SN	NM	1970→Present	All around good-to-average disc	Very slightly unstable	Still in Wham-O Production
15	NM	1968→Present[8]	Lowest profile and *fastest*. See 9	Early 15's were least stable of all Pros[10]	Still in Wham-O Production
16 SD	NM	1970 Only	High Profile. Holds curve. Most stable Pro.	Slow Velocity	Retooled to 16SN in late 1970
16 SN	Retooled from 16 SD	1971→Present	Stable	Light! Range 99 to 112 grams	Retooled to "91" in 1972" Sent to Germany[11]
17	NM	1973→Present	Fairly good. Performs like 14 SN	The moldless [12] Frisbee	Still in Wham-O Production

Legend

NM = new mold
SD = split digit
SN = small numeral

Performance factors are the same as in Flying Disc Performance Table

Performance / Colors

Distance	Catching	Accuracy	Velocity	Turnover	Curve	Bounce	Break	Hover	Run	Raw Score	Weighted	Rank	White	Maroon	Turquoise	Purple	Chartreuse	Moonlighter	Fire Orange	Green	Yellow
92	76	86	76	92	84	90	69	79	92	836	800.4	2	Yes	Yes	Yes	Yes	Yes	Yes	Yes[3]	No	No
80	79	79	72	88	80	85	69	69	90	791	752.5	9	Yes	No	No	No	Yes	No	No	No	No
90	76	85	71	93	88	83	72	78	92	828	792.5	5	Yes	Yes	Yes	Yes	Yes	Yes	No	No	No
95	74	81	75	91	88	91	75	80	92	842	803.5	1	Yes	No	No	No	Yes	Yes[5]	No	No	No
90	75	81	74	89	83	91	75	75	91	824	783.3	7	No	No	No	No	Yes	Yes	No	Yes[6]	Yes[7]
93	70	78	84	87	86	93	77	69	93	830	786.6	6	Yes	Yes	Yes	Yes	Yes	Yes	No	No	Yes[7]
87	79	86	69	94	85	85	78	81	91	836	795.1	3	Yes	No	No	No	No	No	No	No	No
90	79	82	71	92	85	92	78	75	92	836	794.3	4	No	No	No	No	Yes	Yes	No	No	No
90	75	81	69	92	83	91	78	75	91	825	783.1	8	No	No	No	No	No	No	Yes	No	No

Footnotes

1. There were several Pluto Platter molds. The one largest in diameter was transformed into Pro mold One.

2. Controversy here. May have happened sooner or several times. Injection molds require reworking every-so-often. And while mold designers are adept at mirror image writing, i.e. 16 produces ∂l, mold re-workers occasionally make mistakes. The backward one's were the first such mistakes in Pro making.

3. Made for 1969 International Frisbee Tournament competition. Some of these have the word "straight" misspelled in the "flat, flip, flies straight" logo.

4. Perhaps one of the several 10 molds was the old "One" mold retooled after foreign service.

5. Made for 1970 International Frisbee Tournament.

6. The rare Wolfschmidt green premium. There are probably other premium Pros.

7. The already famous 1974 Rose Bowl Frisbee, extra heavy 118 to 120 grams. Highly prized, excellent performer, especially made for that tournament.

8. Wham-O considers their 15's the best Pro mold, now after reworking the balance. Current 15's have raised letters 11/32 in.; all other current molds are 13/32 in. See footnote #9.

9. 1968 and early 1969, 15's were extra stiff and heavy. Called "Brickbats."

10. Current 15's are more stable; the distance record at 1974 W.F.C meet was made with a 15 mold.

11. Another of those mirror image mistakes. The "91" was "domy" i.e. the central height is disproportionate-too tall-for the Morrison slope factor. Makes for an unstable flyer.

12. Sometime in mid-1974 after a minor mishap and quick reworking, the 17 mold number was accidentally left off, producing the very rare "moldless" Frisbee.

HOW TO DATE A WHAM-O PRO

The time of production of a Wham-O Pro can be deduced from the color, label, plastic rings, and several miscellaneous elements. For example, a white, number 4 mold, with one wide black ring and a weighted label (i.e., 108 grams), would have to be made in late 1968 or early 1969.

The chronological table shows some of the special periods in Wham-O Pro making, such as the "Magic Moonlighters," the "Brickbats," and the "Lean Period" when plastic sources diminished during the 1973–74 energy crisis.

Legend

- ● = start or stop in production
- U = uncertain when production started
- ? = uncertain if still produced
- R = mold retooled
- ∿ = special or unusual production period
- SD = split-digit mold number
- SN = small-numeral mold number
- → = still produced

Footnotes

1. *Made especially for Rose Bowl World Frisbee championships on 14 SN and 15 molds.*

2. *"Lean period" of available plastic secondary to energy crisis–much variation in plastic used.*

3. *After retooling "1" mold the number was accidentally turned around ("Ɩ").*

4. *Number one mold may have returned to the States and been retooled to be a ten mold. At one time there were at least two, maybe more, ten molds.*

5. *This was the period of the Magic Moonlighter, the late 1968, early 1969, SD14, 130 gram plus models. Many players favor this Pro above all others.*

6. *During this period there were some very heavy colored Pros made on the 15 mold, the Brickbats–extra stiff.*

7. *The 16 SN was retooled and became the short-lived "91" mold. It was in use for a few months only. It was not an outstanding performer.*

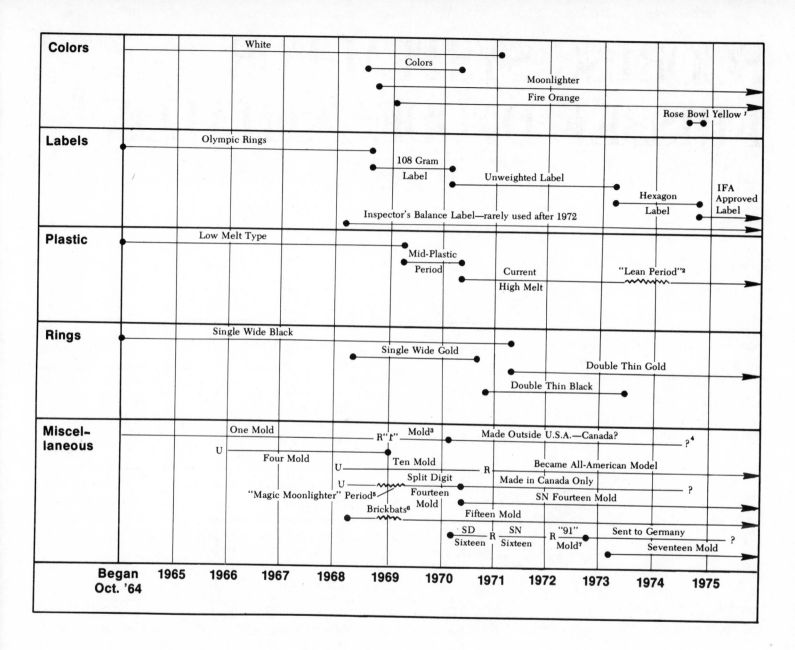

SCORING SYSTEM FOR FRISBEE DUODECATHALON

Scores of each of the twelve events are weighted in the following manner to produce a total point score for the duodecathalon.

No. Event	Scoring Method & Example	Sample Score
1. Distance 5 throws	Best throw in feet × 2 e.g., 250 ft. × 2	500
2. MTA 5 trials	Best time in seconds × 50 e.g., 10.1 sec × 50	505
3. TRC 5 trials	Best distance in feet × 3 150 ft. × 3	450
4. Accuracy 10 throws	Through target = 50 pt. Touch target = 10 pt. 6 throughs × 50 = 300 2 touches × 10 = 20	320
5. Medley Accuracy 10 throws OR	same scoring method as Regular Accuracy e.g., 4 throughs, 3 touches	230

No. Event	Scoring Method & Example				Sample Score
Trick Throw Accuracy	(Number through target at each of eight stations × 5) × station value (sv)				

Station In Yards	Throughs		SV	Score	
10	5×5=25	×	1.0	25	
15	4×5=20	×	1.5	30	or
20	3×5=15	×	2.0	30	
25	4×5=20	×	2.5	50	
30	3×5=15	×	3.0	45	
35	3×5=15	×	3.5	52.5	
40	2×5=10	×	4.0	40	
45	1×5=5	×	4.5	22.5	= 295

No. Event	Scoring Method & Example	Sample Score
6. Bull's-eye Accuracy 5 throws	Target Rings of 100, 50, 25, 10 point values e.g., Points for Five Throws: 100 + 25+ 0 + 100 + 100	325
7. Golf 18 holes	$(100 - Score) \times 15$ e.g., $(100 - 78) \times 15$ 22 x 15	330
8. Guts Individual Single Elimination Round Robin	(Your Score) × (20) + (your score −loser's score) × 10 ÷ number of games	413

Game 1: 21 to 20 $21 \times 20 = 420 + 1 \times 10 = 430$

Game 2: 21 to 14 $21 \times 20 = 420 + 7 \times 10 = 490$

Game 3: 16 to 21 $16 \times 20 = 320 + 0$ $= \underline{320}$

                                                    1240

        $1240 \div 3 = 413$

No. Event	Scoring Method & Example	Sample Score
9. Courtsbee Individ. Single Elimination Round Robin	Same method of scoring as No. 8 above except total score is multiplied by 17 instead of 20	
Game 1: 25 to 20	$25 \times 17 = 450 + 5 \times 10 = 500$	446
Game 2: 25 to 20	$25 \times 17 = 450 + 5 \times 10 = 500$	
Game 3: 20 to 25	$20 \times 17 = 340 + 0 \qquad = 340$	
	$\qquad\qquad\qquad\qquad\qquad\quad 1340$	
	$1340 \div 3 = 446$	

10. Free Style

Three-minute exercise performed in pairs at a distance of at least twenty yards. Four subjective scales with point awards of up to 75 points each:

1. Style and grace of play
2. Agility of movements
3. Inventiveness of program
4. Cooperativeness with partner

In addition to overall scores in the above four categories, each handling of the disc may be awarded up to 20 points for complexity and execution. A simple catch and return would receive no points, whereas a toe tip and spinning behind-the-back in-air, thumbs-up catch blending into an accurate Boda might receive from 15 to 20 points depending upon the execution.

e.g.,		
Style and Grace	68	
Agility	71	
Inventiveness	63	
Cooperativeness	58	
	260	

Fifteen point-making handlings with total score 246

$246 + 260 = 506$ 506

No. Event	Scoring Method & Example	Sample Score
11. Discathon	Distance in feet ÷ Run of time in seconds × 35	
	e.g., $10,560 \div 840 = 12.57$ 12.57×35	440
12. Double Disc Court Single Elimination Round Robin	Same scoring as No.8, Individual Guts See example No.8	413

TOTAL   4,878

(Using Trick Throw
Accuracy for Event No.5)

ADVANCED NOTATION SYSTEM FOR THROWS AND CATCHES

The practice of naming throws by their grip is obsolete for the accomplished player who can make an underhand throw with a sidearm grip or use a hooked thumb grip to deliver an upside-down backhand toss. And thumbs down, thumbs up, tip, between the legs, or behind the back is not enough to describe the complexity of master catchers.

The following is a system of notation for both throws and catches. The area around the player's body is divided into segments called zones—eight for throwing, seven for catching. Each zone has a name and a number. This facilitates both narrative descriptions of disc play and more formal written resumés of, say, Guts games.

With this system a free-style demonstration between, say, Victor Malafronte (M) and John Kirkland (K) could be written as follows:

$$M: R\text{-}2\text{-}3 \longrightarrow K: L\text{-}2\text{ - TD}$$

Malafronte throws right-handed with a sidearm grip (2) from zone three, and Kirkland catches left-handed in zone 2 with a thumbs-down catch.

$$K: L\text{-}3\text{-}8 \longrightarrow M: R\text{-}1\text{-}FT^3 \text{ - \$; } L\text{-}1\text{-}TU$$

Kirkland throws left handed* with thumb grip (3) in zone 8 (an upside-down throw) to Malafronte, who makes three right-handed finger tips and then does a body spin, completing a zone-one left-handed thumbs up.

This playing language should prove valuable in recording future games and contests.

In the resumé below the system is slightly modified to describe a Guts game between Library Bar (LB) and Highland Avenue Aces (HAA).

↓ = dropped   ↑ =deflected

Guts players are numbered 1 through 5, left to right.

					Score	
					LB	HAA
LB-3	R-3-7	HAA-3	R-2-TU		0	0
HAA-3	R-3-7	LB-1	L-4-TU	↓	0	1
LB-3	R-3-6	HAA-2	R-1	↑	0	
		HAA-4	R-1-TU		0	1

*Remember throwing zones 2, 3, 4, and 6, 7, 8 change sides for left-handed throws.

A throw is named on the basis of which zone the release (whelm) occurs in.

Catching zones take their name from the area in which the catch occurs.

The complete description of the catch also includes whether right (R) or left (L), thumbs up (TU) or thumbs down (TD) or tips (T) are used. The description R-FT³ would be right-handed finger tips, three in a row. Other possible tips: Head tips (HDT), Elbow (ET), Knee (KT), Toe (TT), Heel (HLT). Tips can include body spins and somersaults designated T$ or T⑤ respectively.

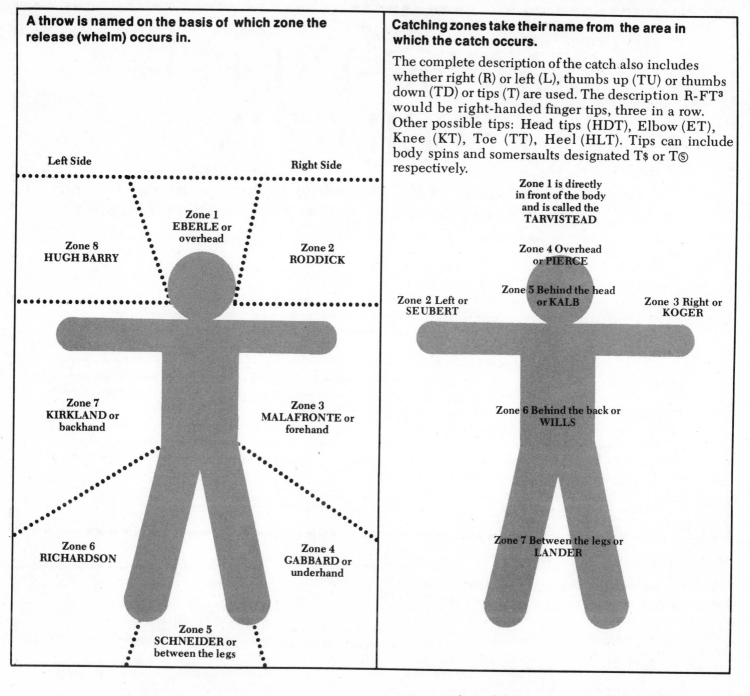

Left Side

Right Side

Zone 1
EBERLE or
overhead

Zone 8
HUGH BARRY

Zone 2
RODDICK

Zone 7
KIRKLAND or
backhand

Zone 3
MALAFRONTE or
forehand

Zone 6
RICHARDSON

Zone 4
GABBARD or
underhand

Zone 5
SCHNEIDER or
between the legs

Zone 1 is directly
in front of the body
and is called the
TARVISTEAD

Zone 4 Overhead
or PIERCE

Zone 5 Behind the head
or KALB

Zone 2 Left or
SEUBERT

Zone 3 Right or
KOGER

Zone 6 Behind the back or
WILLS

Zone 7 Between the legs or
LANDER

OLYMPIC FRISBEE FEDERATION

We, the undersigned, petition the International Olympic committee and the Canadian Olympic committee for the Summer Olympics 1976 to include Frisbee in the olympic games.

Name	Address

Mail Petition to:

Olympic Frisbee Federation
Stancil E.D. Johnson, M.D.
Acting Secretary
178 Central Ave.
Pacific Grove
California 93950

☐ Please send more petitions.
☐ I would like to be an associate member of the Olympic Frisbee Federation, receive a membership card, and all future miscellany as we work for the cause: Frisbee in the Olympics

I enclose $1.00 as my membership fee.

Signed _____

Address _____

_____

216   Olympic Frisbee Federation

FRISBEE ETERNAL

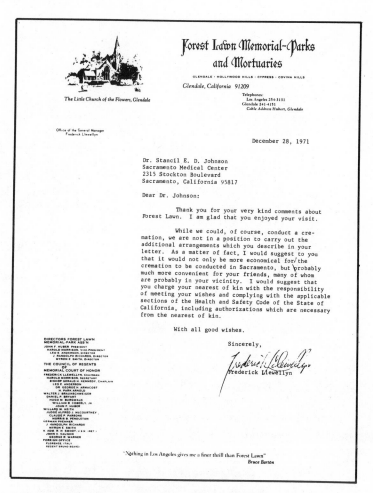

STANCIL E. D. JOHNSON, M.D.
Psychiatry

December 16, 1971

Forest Lawn Memorial Park
1712 South Glendale Avenue
Glendale, California 91209

Gentlemen:

Very recently I had an opportunity to visit Forest Lawn in the Glendale area, and let me say I was appropriately impressed with the many attractive features and facades that you have developed. Equally was I in note of the quiet yet splendid milieu that both grounds and keepers maintain.

As I approach middle years, I know that I must make plans for my eternity. Therefore, it is to you now naturally that I first think and turn.

Because my needs are special, I wish to early outline them for you and work towards their complete understanding. They are as follows:

Upon my demise, I wish to be quietly and simply cremated. Then I would that the ashes would be taken to 13222 Estrella Avenue in South Los Angeles to the offices of Alfa Manufacturing Company, delivered into the hands of Mr. Charles and George Galloway. They in turn will equally distribute the final remains into the melting pot of an injection mold machine along with their finest grade raw industrial polyethylene. Then by previous instruction, they will appropriately disperse the mix and see that the melt is finished into twenty-five highest grade number one mold, professional model Frisbees. As you may already know, I am the historian for the International Frisbee Association and Tournament and author of the book, Frisbees. Therefore, it is only natural that I would wish that my last vestiges would be contained in what I consider to be the finest Frisbee yet, and possibly ever made. The Galloways will then deliver the entire run into your hands, probably within three days of their receipt. And at this time, under the direction of Mr. George (Thor) Anderson, of Gary, Indiana, at a small, and I insist, intimate gathering, each Frisbee will be distributed to the twenty-five players and friends that I hold most dear for their personal use. As I think towards the future, and envision that scene, and the hours, perhaps even years, which my remains will waft through the air between the hands of those whom I have loved so much; my heart even now rises in anticipation.

I hope that we will have no difficulties in engendering this program of final resting (although I like to think of it as the opposite of resting, obviously), and await your reply of acceptance and agreement.

Sincerely,

Forest Lawn Memorial-Parks
and Mortuaries

GLENDALE · HOLLYWOOD HILLS · CYPRESS · COVINA HILLS

Glendale, California 91209

The Little Church of the Flowers, Glendale

Telephones:
Los Angeles 254-3131
Glendale 241-4151
Cable Address Hubert, Glendale

Office of the General Manager
Frederick Llewellyn

December 28, 1971

Dr. Stancil E. D. Johnson
Sacramento Medical Center
2315 Stockton Boulevard
Sacramento, California 95817

Dear Dr. Johnson:

Thank you for your very kind comments about Forest Lawn. I am glad that you enjoyed your visit.

While we could, of course, conduct a cremation, we are not in a position to carry out the additional arrangements which you describe in your letter. As a matter of fact, I would suggest to you that it would not only be more economical for the cremation to be conducted in Sacramento, but probably much more convenient for your friends, many of whom are probably in your vicinity. I would suggest that you charge your nearest of kin with the responsibility of meeting your wishes and complying with the applicable sections of the Health and Safety Code of the State of California, including authorizations which are necessary from the nearest of kin.

With all good wishes.

Sincerely,

Frederick Llewellyn

"Nothing in Los Angeles gives me a finer thrill than Forest Lawn"
Bruce Barton

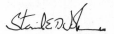

Frisbee mania may have reached its peak in the following exchange of letters with a well-known Los Angeles firm.

BIBLIOGRAPHY

Barrett, R. W. *A Vestpocket Guide to Frisbee Selection.* B.F.G. Publications, 1972.

—*Catalogue of the Postal Flying Disc Auction.* Barrett, 1974

Bauerle, R. F. *The Origin of Frisbee and Related Terms.* Unpublished manuscript.

Benhari. "The Cosmic Art of Frisbee," *Good Times,* Vol. 4, no. 24, 1970, pp. 14–15.

Carroll, Jon. "Everyone Loves Frisbees," *West* (Sunday Supplement), *Los Angeles Times,* pp. 10-13, December 19, 1971.

Chapman, R., Johnston, P., and Keenan, D. *Experiments With Frisbees.* Unpublished manuscript.

Couzens, E. G. *Plastics in the Modern World.* Pelican Original, revised, 1968.

de Roos, Robert. "The Eighty-Four-Pound Jake That Became Frisbee," *San Francisco Examiner and Chronicle,* January 10, 1971.

Doust, Dudley. 'Tony Jacklin– Mystical Perception in Sport." *The* (London) *Times,* November 4, 1973.

Faaberg R. F., and Keenan D. *Flight Dynamics of a Frisbee.* Unpublished manuscript.

"Flipped Discs," *Time,* July 17, 1972, pp. 52—53.

"The Frisbee Phenomenon," *Peninsula Living, Palo Alto Times,* May 4 and 5, 1968.

Hellring, Buzzy, Hines, Jonny, and Silver, Joel. *Ultimate Frisbee– Official Rules.* 4th edition, 1973.

Herrigel, Eugen. *Zen in the Art of Archery.* Vintage Books, 1971.

Hidgon, Hall. "Gentlemen, Start Your Frisbees," *Ford Times,* April 1970, pp. 9–43.

Hodemaker, E.H. *Prevention and Cure of Frisbee Finger.* University of California Press, 1962.

Jares, Joe. "It's a Beer Bratwurst and Guts Game," *Sports Illustrated,* August 3, 1970.

Johnson, Stancil. "Frisbee—The Once and Future Sport," *American Medical News.* September 2, 1974.

Katz, Paul. "The Free Flight of a Rotating Disc," *Israel Journal of Technology*, vol. 6, nos. 1–2, pp. 150–155.

Kukuk, Harvey. *Frisbee as a Way Of Life*. Out of print.

La Bel, Thomas. "The Thirteenth Invitational Frisbee Tournament." *Wonderland Magazine*. Grand Rapids Press, July 19, 1970.

La Roche, Mike. "Frisbee—The First Space Age Sport," *American Girl*, June 1972, pp. 142–143.

Leonard, George. "Games People Should Play," *Esquire*, October 1974, p. 6.

Mc Lean, Dan. "The Crowd Pleaser: Twenty-one Inches of Spring," *The Daily Breeze* (Torrance, Calif.), December 29, 1974, pp. C1 & C3.

Manual for the Development of Frisbee Clubs. I.F.A. Press. October 1967.

Morrison, Shelly. "Frisbee: First Fling at the Rose Bowl," *Women Sports*, March 1975, pp. 15–16.

Murphy, Michael. *Golf in the Kingdom*. Dell Publishing, 1972.

Norton, Goldy. *The Official Frisbee Handbook*. Bantam Press, 1971, p. 86.

Official I.F.A. Proficiency Manual. I.F.A. Press, 1967, p. 10.

Petersen, Jim A. "Zen and the Art of Frisbee." *Oui*, May 1975.

Peterson, Harry. *Calculation of Self-Suspended Flare Trajectories*. A.D. Publication No. 731866.

Pinkerton, W., and Stewart, Jr. *The Wall Street Journal*. Pacific Coast Ed., July 2, 1969.

Reed, J.D. "They Are My Life and My Wife," *Sports Illustrated*, February 24, 1975.

Renner, Michael. "The Great Frisbee Episode," *The Shopping Bee*, Claremont, California *Courier*, May 8, 1968

Severn, Bill. *A Carnival of Sport: The Frisbee Fling*. David McKay Co., 1974.

Soucheray, Joe. "Frisbee," *Northliner Magazine*, Spring 1973, pp. 6–9.

Stilley, G. D., Lartsens, L., and Sanders, K. *Aerodynamic Analysis of the Self-Suspended Flare*. A.D. Publication No. 740117.

Trillin, Calvin. "Yale Frisbee Team," *Yale Alumni Magazine*, November 1970.

Ultimate Frisbee. Official Rules. 4th edition, 1974.

Weeks, Albert L. "Frisbee: A Toy for All Seasons," *The New York Times*, August 2, 1971.

Westerfield, Kenneth R., and Kenner, James F. *Courtsbee*. 1974.

Wham-O Manufacturing Company. *Guts Frisbee Instructions*, 1971.

Julius T. Nachazel congratulates the author.

ABOUT THE AUTHOR

Stancil E.D. Johnson is the world's recognized authority in Frisbee. He is the historian for both the International Frisbee Association and the International Frisbee Tournament, and played on the world championship Frisbee teams in 1968 and 1970, and the runner-up teams of 1969 and 1971.

Doctor Johnson is also an avid rhinocerphile, umbilicalogist, LOLolgist (little-old-lady expert), safety-razor collector, and slap-hand champion of the Pacific coast. In his "working" hours he is a psychiatrist with a practice in Pacific Grove, California.